An Imaginal-Vig.

SEMINAL BEING

Primordial Self

MIRRORS OF THE GODS

Reflections of a Sacred Vision

Joan Parrish Morency

A NOVEL FROM A SOUL'S PERSPECTIVE

EPIPHANY
ARTISTIC
LICENSE,
PUBLISHER

An Imaginal-Vignettes® Novel

Published by
Epiphany Artistic License, Henderson, Nevada.

Production Team
Patricia Beaulieu, editorial project manager, Ida Gamban, editor,
Nancy Ratkiewich, cover design and book production, njr productions.

978-1-7364923-0-7   Paperback
978-1-7364923-1-4   e-Book

Printed in the United States of America

10 9 8 7 6 5 4 3 2 1

I dedicate this book to Mark Spirtos and Jerome Downes

for encouraging me to take bold actions toward fulfilling

my vision—the return of my soul to its original Self.

—Joan Parrish Morency

CONTENTS

Joan Parrish Morency

In the spring of 1993, I was living in Los Angeles and participating in a profound personal development program about inventing oneself. During that program I experienced a vivid dream involving a multidimensional being that was more impressive than my own life. When I awoke, I felt as though I had embodied a spiritual realm seen through the eyes of the ethereal being. What was communicated to me altered my perception of reality and elevated my awareness to include the "Seminal Being" Soul—the Primordial Self and its intent that accompanies me throughout each incarnation.

ACKNOWLEDGMENTS

Joan Parrish Morency

My most heartfelt thanks to:

Greer Williams and Jodi Ann Lowe, Harry Sandhu, and Jason Jones (Trademark Attorney) for their unwavering love and powerful listening for the fulfillment of my life's work.

All my friends, who have a deep appreciation of life's great mysteries within the natural order of the universe: Margo Piper, Vernon Quever, Jackie Wilson, Claire Morency, Pat Finn, and Patricia (Trish) Beaulieu.

I would also like to give special thanks to everyone who wished me success in my 18-year commitment to have my story adapted into a movie or miniseries.

CHAPTER ONE

A Place of Foundation

Baile Movimiento "Dancing Movement," a divine-messenger, stood motionless in anticipation of meeting Chalchiuhtotolin "Blood-Jeweled Fowl, Long-Nose Turkey," the Toltec Deity of Karmic Debt Removal-soul retrieval. As we waited inside "The Chamber of Mirrors," a subterranean grotto, I tried to discern the sun's whereabouts. Void of all-natural light, I was unable to judge the time of day and became impatient. What must have been minutes felt like an hour. This was the way time occurred in my disembodied state.

"Do you suppose he's forsaken us?" I asked the emerald-green, androgynous, spirit-being.

"No, Quetzal!" Dancing Movement informed me telepathically. "Once provoked, the Toltec Deity must comply."

A moment later, I watched in amazement as Blood-Jeweled Fowl, Long-Nose Turkey emerged from a black obsidian scrying mirror embedded in a rock formation. Initially, the reflective surface did not produce his image but rather seemed to absorb it, creating an embossed likeness of a half-man, half-fowl creature. During this stage of his transfiguration, the Toltec Deity exhibited great volition and dexterity. He liberated himself from the misshapen outwardly appearance of Black Tezcatlipoca "Smoking Mirror."

Smoking Mirror, the Lord of Ancestal Memory and Master Instigator of Conflict, delighted in his longstanding achievement—the all-pervasive despair felt by a community when a person's intent (virtue) failed repeatedly in achieving self-actualization. The intent, which dwells within the individualized soul, emulates the "divine spark" of the Godly Soul, Seminal Being. *Therefore, restoring the integrity of* Seminal Being *is paramount in the spiritual evolution of the human soul as it assimilates "Supernal Light," the movement of grace through vibration. This is how it was presented to me by "Dancing Movement," back in the 10th century AD.*

A minute before Smoking Mirror withdrew into the black obsidian scrying mirror—a gateway to the Akashic Records—the hunched over Toltec Deity dipped in black, with two broad yellow bands across his face, cast a spell upon the mistress of ceremonies.

"You come from Heaven and look what prevails,
Unanswered prayers said long ago.
A silent tongue offers no conversion,
Ignorant of you, she will die."

Dancing Movement floated over to Blood-Jeweled Fowl, Long-Nose Turkey as he completed his metamorphosis, and I followed in his wake.

"Only by way of the Self-Correcting Principle 'Recapitulation' will the mixed-heritage American recognize you as an aspect of her Godly Soul," the Toltec Deity of Karmic Debt Removal-soul retrieval explained to me.

"During these past twenty-one years, I was led to believe that I was acting on behalf of Noelle," I said.

"So we thought, Quetzal Hunahpu 'Sacred Bird, One Marksman, Lord Eternal.' "

"What am I up against?" I asked the Toltec Deity.

"It seems from the moment you became involved, Smoking Mirror clouded Noelle's memory through short bursts of traumatic event recall. You must be watchful and discerning of any unsettling disobedience. It is a sign 'the devil' is in the vicinity!"

"You mean to tell me the 'dirty dog' has been following us this whole time?"

"Correct! And, as a result, her condition has worsened."

There was a long pause before either of us spoke. Dancing Movement had stopped his free-form animation completely.

"If the spirit is weak, the soul is vulnerable to attack; if the soul is vulnerable to attack, the spirit is weak," Dancing Movement advised.

"What do you have in mind?" I asked, showing my disappointment.

It had been centuries since I had questioned the intentions of the Toltec Deity of Karmic Debt Removal-soul retrieval.

"I have managed to make the 'Recapitulation Process' more to your liking," he said cajolingly.

"I doubt that," I mumbled under my breath while glancing over at Dancing Movement.

Recapitulation—the reliving of past events to gain valuable insight into erratic habitual behavior—had never been my forte. I tended to become disoriented, isolated, and then overwhelmed. Repeatedly, I thwarted my own stated intention to be well, as in complete and whole, and instead turned the entire process into a life-threatening ordeal.

In retrospect, I should have known that the fracturing of Amrit Sandhu's soul in the second century BC produced a diminishing effect on our Godly Soul. Amrit's neglected soul, still to this day, has interfered with three subsequent souls: Noelle, Immokalee, and I, from recognizing and producing our intent for the benefit of all.

Within a matter of seconds, my expression must have revealed my self-absorption. A loud fluttering sound coming from Blood-Jeweled Fowl, Long-Nose Turkey brought me back to the conversation.

"Quetzal, you are simply to restore Noelle's memory this evening," he said. "Dancing Movement will cause the shift to occur, and a new perspective will reframe her reality. Thereafter, the Intent will communicate to Noelle the specific virtue that will miraculously heal her soul from the debilitating effects of your accumulated trauma."

"And what if I should fail?"

"By this time tomorrow, Noelle Intaglio Leandre's 'Day of the Lord, Incised Image, Lion-like Man' will have been given every opportunity to restore the integrity of her Godly Soul."

"Will you be nearby if I sense she is about to succumb to an inferior resolution?"

Dancing Movement nodded 'Yes' and then joined the Toltec Deity inside the scrying mirror, activating the portal to Noelle's memory vortex.

High above sea level in the municipality of Pátzcuaro Michoacán, Mexico, stood the Mayan-Toltec Estate Moyocoyotzin "The Inventor of Himself." Encased within a curtain of mature pine trees, reinforced by wetlands, the terra-cotta estate situated on Lake Pátzcuaro remained hidden for hundreds of years by the surrounding volcanic steep mountains. It was predawn on November 1, 2015, when the master of the estate, Saltire Daghda McKenna Celestino "Sacred Cross (X), Protector of the Tribe, Ardent Love, Secret of Heaven," age sixty-seven, walked along a second-story hallway wearing cargo shorts and an authentic looking papier-mâché facemask of the Mayan-Toltec Deity Chaac/Tlaloc. The Long-Nose Mesoamerican Deity of Lightning and Thunder would soon spark a spiritual transformation unique unto its kind.

Saltire, an attractive vibrant man of virtue, was forever changing and mixing up his physical appearance. This allowed him insight into others while keeping them at a disadvantage. They were never quite sure who he was, and only a select few ever got to know the man behind the mask.

Hung on whitewashed plaster walls were ten Huichol Indian Prophetic Yarn Paintings. Saltire hesitated momentarily under a dimly lit animal-shaped iron lock plate sconce and removed one of the yarn paintings in exchange for the facemask. A whiff of copal incense informed his next move. Saltire addressed the yarn painting in the native Nahuatl language of his forefathers and then in English. It was an ancient invocation he often used before speaking to Spirit.

"Heli Lamah Sabac Tani. Now I immerse myself in the Predawn of Your Presence."

Without further adieu, Saltire ducked into Paloma's bedroom, rich in family heirlooms and indigenous artifacts. For a moment, he was taken aback by the beauty of the portrait paintings, landscape photographs, and handcrafted Talavera pottery. He then placed the yarn painting beneath a five-foot-tall were-quetzal bird (sacred man-bird).

Sitting upright in a bentwood rocker was the phantom of Paloma, the half-sister of Saltire. Flanking the giant bird was two ten-year-old Belgian Malinois, a male Naoki (honest tree), and a female Mayu (true). They were a birthday gift from her niece, Xochitl, two years prior to Paloma's unforeseen departure.

On October 29, 2007, Paloma Balam Celestino, 'Peaceful Dove, Jaguar Prophet, Secret of Heaven,' shed her body in order to retain her 'divine spark.' Torrential rains had submerged eighty percent of Tabasco in Southern Mexico, and the entire Celestino family were involved in the rescue efforts on their 20,000 acre cocoa plantation. Late that afternoon, as the waters swelled, so did the element of fear. Xochitl had accidentally slid down a riverbank and into raging waters. She was nowhere in sight.

Paloma's pups Naoki and Mayu, with their perfect scent, quickly located Xochitl. Facedown, she was drowning in a sinkhole made of swirling mud and debris. Having "the presence of mind," Paloma was able to rescue Xochitl in one energy-efficient maneuver. She grabbed Xochitl by her ankles and flung her fifteen feet into the hurricane winds. The gesture forced Xochitl to come to her senses and land safely away from the mudslides and rolling boulders. Hearing a shrill scream, she watched in horror as her beloved aunt plunge headfirst into the unforgiving and life-threatening river. Miraculously, instead of dying in the harrowing incident, Paloma managed to ward off "terrible beauty" and transform into a winged creature. First shape-shifting into a were-eagle (man-bird of prey), and then into the sacred were-quetzal bird (man-sacred bird), Paloma transcended physical death and ascended into Heaven, the "Otherworld."

The *Otherworld* comprised of an infinite number of souls, angels, and enlightened beings rejoiced in Paloma's recovery. Dancing Movement, who had been her closest confidant on earth, was the first to welcome her. Together, they devised a plan, which allowed Paloma to remain active in her family's spiritual practices. Once every year, Dancing Movement accompanied Paloma as she made the flight from the *Otherworld* to The Chamber of Mirrors. There in the subterranean cavity, she helped conduct the Toltec Secret Eagle Knight Council's Initiation Rites.

The Toltec Secret Eagle Knight Council, "An Archetypal Creative Order," was the dream child of a devout partnership. The Council was formed in the late 900s at Tollan, the Toltec capital. The King-Priest Ce Acatl Topiltzin-Quetzalcoatl "One Reed, Prince, Feathered Serpent" and Quetzal Hunahpu co-founded the Council to counter the depraved "Black Jaguar Cult" of Black Tezcatlipoca, the evil twin of the Toltec King-Priest. Initially, the Council was triumphant, and the people thrived under the tenets. However, in 987 AD, the Black Jaguar cult, thirty-two black were-jaguars who had sworn to extinguish the Toltec Secret Eagle Knight Council, succeeded in infiltrating the Council through Smoking Mirror's magical spells. In response to the threat, Ce Acatl Topiltzin-Quetzalcoatl gave the order, which allowed for two possible escape routes. The King-Priest and the Council optioned to travel by moonlight on a southerly trail to Chichen Itza on the Yucatan Peninsula. Upon their arrival, they were graciously welcomed by the Mayan Lords, who had arranged for their safe journey.

As Quetzal Hunahpu, the Toltec Atlantean Warrior, my soul's purpose took me on a dramatically different path altogether. A band of tawny-yellow were-jaguars accompanied me eastward to Veracruz on the Gulf of Mexico. There in one simple movement, I answered the challenge set before by my King, "Can you be trusted in the matter of another person's life?"

After giving the were-quetzal bird the yarn painting, Saltire stepped around the bentwood rocker, picked up a large banner at the foot of Paloma's Mexican Colonial oak queen-size bed, and took it over to a trio of opened recessed windows. Attaching each end of the banner to exterior hooks, he boldly displayed it across Moyocoyotzin. The banner was emblazoned with the Celestino family Crest.

At its "Chief Field" or center was an indigo blue Mayan Hunab Ku Butterfly encapsulated in a chestnut brown bulls-eye. In a second concentric circle in silver were two emerald-green and red Quetzal birds facing one another. "Speech Scrolls" at the tip of each beak indicated the utterance of five Mayan glyphs. The characters creating a five-pointed star in the space designated "Helmut," spoke to the Celestino family's motto:

Transcending fear the serpent learns to fly,
Quickening her soul retrieval.

A third concentric band, a narrow ribbon of jade, was adorned with eight purple St. Andrew's Crosses (X) separated by eight golden brown eagles in various stages of flight. Having the symbols evenly spaced around the perimeter suggested inner strength and containment.

Above the family crest, complemented by a purple field of canvas, was the name CAELESTIS—Latin for "Heavenly." Below the family crest fixed a reference to the eternal nature of *Seminal Being:* ET IN SAECULA SAECULORUM—Latin for "A World Without End."

On the "Dexter," right side, and "Sinister," left side, of the family crest, were six male jaguars, three per side stacked horizontally. The two Jaguars at the bottom of each side were in shades of black, accentuated by black paw prints. The middle jaguars were orange imprinted with black rosettes. The two remaining jaguars at the top were were-jaguars in tawny-yellow with large black rosettes signifying a successful integration of the soul.

The glyphs above the were-jaguars to the right represented the creator deities: Quetzalcoatl and Tlaloc. The glyphs above the were-jaguars to the left were depictions of the transformative deities: Tezcatlipoca and Chalchiuhtotolin. Each of the glyphs symbolized the journey of the birth, life, death, and rebirth of the eternal *Seminal Being*—Godly Soul.

Paloma Celestino's soul, as the were-quetzal bird, leaned forward in preparation. She was to decipher the meaning depicted in the Huichol Yarn Painting inspired by my Prophetic Resurrection Hymn *In the Presence of the Lord of Dharma.* All that remained of the hymn was the middle section. Chapters One and Three were mysteriously absent when the copy of the codex was given to Saltire by his adopted father, Lucius Antonio Celestino.

The yarn painting consisting of brightly colored yarn pressed into warm beeswax spread on a plywood panel began to vibrate in the claws of the were-quetzal bird.

Paloma's Godly Soul spoke in a low, deliberate tone, first the title of the hymn and the chapter head, then the title of the middle part and the four stanzas with a refrain that followed:

"IN THE PRESENCE OF THE LORD OF DHARMA
CHAPTER TWO
SEMINAL BEING: MIRRORS OF THE GODS

Eagle Knights to summon Dancing Movement,
Loathsome creatures signal terror.
Mirrors of the Gods will too intervene;
The Morning Star is ill at ease.

Beholden is the Master of Intent,
To the fate of the one transfixed.
Immutable Wind, living memory,
Restores what has been forgotten.

I am a rock in the River of Light,
Emerging as Falling Waters.
Transcending fear, the serpent learns to fly,
Quickening her soul retrieval.

Now the Door of Life opens up to all,
Toltec Atlantean Warrior.
Let my presence transform your body and mind,
I AM that you shall be reformed.

Refrain: As Archetypal Creative Order,
Retrieving souls is our passion.
We are the archrivals of ill-intent,
Our kind will not be extinguished."

At the close of the quatrain, Saltire leaned against a double-door cypress shutter and said kindly, "I am that you fulfill your Soul's Intended Future."

In the distance, the cadence of a single drum was echoing from a volcanic cliffside sheltering a cenote. The well used in ancient Mayan-Toltec human and animal scarifies still harbored some sacrificial bones and precious artifacts. The reverb made its way into the bedroom, filling the space. Saltire disengaged from the open windows and left his sister's bedroom without another word. He then hastily retreated past the gallery of Huichol Yarn Paintings and backed down the front sweeping limestone stairway.

Clouds outfitted in fiery tones announced the arrival of another day's invention. Lake Pátzcuaro, the place where life and death converged and spirits reawakened at dusk, reflected the surrounding wetlands and cattails. As shadowy formations stretched across the face of irrigation canals, a young Mexican woman, wearing a yellow-ochre cropped linen jacket and matching pants, was loading baskets of fresh produce onto a horse-drawn cart. Attending the vegetable garden was Xochitl Ixbalanque Celestino, age twenty-nine. She was accompanied by her one-year-old Belgian Malinois named Ceiba. The female was in training to become a search and rescue dog for the family.

Overhead and within earshot, the were-quetzal bird flew counterclockwise—which set in motion the "karmic debt removal" process to take place later that evening. Xochitl watched the were-quetzal bird's flight pattern twice around, and then spoke into existence the clearing into which the Toltec Secret Eagle Knight Council would be listening from.

"I am, that WE shall be reformed," Xochitl decreed.

Stationed alongside a large bas-relief fountainhead adorned with Ceiba trees, jaguars, eagles, and human skulls, was an electric dirt bike: license plate number PARVULO X 20-15. The were-quetzal bird whooshed by the dirt bike, through a grove of mature pine trees, and into the belly of a volcanic cave dwelling.

CHAPTER TWO

Life as Art

Twenty-one years earlier, Noelle, age thirty-six, was deposited at Cheryl Bekenkol's modern tri-level storybook home located off Laurel Canyon, in the Hollywood Hills of California. The 1950s white stucco estate sat diagonally on a two-and-a-half acre parcel with its Mexican Colonial front door facing southwest. In contrast, to the expansive vista looking out over the valley, the house was hemmed in on three sides by overgrown terraced gardens encased in a five-foot-high stonewall. A complimentary prickly desert landscape ran parallel with Cheryl's private driveway and acted as an additional natural barrier. The second-story picture window overlooked a two-car garage with a significant parking area. Cheryl, who enjoyed basking in the limelight, had the reputation of throwing outlandish dinner parties that led to sleepovers from time-to-time. Sufficient parking signaled "more-the-merrier."

Noelle graciously thanked her neighbors, Mr. and Mrs. Joffy, and headed in the direction of the main entrance. A seemingly prudent American artist, Noelle wore her good looks and athletic physique the way a warrior wears his armor as a defense mechanism against mortal injury.

When Noelle reached the front gate, she jangled the metal galvanized gate bolt open and let herself onto the property. Where is Lily? Noelle thought to herself. She then proceeded to jog up the flagstone footpath in search of the four-year-old red and white Havanese.

"Lily, Where are you girl?" Noelle shouted.

Around and to the left side of the house, a faint whimpering caught Noelle's attention. Without hesitation, she ran through Cheryl's colorful rose garden, which overlooked the valley.

Exposed chicken wires attached to shredded pieces of papier-mâché were all that remained from Cheryl's early childhood.

Unwittingly, Cheryl was about to awaken the "Underworld." Her prefabricated pumpkin patch provided perfect hiding places for less than benevolent spirits, as I recall.

Earlier that morning, Cheryl had lined the inside of the pumpkins with wax paper and filled them to the brim with dog treats. It's a wonder that more animals hadn't thought to trespass and score a piece of candy. At some point, Lily, in her Halloween hoodie disguised as a turquoise-blue Narwhal, had gotten the unicorn-shaped tooth wedged inside one of the Halloween pumpkins. Try as she might, she was unable to uncoil the twisted horn from its eye socket.

Noelle quietly reassured the frantic pup that she was all right. She then reached inside her handbag and grabbed a set of keys. Only one object was required, it was her father's Swiss Army knife. In a flick-of-a-switch, Noelle freed Lily by slicing off the ensnared appendage. Noelle immediately inspected the dog for puncture wounds and broken limbs; fortunately, none were found.

Noelle had grown up in a household of animal trainers. Her father, Julien, was a K-9 Officer, and her mother, Francis, a professional Animal Communicator. Both her older siblings, Emilie and Douglas, worked at several animal shelters rescuing and retraining traumatized dogs and cats for adoption. Noelle had the uncanny gift of seeing the whereabouts of lost and/or injured animals and the know-how to relieve their critical situation with minimal effort.

Lily leaped into Noelle's arms, and the two advanced quickly over to Cheryl's house. The front doors to Cheryl's house were propped open with segments from the LA Times Saturday Morning newspaper dated October 29, 1994. Noelle caught her breath at the top of the stairs, hesitated, and then read the headline of the Travel section:

WILL WITCHES, GHOSTS, OR GUARDIANS
TAME THE STORM IN TIME?

Noelle responded as if the question was being posed to her. Speaking to herself, she misread the headline. "Will witches, ghosts, or guardians tame the storm inside?"

Pressing forward at the threshold, Noelle hollered, "Cheryl! Cheryl! Mrs. Bekenkol!"

Cheryl Vanzetti Bekenkol "Beloved, Advance, Cabbage Farmer," age fifty-two, was an only child of a distinguished land developer in Southern California. When she was born, Cheryl's parents established a four million dollar trust fund that provided her with a sense of entitlement.

Cheryl has never felt the burden imposed by financial restraints and consequently gives little weight to the needs of those around her. In her youth, she was considered a "showstopper," who was never in short supply of male suitors. As the years marched on, however, the three-time divorcee would have to rely on her wit and her reputation, as the perfect host, to win over new friends and secure old ones. Somewhat aware of her deprived sense-of-self, Cheryl spent the majority of her waking hours seeking comfort in purchasing unusual antiques from far away exotic lands.

Cheryl flew from around the corner, wearing a witch's costume, and proceeded to drop in Noelle's hand a heavy-duty measuring tape.

Reaching out to take hold of Lily, Cheryl barked, "Alright there lassie, let's get to it. I need this entire foyer measured, ASAP!"

Noelle reluctantly handed Lily over to her unappreciative and irresponsible guardian. Then, against her better judgment, she asked to be paid for the work completed the day before. Cheryl dismissed Noelle's request and headed in the direction of her botanical garden, to her immediate right and past the kitchen picture window. Magnificently festooned in Halloween ornaments and rose bushes, Cheryl successfully blocked the pumpkin patch below in a feeble attempt to shut out painful memories.

Accepting defeat, Noelle made a half-hearted attempt to measure the foyer surround before she walked into the nearby kitchen, removed a phone from its receiver, and dialed a friend. She appeared anxious and annoyed.

"If she does this to me one more time, I swear I'm going to have an F 'n come-apart! Yeah, it's me."

Before Noelle had time to respond to her friend's advice, she caught Cheryl looking at her through the set of French glass doors to the kitchen. Her voice began to escalate, "Okay—I will—Got to go!" Noelle placed the dial-up phone quickly back in its receiver.

Returning to the foyer surround, Noelle picked up an entry table along with a shoebox of Polaroids and headed toward a sunken living room enclosure—the heart of the house. A second later, Cheryl burst through the French glass doors, which caused Noelle to lose her footing on the shallow landing below.

"Here, give those to me!" Cheryl demanded as she set down her gardening shears on the kitchen counter, crossed the kitchen floor, and entered the sunken living room.

"Who were you just talking to, your boyfriend?" Cheryl asked.

Noelle waited for Cheryl to take the entry table and shoebox of Polaroids off her hands before she answered, "No, I don't have a boyfriend."

Cheryl confiscated the entry table and shoebox and then stormed through the sunken living room and into a guest room, leaving a trail of Polaroids on the carpet. Except for antiques, the bulk of the living room was furnished in pastel colors by Shabby Chic Boutique in Santa Monica, CA. When it came to décor, no one could say she didn't have style.

Cheryl pressed on, "Didn't you use to have a boyfriend?"

Noelle took in a deep breath, "Yep! He took me to 'the farthest part of the Rich Indies.' " (A Salem, MA Motto).

It seemed to me Cheryl Bekenkol went off-topic. Wasn't it Cheryl who caught her boyfriend in bed with her best friend on her twenty-first birthday and ran screaming from his apartment? Then wasn't it later that same day that she drove to another county to stay with her parents. As I recollect, the following week, her father moved all her belongings into his carriage house. Cheryl lived with her parents until she got married. Some would say her behavior was understandable. Upon closer examination, however, I would say she had it coming.

In an attempt to override her disgruntled disposition, Noelle re-entered the kitchen, poured herself a glass of lemonade, and turned on a small television sitting next to the pair of gardening shears. Plastered across the TV screen was a NEWS BULLETIN:

"WE INTERRUPT THIS PREVIOUSLY SCHEDULED
PROGRAM TO GIVE YOU THE LATEST UPDATE
ON THE STORM SURGE THAT IS
THREATENING THE PACIFIC SEABOARD."

A newswoman was at the forefront of the scene displayed on the TV screen. In the background, the disaster was unfolding, as 95 miles per hour winds ravished the Long Beach Shipyard in Southern California. Unbeknownst to the newswoman covering the story, her microphone was experiencing transmission problems. The station's cameraman, however, had been alerted to her audio malfunction and suggested she air the previously recorded video of the hurricane-force winds as they touched down along the Long Beach Shipyard. The newswoman looked relieved and did what he recommended. The previously recorded video followed a specific accident of a deliveryman right as it happened. Noelle, looking intrigued, kept her eyes glued to the TV.

Garbage cans were rolling, and streams of papers were swirling as seagulls struggled to find shelter. The heads of hundreds were lowered as men and women, longshoremen, and security personnel worked the loading docks, separating merchandise into various delivery trucks. Two longshoremen were joking around making fun of a deliveryman; it was their friend, an American Indian named "Moonlit Bear," who was in his mid-fifties. Suddenly, a gust of wind tripped Moonlit Bear, and he slipped off the loading dock, massive headboard in hand, and landed on the concrete below.

"Aah crap, Bear!" An old Stevedore hollered.

Pressed under the hand-carved Andean Condor headboard, Moonlit Bear was immobile; a gash was oozing blood from his hand.

"Get this thing off me!"

Quickly a group of longshoremen removed the headboard and carried Moonlit Bear into the onsite office. A Coppertone sign read: SOVEREIGN NATION FREIGHT CO—Native American Owned Since 1924.

The sound of a were-eagle's cry was recorded, "Kee! Kee! Kee!" The were-eagle dropped into view, played catch with a rock, and proceeded up the coastline.

Noelle left the kitchen when the local news station went to a commercial; then resumed measuring the foyer surround. As soon as she reached the threshold, the phone rang. Noelle watched Cheryl, out of the corner of her eye, as she scampered from the guest room into the master bedroom.

Cheryl circled the master bedroom, with the phone pressed tightly to one ear. The caller was notifying her that an accident involving one of the deliverymen had delayed the transfer of her one-of-a-kind antiques.

As soon as Cheryl hung up the phone, she attempted a telephone call to her exotic landscape designer, Octavio "Sally" Salvador Celestino "Eighth, Savor, Secret of Heaven," age forty-six. Octavio's physical appearance was enhanced by his tempered expression, dark hair, and tall stature. In contrast to the rest of the members of his immediate family, he preferred to communicate through a direct inquiry. Octavio was known to his community as a "Master of Intent" and as such, could both imagine and manifest from the final outcome.

It was 8:15 a.m., and the fog was wrapped partway up the Santa Monica Mountains in the small coastal city of Malibu, California. Inside his handcrafted 1980's hacienda, Octavio was stationed below and in front of a wall-mounted cordless speakerphone. Sitting in his hand-honed wooden chair, squeezed between a terra-cotta plaster wall and a rectangular kitchen table, he waited patiently while the operator reconnected him to his brother Saltire.

Saltire was standing outside on a raised wooden deck facing Banderas Bay in Puerto Vallarta, Mexico. His unique appearance was enhanced by his unruly black wavy hair and disquieting gleam in his eyes. From his antiquated boathouse named TA ESO "The Inner Things," he had a 180-degree view of the surrounding beachhead. On one hand, he propped up an old plaque depicting a family of mermaids. Paintbrush between his thumb and index finger, he was meticulously restoring Grandmother Mermaid's tail in the sea-foam-green paint. Saltire had positioned himself near a jimmy-rigged callbox fastened tightly to wood siding in anticipation of his brother's phone call. When the phone rang, he placed the brush behind his left ear.

Octavio informed Saltire of his updated travel arrangements; his voice was clearly heard through his brother's crude communication device.

"Saltire, you got a minute?"

"I can hear you just fine; go ahead," Saltire said.

Octavio rose, shouldered the wooden chair to a nearby spot under the kitchen table, and proceeded to pace back and forth in front of a wall-mounted speakerphone. He then informed Saltire that there had been a change of plans.

"I need you to book three flights from LAX into Puerto Vallarta for Monday . . . Yes, the 9:00 a.m. flight will do . . . No names as yet, I'll give them to you tonight . . . Hold on a second, I've got another call coming in, I think it's Bekenkol."

Octavio switched over and listened patiently as Cheryl told him of the delivery company's dilemma. He agreed that his assistance would make things go more smoothly and offered to stand in for the injured man. Octavio assured Cheryl that he would be leaving momentarily, after which, he clicked over and was back online with Saltire.

"I'm back!" Octavio said joyfully.

Saltire, with Mermaid family in hand, turned his head in the direction of Octavio's voice.

"Continue, Bro."

"Paloma flew in last night. Yeah, plumage 'n all. She found Quetzal Hunahpu's original codex in the Malibu Chamber. Oddly enough, the text was right where Immokalee had told great-grandfather it would be."

Saltire leaned into the speakerphone and asked, "Have you had an opportunity to see it?"

"Yes!"

"What's on the cover?"

"A glyph of "The Spirit of the Voice," Octavio said proudly.

"What a fiasco that was," Saltire emphasized. "First, she's accused of stealing the book, and then we never see her again."

"After the mudslides, I searched every inch of that cave but never found it," Octavio added.

"A *Seminal Being* ensepulchered within a sacred text has been known to cloak itself when under attack." Saltire surmised.

"Yep! That appears to be the case."

Octavio stopped in front of the speakerphone, and then flicked it to the off position while raising the cordless phone to his ear.

"Paloma must have an idea of the whereabouts of Immokalee's *Seminal Being* Soul. She wouldn't have made the trip otherwise," Octavio said assuredly.

"So Paloma is planning on taking you to 'an aspect' of the same *Seminal Being* Soul as Immokalee's this morning?" Saltire asked.

"For all I know, she's at Bekenkol's." Octavio chuckled.

With a string of mango slices balancing on an obsidian-tipped knife, Octavio had a sudden recollection, the main reason for his call.

"Hey, that reminds me. You'll need to drop by Rosita's Monday morning and get a letter from her. Look for the one with the butterfly insignia. Paloma's insisting that you deliver it at noon to our three indian friends. They'll be at the Parish of Guadeloupe; they're expecting you."

Saltire placed the mermaid plaque over the screened-in backdoor before asking, "Anything else?"

Octavio covered the phone's mouthpiece with the collar from his shirt, just long enough to clear his throat before responding.

"Just something to carry me the distance," Octavio said wistfully.

Saltire, with his lips just a few inches away from the voice box, pronounced unequivocally, "I'm seeing Cousin Victor on Sunday, and I'll get a bag of crystal charged remedies for you. Follow the bird, find the soul, and get it to Puerto Vallarta. I'll handle the rest."

Octavio clearly enrolled, expressed his thanks, dropped his cordless phone in its charger, and snatched a container of water from the refrigerator. Before leaving for Cheryl's, Octavio stopped and looked at himself in a wall mirror. Taking a swig of water, he moistened some flakes of dried blood crusting in the corners of his mouth. Wiping the area clean with his fingertips, he made his way out the side door, past a neglected horse stable and over to a 1990 Ford F-250 Extended Cab, white pick-up truck.

Octavio was born at the Celestino's Mayan-Toltec Estate on Lake Pátzcuaro, Michoacán, Mexico. His adolescence was spent in mimicry while observing the energy fields of sentient life forms alongside his two older sisters: Paloma Balam and Rosita Maria. Summers were, for the most part, spent at the Celestino's three-story Spanish B&B named Mar Casa De La Concha overlooking Banderas Bay in Puerto Vallarta, Mexico.

The fall of October, when he was eight years old, proved to be one of the most rewarding times of young Octavio's life. He met his half-brother, Saltire Daghda McKenna, for the very first time on Halloween night at the B&B. They greeted each other in brightly colored feathered costumes, denoting two significant aspects of the Toltec Deity Quetzalcoatl: Octavio was Feathered Serpent, the red-breasted green-tailed Quetzal Bird Deity, while Saltire was Blood-Jeweled Fowl, Long-Nose Turkey, with the black 'n white elephant-like trunk. That evening the two established a friendship that would forever transcend every ordeal and transgression.

In the summers spent playing by the Pacific Ocean with Saltire, Octavio broadened his understanding of energy to encompass both visible forms of ethereal light as well as invisible rarefied electro-magnetic fields. Octavio's father encouraged him to share his ability to perceive awareness directly with his half-brother. Octavio solidified his relationship with Saltire by introducing him to the Celestino's long-held relationship with Mayan/Toltec spiritual practices.

When Octavio and Saltire were teenagers, they spent their summers at their second cousin Victor Ruiz Celestino's horse ranch located inland in the hills of Tonala, Mexico. There they worked in the stables, trained horses to dance to Latin music, and expressed a keen interest in learning the ancient Art of Karmic Debt Removal and animal familiar shape-shifting. Under the tutelage of Victor, a renowned horse breeder in Central and North America, the two young men quickly excelled in the long-forgotten Magical Arts of Mesoamerica.

At age twenty, they expanded their spiritual development to include teachings from the "Chilam Balam"—three Huichol Indians and one Toltec Shaman residing in Old Town, Puerto Vallarta. Under their instruction they learned how to listen for, have access to, and assimilate "Silent Knowledge"—Universal wisdom that was transferred from the Milky Way, the generator, to Mother Earth's Sun, the receptacle/transistor. The knowledge was released through the Sun's flares, whose trajectories then comingled with the Earth's atmosphere. This allowed

Octavio and Saltire to perceive the fourth dimension and the Universal Laws of Causality and Creation; furnishing them with the tools to commune with God, the Prime Mover, directly.

By age twenty-six, Octavio experienced a quantum leap in his personal and professional life. His mother, Melita Eztli, age fifty-two, insisted he settle down and legitimize his relationship. He married his longstanding, pregnant girlfriend Maribel and legally adopted her illegitimate son Reynaldo, age three. Octavio labored six days a week as a landscaper working his way up the ranks to Forman and then Supervisor. At night he stretched canvases for his father Lucius Antonio's second love—family portraits in all manner of expression. By the age of thirty-three, he became Senior Designer and was responsible for twelve crews of six specialized landscapers throughout Central Mexico. The owner of the landscaping company was so impressed with Octavio's management and design capabilities that he established a landscaping business in Southern California for him to oversee.

Octavio moved his wife, Maribel, and their two young boys, Reynaldo, age ten, and Sergio, age six, to the most northwest community of Malibu, CA in 1981. Affordable housing was still available then, so he purchased a five-acre parcel and built a hacienda with an adjoining horse stable. His entire family flourished in their new environment until his wife Maribel, age thirty-nine, died in a car accident. On September 21, 1990, Maribel swerved to avoid hitting a neighbor's golden Labrador retriever and was struck by a Jeep head-on; she was declared dead at the scene of the accident. Octavio and the entire Celestino family were devastated by the news of Maribel's unexpected passing. The untimely nature of her death caused them to re-examine their core values and imaginings. What arose from the family's inquiry was a greater appreciation of the importance of cleansing the link of their traumatized rich past to free their everlasting *Seminal Being* Souls.

Cheryl was wiggling out of her witch's costume when she approached Noelle who was finishing up measuring the foyer surround. Cheryl relished in getting other people to do things for her free of charge. Their loss was her gain. She only contributed to others if it somehow benefited her directly.

"He'll be here within the hour," Cheryl reported as she picked up the folding ladder and shuffled it over and into the pantry closet.

Noelle curious as to who he is, asked, "Who's so important that you don't want to offend?"

"Sally, that's who!"

Noelle followed Cheryl into the kitchen and listened.

"Apparently, there's been an accident with the delivery man. They're one man short, so Sally has agreed to come and help me."

"Oh, so is this what this guy does for a living?" Noelle asked.

"Not hardly; he's a landscape designer who's done quite well for himself."

"He's good at what he does, is he?"

"He's the best!"

And with that, Cheryl whipped off her Halloween costume, rolled it up into a ball, and then stuffed it in the corner on the top shelf of the pantry.

"It's rather sad," Cheryl continued from within the pantry. "He told me his wife was killed in a head-on collision. It had something to do with a dog!"

Noelle lowered her eyes and looked uncomfortable.

Cheryl then proceeded to tell Noelle that if she wanted to hear more about her friend, Sally, she would have to join her while she gets dressed. "I can't be seen hanging out in my undies," Cheryl said, striking a pose.

It didn't much matter either way to Noelle. She had come for services rendered and had been dismissed. Noelle was held hostage to Cheryl's whimsical desires until the time Cheryl paid-up.

Cheryl led Noelle through the sunken living room enclosure and into the master bedroom. The room was packed to the hilt in one-of-a-kind antiques from all around the globe. Cheryl took to her spacious walk-in closet as Noelle respectfully waited for her on a Fantasy Shell Vanity from Paris, mid 1700s. Her voice could easily be heard from anywhere in the bedroom; it seemed to travel effortlessly, as if in an echo chamber. Lifting a smart looking outfit from the rack, Cheryl proceeded to share firsthand knowledge of Octavio.

"To hear Sally tell it, you'd think he was 'Old Soul.' "

Noelle looking puzzled, asked, "So what did he say that made you think that?"

"He said that his family goes back over 1,000 years and that they—"

"Mine can be traced back over 6,000 years," Noelle interjected. "What of it?"

"Let me finish. I hate it when you interrupt me!"

Noelle stood up and walked over to a bay window located just to the right of the French Rococo vanity.

Cheryl emerged from the walk-in closet and stood in the doorjamb wearing a pair of green silk slacks and holding a red turtleneck up to her chest.

"Apparently, they were the founders of an ancient secret cult in Mexico," said Cheryl.

Noelle glancing back over her shoulder, asked, "What? Which cult?"

"I don't remember. It had some funny-sounding name."

"Well, what did Sally say that they did?"

"Sally said his ancestors practiced the teachings of Christ Jesus long before Cortez and the Spanish invasion brought Christianity to the Americas."

Noelle shrugged her shoulders and winced. Turning back around, she gazed out the window.

Cheryl, noticeably disappointed with Noelle's lack of interest in her story, ended the discourse in favor of a business matter.

"Hop-to-it, girlie!" Cheryl insisted. "You can get into all that when you meet him. The doors still need to be double-sealed!"

Beautiful white sand was creating singing sounds as a Mexican family, consisting of several teenage children and four adults dragged palm leaf baskets filled with white miniature lights. They passed Saltire as he stood on the deck of his boathouse. They were on their way to an abandoned burned-out beach house on the shoreline in Banderas Bay in Puerto Vallarta, Mexico. Saltire leaped off the deck, overshot an ocean canoe perched on support beams, and followed after the Mexican clan.

A self-made multimillionaire, through importing and exporting customized motorcycles and luxury cars, Saltire is an artificer reinventing life from his highest vibration. If asked what his greatest accomplishment to date is, he would reply, "My greatest work of art is my eight-year-old daughter Xochitl."

About fifty yards away, Saltire spotted the arms and torso of his daughter and a small boy mimicking swimming movements in front of a large picture window. The five-year-old boy screamed when he saw the Mexican family nearing the burned-out beach house and ran over to them. Saltire's little girl, Xochitl Ixbalanque Celestino, "Queen, Parvulo flower, Secret of Heaven," waited patiently for her father. Xochitl was an enchanting eight-year-old Mexican girl. Adorable and unpretentious, she had large brown eyes that drew you in, framed by black curls that complimented her pixie image.

Saltire, now within range, yelled up to his daughter, "Xochitl, it's time for your fitting!"

Xochitl stopped abruptly, turned her head, and yelped, "Papi!" She then scampered across an embankment and over to her father's side. Xochitl had the physical hand deformity called Ectrodactyly, commonly known as "lobster claw" syndrome. Except for her family, the little girl kept her hands hidden until she felt she could trust the person in question.

Octavio's pick-up truck skated by an elementary school playground and trailed with it the attention of the were-eagle, Paloma.

As Octavio approached his meeting with Cheryl, he noticed the were-eagle and softly remarked, "There seems to be a divine plan unfolding."

A true force of nature, Paloma Chilam Celestino, "Peaceful dove, Jaguar prophet, Secret of Heaven," age fifty-four, was the matriarch of the Celestino family. Four years earlier, in 1990, at the request of her mother, Melita Eztli Celestino, Paloma has also appointed the gatekeeper of the Celestino family's Mayan-Toltec artifacts: Prophetic Huichol Yarn Paintings, sacred codices, musical instruments, and other family treasures. At that time, Paloma had no plans of marrying her longtime boyfriend of eleven years, Edmundo. This was, in part, due to the sudden exit of Xochitl's mother, Leah. After Leah walked out on Saltire and abandoned Xochitl, Paloma was proclaimed the other official legal guardian of her, aside from Saltire. The private event took place at his Mayan-Toltec Estate on Lake Pátzcuaro.

It was during her stay at the Saltire's estate that Paloma mastered the shamanic ability to shape-shift and create a body-double in the form of a were-eagle. In an altered state of consciousness, Paloma encouraged her ethereal body to lift off as-it-were and shape-shift into the were-eagle. The were-eagle was for a short time a holographic 3-D aspect of Paloma's animal spirit, while her physical body rested peacefully in her bedroom at Saltire's Estate. Shape-shifting granted Paloma the ability to examine a situation from a different perspective and gave her a new approach to an age-old spiritual dilemma.

The wind was gaining force and blowing leaves and empty water bottles about. Noelle was outside Cheryl's storybook home preparing the series of solid oak French doors for their final coat of sealer. Noelle's mood was expressionless as two Mexican gardeners sent lingering glances in her direction. She was wearing a pink T-shirt, tightly fitted black jeans, complemented by a pair of Sperry Top-Siders. This outfit closely resembled the one she damaged as a child.

When she was only nine years old, Noelle had been sexually assaulted by a known juvenile delinquent in the neighborhood. She managed to escape with just a broken zipper, torn shirt, and bruised left shoulder. The attack, unfortunately, did leave an impression and make her question whether she was safe. Noelle had been told time and again to tell someone where she was going before stepping out of the house. That particular morning, she left without a word and ventured into Jim Franco's backyard to climb a maple tree. When Noelle returned home, she lied about her injuries. "I fell from a tree; it's no big deal!" she told her mother. In turn, her mother told the entire family what had happened and to not be concerned. This would be the first of many lies Noelle would tell herself so as to deflect the pain of being afraid.

Octavio pulled up alongside the curb, caught sight of Noelle, and was instantly intrigued by the lack of interest she was showing the young men. Stepping out of his pick-up truck, Octavio was warmly greeted by the Mexican landscapers; together, the three of them walked over to Noelle. Distracted by the young men and their persistent flirting, Noelle did not see Octavio slither around a pillar and out of sight. Rolling a smooth rock across the top of his fingers, Octavio watched as Noelle failed to combat the young men's advances.

Frustrated and annoyed, Noelle yanked her canvas book bag and paint tray up off the ground and quickly disappeared inside Cheryl's house.

Octavio spoke to the young men who were his sons, Reynaldo Antonio Celestino, age twenty-three, and Sergio Mateo Celestino, age nineteen. Reynaldo Antonio Celestino had a broken nose, which was upstaged by the signature scar that ran the length of his left cheek to his chin. He received the scar in a street fight. While Sergio Mateo was getting wailed-on, Reynaldo stepped in to stop another guy from potentially killing him. He loved his little brother the way his father loved him; he organized his free time around what they enjoyed doing together. Generally speaking, he was an attentive and hard-working young man; the backbone of his father's landscape business.

Sergio Mateo Celestino was a fun-loving, easy-going, "don't give me more than I can handle" kind of guy. He was the jokester in the family and loved making people laugh, especially his older brother Reynaldo Antonio. The girls liked him because he was cute, fun to be with, and considerate. Sergio found girls to be very entertaining, but as yet, he had not fallen in love.

After discussing the landscaping job briefly, Octavio said goodbye to his sons and walked directly over to a commercial delivery truck. The delivery truck was attempting miserably to back into the driveway. A blur of red and green came screaming in Octavio's direction—Cheryl was objecting to the deliveryman's choice of a parking spot.

"Stop! Not there, Sally!" Cheryl protested. "It's going to block my car!"

"Oh, I wasn't aware; you plan on going somewhere?" Octavio calmly responded.

Cheryl looked away, embarrassed, and said, "Well, no, not exactly."

Octavio gestured to the driver to leave the delivery truck where it was.

Sipping on a glass of lemonade, Noelle strolled over to Cheryl. In her other hand, she carried a glass she had prepared for her client, Mrs. Cheryl Bekenkol.

Octavio took his eyes off Cheryl and rested them gently on Noelle. Cheryl whipped her head around to see who was behind her. When she realized that it was Noelle, she readdressed Octavio and shamelessly attempted to impress him with a quote from a book she had memorized.

"Human power is limited only by the poverty of its imagination and the pettiness of its will."

In a gesture of one-upmanship, Noelle proceeded to walk past Cheryl and offered the glass of lemonade to Octavio. In her best impersonation of Cheryl, Noelle was more than happy to state the author's true identity. "Why that'd be William Wynn Westcott."

Noelle was familiar with Cheryl's obsession with memorizing quotes from somewhat well-known figures. Noelle disapproved of how Cheryl slighted her at every opportunity and found it amusing when she had a chance to identify the correct source before her client.

Octavio accepted the refreshing drink and told Noelle to stay. He then dismissed Cheryl after they had agreed that her shipment would best be stored in the garage.

Cheryl quickly returned to her home in response to the phone ringing.

While running back inside, she hollered. "If you'd like some more lemonade, Noelle will get it for you."

CHAPTER THREE

Wounded Heart

oelle and Octavio were alone in the commercial delivery truck container, removing shipping boxes blocking the massive hand-carved Andean Condor headboard. Octavio had begun a line of questions designed to stir-up Noelle's emotions and uncover the source of her suffering. He asked Noelle about her family and where she came from. "I was born and raised in Lexington, MA; I'm what you might call a product of the fifties." Noelle said.

Noelle's parents, Julien Chisholm Le Havre Leandre and Galilani Francis Degataga, had ancestral roots that went as far back as to the Native Americans of the late Desert Archaic Period (1200 BC–AD 100). Julien's side of the family was a combination of African slave from the West Indies, Arawak Indian from the Amazon Jungle in South America, and the comingling of the Quallatown Cherokee Indian and French Huguenot from the Great Smoky Mountain Range in North Carolina. Galilani, on the other hand, was a mixture of the Hohokam, Cherokee, and Northern Toltecs from Alta, CA to Arizona. After WWII, both Julien and Galilani's parents, the Leandre's and the Degataga's, moved from Lexington, MA, and settled in the seaport of Salem, MA. Shortly after graduating from high school, they became assistant managers of a home healthcare business catering to Salem's wealthy seafaring folk. It was but a short time before the two fell in love, married, and began a family.

At the stroke of midnight on December 31, 1958, Noelle was born. Her mother, Galilani, spent New Year's Eve icebound in a ski lodge in Killington, VT. The Leandre family was staying with the son of one of their parents' healthcare clients when Galilani's water broke. Fortunately, Dr. Richard Sniggler was nearby inspecting the medical facilities at the new Killington ski resort and assisted in the delivery. Noelle was the youngest of three. Emilie Marie, seven years her elder, and Douglas Thomas, two years her senior, both exhibited displeasure over her arrival. In response, she learned how to occupy herself and keep out of trouble by playing with her troll dolls, plastic toy horses, coloring books, and pick-up-sticks. As a preteen, Noelle was not particularly close to either sibling and much-preferred playing with her friends over tedious family excursions—someone inevitably forgets to bring something they need, so they have to return home and start again. This would prove to be a valuable coping mechanism for Noelle; she was very capable of starting something over with fresh eyes and a positive outlook.

When Noelle reached high school, she distinguished herself as a standout mural artist in the public school district of Salem, MA. She received a scholarship to a prestigious East Coast university. After graduating from Pratt University's School of Art and Design in Brooklyn, NY, she moved into a third-story attic apartment in a Victorian home in Lexington, MA. Within a week, Noelle turned the nondescript one-bedroom living space into an art studio featuring her abstract charcoal renderings and 18th-century pastoral murals. Through word-of-mouth, she launched a successful business that endured twelve years. Then on November 1, 1991, Noelle moved cross-country to Los Angeles, CA, in an attempt to escape from her failed relationship with ex-fiancé Avery Emmett Millstone.

Octavio smiled and then asked if Noelle was married.

"Second time today, he's come up," she grumbled. "No, I'm not married. I was engaged once, but that ended abruptly with no chance of reconciliation."

Noelle's mood was becoming melancholy. She set her empty glass of lemonade down and said, "It's why I'm in this 'state.' "

Despite her innate ability as an artist, Noelle was weak in spirit; she had succumbed to a modest and disingenuous way of relating to herself and others. She had forsaken her desire to know and experience the mystery that sustained life in exchange for a life motivated by obligation and fear. Most disturbing, she continued to allow herself to remain stifled and oppressed by the limiting views others had of her. It was apparent that Noelle's demeanor was still responding to traumatic events that had left her both acting and feeling disillusioned with life.

Octavio, still tugging at the chain fastened to Noelle's heartstrings, sang, "Ahh, the wounded heart, the one that never sees his part, in his own demise."

Noelle turned her back on Octavio to avoid his line of questioning. Octavio took notice of a deep scar on the back of her neck and blew on it.

"Someone catch you off guard?" Octavio asked.

Sounding perturbed, Noelle said, "No! Why?"

Octavio leaned in for a closer look and whispered, "Gotcha!"

Noelle's body ghouled-up as the color in her face turned to ash.

"Tell me, what's a brown recluse doing in New England?"

"Salem."

"This is the mark of a rogue and his lover," he speculated.

Noelle's breathing became shallow and sporadic.

"What do you suppose became of those two?"

Noelle's legs began to wobble uncontrollably. She jetted out her arms to stabilize her body and grabbed onto Octavio's arm for support.

Octavio's keen sense of underlining truths either put people at ease or on edge. The mere inquiry into her ex-fiancé, Avery Emmett Millstone, caused Noelle to be transported back in time.

Noelle's 1994 *Flashback Sequence* began with her standing at the backend of the delivery truck. The year was 1990, and she was in the throes of a near-death experience on Halloween night. Noelle was being cared for by the Thorndike's at their two-story historical Federal-style brick manor in Lexington, MA. Mr. and Mrs. Thorndike were dressed in 18th-century clad regalia—Prosper was William Blake, the poet, and Sophie, his wife, was Prosper's wife, Catherine.

A plateful of white candles from inside the parlor shed light on a lowdown invalid character. Dripping sweat and hunched over a footstool, Noelle had seen better days.

"Come, let's get her over to the bed." Sophie raised concern to Prosper. "We certainly don't want her to wind up face-first on the floor!"

Noelle was escorted over to a cast-iron canopy bed by Sophie and Prosper and immediately fell victim to a bacterial infection ragging havoc on her body, mind, and soul. Sophie then lowered Noelle onto the guest bed and saw the red, inflamed spider bite. She knew its origin immediately.

"She's been bitten by a recluse," Sophie concluded. "Michael Jean, stop what you're doing and get my IV drip from the pantry, then get me some of that "blue blood" we keep in the small freezer in the tack room. Go right quick!" Sophie said. "This girl's spirit is leavin' us!"

Octavio was positioned face-to-face with Noelle. He was looking at her ethereal body, her aura field of energy in the fourth dimension. Noelle's entire physicality reflected the way she looked on the evening of her near-death experience—that of a tawny-yellow were-jaguar with large black rosettes. Octavio believed he had identified an archetypal divine aspect within Noelle's nature. This aspect was that of the *Seminal Being* Soul of an ancient Toltec Atlantean Warrior who lived over 1,000 years ago. Quetzal Hunahpu had stirred inside Noelle and was vying for dominance.

Octavio called out to the appearance by its sacred name, Chilam Balam?"

I remembered vividly the Chilam Balam. They were Mayan and Toltec sacerdotal priests—interpreters of messages from the Gods that appeared as four were-jaguars or four shamans. When Noelle did not respond as he had anticipated, Octavio transferred the gift of Intent from his ethereal body—a 4-D holographic image of himself to her. In doing so, he was able to awaken in Noelle a spiritual process called Karmic Debt Removal-soul retrieval—the Self-Correcting Principle. This was to be the first of seven initiations into the Toltec Secret Eagle Knight Council that Noelle would undergo, as an active member, before 2015.

Noelle's 1990 flashback became a real living nightmare. Peering out from the dimly lit room was Sophie managing the IV drip mixed with the Horseshoe crab's blue blood. In the flickering candlelight, Sophie lowered herself onto a chair stationed next to Noelle and removed a handful of loosely compiled parchments. Each sheet of paper identified with a logo illustration—an emerald-green androgynous humanoid. As she rummaged through the parchment, a Polaroid of Noelle, Avery Emmett Millstone, and his best friend Blake Samuel Parris fell onto her lap; everyone in the picture was laughing and seemed to be of good cheer. A black face with two yellow bands across it seemed to be focused on the three in the photo's background. Sophie paid no attention to the mysterious entity and placed her entire focus on Avery and Blake.

Sophie looked at the photo and said, "I know these boys; I see them at the Farmers' Market every Saturday getting handouts. Don't tell me she's gotten herself mixed-up with these two?"

With no time to spare, Sophie initiated a time-honored treatment designed to identify Noelle's spiritual affiliation and her attacker. To accomplish this, Sophie first evoked what she perceived to be one of Noelle's greatest allies—"Silent Knowledge."

> *"Silent Knowledge reveals her affliction,*
> *Rise in spirit God-Loving Souls.*
> *Unleash the denizen at twelve tonight,*
> *Dispel the presence of this bite."*

Prosper was standing in the farthest corner of the quest room kitty-corner to where Sophie was seated. His image was reflected in a floor-to-ceiling mahogany English Country Cheval Mirror. Sophie waved Prosper away from the mirror as she stared intensely into its surface. There before her, disclosed in the mirror, was Noelle's face marked in black rosettes.

Concerned by what he saw, Prosper said to his wife, "Careful dear. My God, what's she doing?"

"Noelle is recovering from the flesh-eating bacterial infection brought on by a brown recluse spider bite," Sophie assured her husband.

Noelle shifted her position as the black rosettes on her face became more pronounced. Sophie responded as if hearing a voice inside her head; she then said out loud her interpretation of the events that transpired earlier that evening.

> *"Casting doubts born from false testimony,*
> *The witches, Millstone and Parris,*
> *Conjured up the spider that locks down speech,*
> *Adding insult to injury."*

Suddenly, a loud fluttering of birds caused Noelle to raise her eyes again. She had returned to her original Recapitulation in Process in 1994. She was now standing on the delivery truck-loading ramp alternating back-and-forth slightly between realities. Noelle held her head up with one of her hands. She began to groan; not realizing Octavio was standing nearby.

"I feel sick!" Noelle said to herself.

Octavio reached around Nicole from behind and handed her his open container of water. "Nausea always accompanies hidden truths," he said playfully.

While Noelle was taking a sip of water, she noticed something unusual moving in front of her and shivered. "What on earth is that?" she asked.

Noelle pointed to a bright, emerald-green, low-riding cloud blanketing an old Mesquite tree. Octavio accompanied Noelle and made sure she was stable. Looking up at the cloud, he slowly descended the loading ramp, and sauntered over to the great-grandfather Mesquite tree.

"Take a break; I'll see you in twenty," Octavio yelled back to Noelle.

CHAPTER FOUR

The Chamber of Mirrors

Octavio saw Noelle Intaglio Leandre some twenty-one years into her future. It was November 1, 2015, and she was a modern-day Mayan/Toltec Spiritual Warrior. Noelle, age fifty-seven, was out by a cenote—a sacred pool—protected by a volcanic cliff and aviary. She was leaning peacefully up against a limestone pillar supporting a palapa when Baile Movimiento, Dancing Movement, the divine messenger of the archetypal Toltec Deity Ometeotl/Moyocoyotzin, appeared. The emerald-green alloy of spirit, animal, and human natures walked under a barrel-vaulted archway and gracefully slipped into the pool. Noelle remained in a deep meditative state as a watery plasma-like substance continually redefined Dancing Movement's distinct geometric-like markings. In the distance, an imposing black cloud began to obscure a majestic sunset. Without warning, Dancing Movement rose up out of the Cenote and walked over to Noelle. With a tap of a forefinger on her forehead, he/she informed Noelle, via mental telepathy, that the Toltec Secret Eagle Knight Council was requesting her presence in the Chamber of Mirrors.

Noelle leaped into action and began ringing a large brass bell three times. She then charged past the accompanying gardens and headed swiftly into Saltire's terra-cotta Mayan-Toltec Estate enriched with jaguar and eagle limestone cartouches. Making her way up the sweeping front stairway, past a series of ten Huichol Yarn Paintings, hung symmetrically on whitewashed plaster walls; she entered the master bedroom at the end of the hallway.

Outside Xochitl Ixbalanque Celestino, now age twenty-nine was leading Noelle's Classic Gray Dun Andalusia stallion, named Lexicon, from out of the horse stables. Noelle reemerged from the estate wearing her riding gear while holding in her right hand a papier-mâché Nagual Spirit Costume—an eight-pointed Mayan Hunab Ku Butterfly breastplate with an obsidian mirrored back-plate. Taking hold of the reins in her left hand, she mounted her horse Lexicon. She then tied the Spirit Costume tightly around her waist so that the mirror was facing backward. Noelle quickly opened wide a brown leather bag. She dipped a were-eagle quill into a gypsum clay mixture and then stippled a line drawing of a Toltec Atlantean Warrior glyph across her face. Now marked with the gypsum clay mixture made from earth and sacred plants, Noelle took on the role of a modern-day Mayan/Toltec Warrior and prepared to reveal her affiliation to the Council.

Peering down at Xochitl, Noelle asked, "I've failed them, haven't I?"

"Not as yet!" Xochitl replied.

Tracing a circle around Xochitl, Noelle shouted up at the foreboding sky, "INTENT!"

The black cloud broke apart as thousands of pieces tumbled to the ground. Lexicon jumped out of the circle, leaped across a river tributary, and headed in the direction of silver bursts of light. Lightly trampling on adjoining irrigation ditches, the horse and Noelle raced into a mammoth-sized zigzag lightning bolt.

The Chamber of Mirrors was moments away from being activated. Seven members of the Toltec Secret Eagle Knight Council entered the belly of the volcanic cave at Saltire's estate on horseback. Traditional Mayan-Toltec Nagual Spirit Masks made of papier-mâché along with complimenting costumes disguised their true identities. (The seven members on their way to the Chamber of Mirrors on November 1, 2015, were: Octavio, Saltire, Xochitl, Sergio, Reynaldo, Dahlia, and Cousin Victor.) After dismounting, the group moved quickly along a narrow corridor.

Octavio's son Reynaldo, now middle-aged, said to his Cousin Dahlia, age fifty. "Thirteen years of her ineptitude has really managed to put us at a disadvantage. Spirit may have chosen her, but if I'd been my father, I'd have dismissed her long ago!"

Victor Ruiz Celestino "Conqueror, Renown, Secret of Heaven," an elderly gentleman, said in agreement, "Esta Bien! Unless she's able to shift her perception and distill the oneness of Source, we will all become like those who came before us; indentured servants to Smoking Mirror."

As the seven members of the Council approached the Chamber of Mirrors' entrance, the circular floor directly in front of them began to spin counter-clockwise—a movement that allowed for retrograde time travel. Rising from the center of the spinning floor Baile Movimiento, Dancing Movement, made his/her grand entrance; Noelle was close behind. With no time to waste, Dancing Movement, Noelle, and the seven Council members descended upon the Chamber of Mirrors. On the back wall was an impressive floor to ceiling scrying mirror made from obsidian lava rocks, which permitted time and space travel into the fourth dimension.

Dancing Movement moved first into position while Noelle and the seven members quietly took their places, forming a Tetraktys—a ten-point pyramid devised by the Greek philosopher Pythagoras to symbolize the Cosmos. From the fourth dimension, he/she spoke softly.

"I share with you what the great Milky Way has shown us: Life evolves from pre-existing life; incarnated prior lifetimes preempt our present existence. The source of all eternal life is the Living Soul—the *Seminal Being* Soul—who comes to us through 'The Spirit of the Voice.'"

Dancing Movement's introduction was suddenly interrupted when Paloma's *Seminal Being* Soul, as the were-quetzal bird morphed through the obsidian scrying mirror embedded in the bedrock. Tucked securely under the bird's wing was a Prophetic Huichol yarn painting. Before accepting the tenth position in the Tetraktys, the were-quetzal bird delivered the Huichol yarn painting to Noelle.

Noelle, in the point position, placed the Huichol yarn painting at her feet and then raised her arms, forming a Saint Andrews Cross. The X shape posture in a Mayan/Toltec Recapitulation Guided Tour created a human gesture of emotional equivalence and temperance, allowing the individual to transcend fear and awaken Silent Knowledge held within one's Intent/Spirit/Will. Eyes closed, face and octagon quartz crystal necklace to the stars, Noelle surrendered to the design of a seventh level initiation into the Toltec Secret Eagle Knight Council.

Without warning, the scrying mirror began to ripple and crack, spraying specks of silver particles on the surrounding obsidian walls. The effect caused the reflected surface to shake and form images of current global events within its surface. Noelle bowed her torso exposing the Toltec Atlantean Warrior obsidian mirrored back-plate fastened to her Spirit costume, toward a sky-opening in the cave. Within seconds, the present-day turmoil of 2015 was replaced with newsworthy events during each previous year.

Stopping abruptly on October 29, 2007, the mirrored walls reflected images of the cataclysmic torrential rains that submerged eighty percent of the Tabasco, Mexico. Noelle, now age forty-nine, and the entire Celestino family were assisting in the rescue efforts on their 20,000-acre cocoa plantation nestled between a mountain range and a serpentine river. Paloma, closer to seventy, tumbled into the raging river while saving her niece, Xochitl, age twenty-one, from drowning in a nearby sinkhole. Paloma survived the ordeal by shape-shifting into a were-eagle and catapulting herself into the sky. Once she pierced through the clouds, she shape-shifted into a larger than life were-quetzal bird—an angelic messenger.

On the morning of November 1, 2007, Noelle was seen being taken into a volcanic cave dwelling high on a mountain summit by Saltire, age fifty-nine. There she was instructed to trust her intuition and identify aspects of her soul that she felt were interfering with her thoughts.

With full authority, Saltire instructed the bruised and battered initiate, "Noelle, your soul's intended future is afoot. Keep in mind what you are willing to complete, you won't be required to repeat."

Octavio's Prophetic Waking Dream, of 2015, continued. The obsidian scrying mirror in the Chamber of Mirrors revealed Noelle's failed attempt at the Seventh Level Initiation and rite of passage on the eve of November 1, 2007. Inside the obsidian cave-dwelling, Noelle converted the ten-pointed Tetraktys into ten inverted triangles. She crowned the nine other inverted triangles housing the Council members. Together they formed one vast pyramid 3-D infrastructure. Dressed in rain-soaked attire, the Toltec Secret Eagle Knight Council members attempted to engage Noelle in a line of questions designed to obtain the truth about her *Seminal Being* Soul.

Noelle still resisted; she refused to acknowledge what she had thought for some time—my soul is somehow connected to my Great Aunt Immokalee Awinita Chisholm (1879-1939), who died at the age of sixty from a "wounded heart."

After a few moments, Noelle was asked to step out of her designated position and wait for the Council members outside. Noelle conceded and headed over to the mouth of the cave. She had failed and would not be given another opportunity till November 1, 2015.

"Yes! Yes! We are all aware of what happened." The were-quetzal bird said definitively. "I'm stopping these proceedings because the safety of our community has been compromised. The Stars have revealed there's an intruder! Eight years without incident, how unfortunate it is that on the eve of her Seventh Level Initiation, we face our greatest threat. Smoking Mirror—Lord of Ancestral Memory—was sighted this morning rummaging through the Akashic Records. I suspect he was looking for Immokalee's 'artist book' inspired by Quetzal Hunahpu."

"How is this possible considering we are the Gatekeepers to the 'Library of Souls?' " Xochitl asked.

"How this came to be is not the question we ought to be asking, but rather how do we proceed!" Victor said.

Saltire looking at Noelle, said, "I will do my best to hold him harmless in the matter of your life."

"We must be vigilant!" Victor continued.

"And our Karmic Debt?" Xochitl asked. "What's going to happen to us?"

Octavio, emotionally upset, summed it up, "If Smoking Mirror were to succeed, we would be held accountable for the systematic decimation of the Council."

"Then where would you have me go?" asked Noelle.

"Halloween Night, 1994," Paloma's replied, as the were-quetzal bird.

Noelle dropped her right hand and revealed she had been holding a handmade 'artist book' entitled, *The Spirit of the Voice* by Nicholas Renato Intaglio III and Immokalee Awinita Chisholm. Published in 1913, the antique book filled with photographs, watercolor landscapes, Native American illustrations, and poetry set to music. Inexplicably, the book flew out of Noelle's hand and landed at Dancing Movement's feet, flipping open to the chapter entitled *Quartz Crystal Wands*. There detailed illustrations of quartz crystals in various stages of their development filled the two pages. Suddenly, a bright white light in the shape of a cone beamed down, encapsulating the Council members within an inverted triangle. The images in the scrying mirror were silenced in the presence of JOT—the divine light-set forth by "Prime Mover."

The Toltec Deity Ometeotl/Moyocoyotzin/the Prime Mover's distinct and strident voice announced Noelle's assignment. "You must bring to light the mystery that sustains life so that all the world might see. Demonstrate your devotion and cleanse the link between physicality and pure being—the *Seminal Being* Soul."

Dancing Movement stepped on the open artist book and was enveloped inside its pages, as the divine white light disappeared instantaneously.

As the images from the autumn of 1994 began to fade, Noelle slid outside of her position in the large inverted triangle and ambled over to the scrying mirror. Using her imagination and intention, she moved through a line of demarcation and into the fourth dimension.

The eight remaining members had transformed the inverted triangle into an eight-pointed Mayan Hunab Ku Butterfly. Partway into the reconfiguration, the were-quetzal bird observed with no reservation where the *Seminal Being* Soul had taken Noelle.

"She's gone," said Paloma. "Noelle's gone back to where for her, it all began."

Then in unison, the Toltec Eagle Knights confirmed, "To the Lord of the Star of the Dawn—Ce Acatl Toplitzin-Quetzalcoatl King-Priest of Tollan."

Octavio's Prophetic Waking Dream had ended and he was back in 1994. Octavio left the old Mesquite tree in favor of Cheryl's kitchen situated to the left of the foyer surround. Cheryl was seated at the kitchen counter right below a window. She was talking on the phone with her very pregnant daughter, Lisa J. Webb, age twenty-seven.

"Two more weeks, that's all, Baby Doll!" Cheryl announced cheerfully.

Lisa was living the life Cheryl had always dreamed of. A tight-knit family that included: a loving husband, twin boys, a golden retriever, the neighbor's kitten, and her in-laws. Aside from Lisa, Cheryl had few, if any, real friends. The only other person she could count on was her dear friend Octavio, whom she nicknamed "Sally."

Octavio popped his head through the kitchen window and asked if she had seen Noelle. Cheryl told Octavio she last saw Noelle heading in the direction of the garage. Octavio ventured down to the garage for a look-see.

"I'll call you later, honey. I've got to see what Sally wants," Cheryl told Lisa and rose to her feet.

Noelle was in Cheryl's three-car garage, flipping through the pages of the "artist book" entitled, *The Spirit of the Voice* by Nicholas Renato Intaglio III and Immokalee Awinita Chisholm published in 1913. Noelle carried her family heirloom with her at all times. Stolen a few years back, she could not take the chance of it ever happening again.

Octavio entered the garage and caught a glimpse of Noelle carefully placing the precious book back into her canvas book bag. Noelle, eager to find out about Octavio, mustered up the courage to confront him on his curious affiliation.

"Cheryl was telling me this morning that you're part of a cult."

"Your words, not mine."

"No, really she—"

Octavio objected with a wave of his hand.

"Cheryl said this; Cheryl said that; does she do your thinking for you as well?"

Noelle looked away without answering.

"Don't be looking over there. My answer is in the question."

"Okay, if you're not part of a cult, then who are you?" Noelle desperately needed to know.

Without further ado, Octavio spoke plainly to his naïve mixed-heritage American. "I belong to a Secret Council made up of ten members. Together, we are an "Archetypal Creative Order" that promises to eradicate suffering and heal the debilitating effects of trauma.

"Wouldn't we all like to do that!" Noelle said sharply.

Octavio reevaluated Noelle and then replied, "What if I were to tell you that you're able to be reformed by your own hand?"

Noelle, looking interested, asked, "It makes me wonder if it's possible."

"To be reformed?" Octavio asked.

"Yes! To be reborn."

Octavio crossed the garage and headed over to a side door slightly ajar. Without reservation, he boldly asked Noelle, "Ever been 'South of the Border?' "

"You mean Mexico?"

"In three days, my brother hosts the most outrageous *Days of the Dead* Celebration for the "Warriors of the Spirit" at his 10,000-acre estate."

"What are the Warriors of the Spirit?" Noelle asked while walking toward Octavio.

"The average man acts for profit," Octavio said. "Warriors of the Spirit act not for profit, but for 'The Spirit of the Voice.' "

Noelle glanced down at the artist book with the same title and then asked, sounding half amused, "Is this your idea of an invite?"

Octavio paused, aware that they were not alone. Cheryl was in the room eavesdropping, and he anticipated an unsolicited response from her at any moment. He put it all out on the table.

"Actually, this was all the brainstorm of my sister Paloma. So may we count on you?"

Before Noelle had a chance to answer, they heard Cheryl emerge from her hiding place.

"I've been looking all over for you," Cheryl proclaimed. "Here, Noelle, I have your check."

Turning in Octavio's direction, Cheryl, without hesitation, invited herself to Mexico. "So what's all this about us going to Mexico?"

Octavio directed the ladies outside and told them to pack a bag for a three-day excursion.

"Pack light. We'll be staying with my family, so you don't need toiletries other than a comb and a toothbrush."

Presenting Noelle with a pocket-sized spiral notepad from his shirt pocket and a small carpenter pencil stuck alongside his ear, Octavio dictated to Noelle her next action.

"Jot this down, Noelle. Monday morning, LAX, I'm to be there at 7:00 a.m., Mexicana Airlines, Flight #437, destination Puerto Vallarta, Mexico."

Cheryl waved her finger in the direction of her house and said, "Okay Missy, if you're coming with me to Mexico, then see to it that all those doors are double sealed today!"

"I'm on it, Cheryl. I'll have them done by four!"

CHAPTER FIVE

Lady in Waiting

Octavio headed back to the delivery truck and waited for Noelle. When she was within a few yards of Octavio, she told him she was not going after all. Octavio examined Noelle closely. "So what's the problem? Can't you get Cheryl to give you a lift to the airport?"

"Ah, Okay! I'll ride with Cheryl."

Octavio started to approach the delivery truck driver when Noelle reneged again on his offer.

"You know what? I'm not going. This isn't going to be any fun for me," Noelle said, looking forlorn and unsure of herself.

"You think, it's Cheryl who's preventing you from having a good time?" Octavio asked.

"What's so special about his party?" Noelle demanded.

"The climate!" Octavio said, eyes twinkling.

Not quite sure how to take his last remark, Noelle tilted her head like a puppy.

Octavio raised a finger at Noelle as if to say, just a moment, and took a few steps in the driver's direction. Reaching into the opened cab door, he handed the driver a $20 bill. Then glancing back over his shoulder, Octavio announced to Noelle, "Don't be using up all your bragging rights, but you're about to be my guest on an all-expenses paid vacation!"

Noelle's eyes widened like a small child who has just received a triple-decker ice-cream cone.

Octavio made a dash for it and ducked inside his pick-up truck. Noelle, bemused by his playfulness, could not help but follow.

Octavio peered above the driver's side window, which was cracked three-quarters of the way up. He continued the conversation.

"You'd like me to explain life's little mysteries to you, yes? That's why you've followed me here, is it not?"

Noelle nodded.

"You know, you're not at all what we expected," Octavio said in all seriousness as he rolled the window down. "But I suspect you're as eligible as the next."

"We? Who are we? And, what if anything are we expecting?" questioned Noelle, sounding a-wee-bit incensed.

Octavio overlooked her concerns. With his eyes gleaming, he taped Noelle on her spider bite.

"No curse causeless."

As Octavio leaned in toward Noelle, he noticed her frustration, "Aren't you the least bit interested in finding out more about your friend?" He waited for her response.

Noelle withheld her true feelings and shook her head, "No." Immediately, she took on the look of a stone-faced liar.

"Wouldn't you like to know why you survived the attack while he, I can only imagine, did not?

"What attack?"

"Tell me again where you will be in two days?" Octavio insisted on changing the topic.

Noelle, with a renewed sense of wonder, looked on the pad and read her handwritten note:

- Monday morning LAX; I'm to be there at 7:00 a.m.,
- Mexicana Airlines – Flight #437, and
- Destination Puerto Vallarta, Mexico.

Noelle hesitated at first and then blurted out, "Am I supposed to bring a Halloween costume?"

"Nope! I've got it covered."

Without uttering another word, Octavio raised an eyebrow and then drove away, just as the were-eagle left its perch from the great-grandfather Mesquite tree. The two drift out of sight as they wove their way through the Hollywood Hills.

In the tropical rainforest that surrounded Puerto Vallarta, Mexico, a series of dirt roads cut through the jungle. Situated deep inside its lush terrain were several bungalows randomly spread out over a three-mile radius. The late afternoon sun was kicking up a breeze, disturbing several slumbering creatures.

Hungry, hot, and a bit on edge, the persistent panting of an oscillating were-cougar in its cage forced its jailer, Chargo, to take note. Someone or something was in the vicinity; the ground cover was crackling and snapping every few seconds. Chargo dismissed the disturbance as nothing to worry about. He picked up a garden hose, stuck it inside the were-cougar's rattan cage, and refilled a five-gallon tank with water. The were-cougar lapped up the water laid down near the enclosure's opening and waited for her trainer to arrive. The were-cougar, Mela T. (Terra) Delgado, "Black, Terra, Slender," who was age twenty-six, was the younger sister to her brother, Emilio Garcia Delgado, "Emulating, Fox, Slender," age thirty-three. The siblings had been very close when they were children despite their many differences. As adults, however, they grew to mistrust and deceive one another.

As a kid growing up in Puerto Vallarta, Emilio was a streetwise petty criminal. He voiced no objection to standing out in a crowd, wearing his brown leather-and-hemp spectators and flashy polyester and cotton long-sleeved shirts and slacks. Emilio liked to fashion himself after the renowned Chicago gangsters of the 1930s. As it is with underground criminals, Emilio's thumb was on the pulse of things; he seemed to know who was doing what, where, when, and with whom. His closest relationships were embedded in the merchant class who best profit from the local tourist industry. Superior to most in looks and style; he was beauty in motion.

It was Emilio's carriage that first caught the attention of Rosita and Dahlia while dining in a posh restaurant by the bay. Emilio's interest in Dahlia was primarily monetary; he wanted what he perceived she would inherit from her mother, the B&B on the beachhead in Puerto Vallarta. Emilio also had his sights on owning a large part of the Celestino's ten thousand acres of undeveloped land in Vera Cruz, Mexico. He saw himself as the manager after they were married. Emilio intended to build a housing facility for the Cartel families involved in animal trafficking. Illegal wildlife trade was one of the most profitable industries in the world. It took in over a billion dollars each year and was rapidly growing. With the added Exotic Creature Line: were-jaguars, were-cougars, were-eagles, and exotic birds, he anticipated a hundred percent growth in international sales within the first three years. Emilio figured once his business was established, it would be almost impossible to shut it down without media attention. The last thing the Celestino family wanted was unwanted negative publicity. Neither could they afford to be exposed.

Put politely, Emilio had a disproportionate interest in Rosita's business portfolio. A natural charmer, he used his *devil-may-care* attitude and wit to put women at ease and get them to do his bidding. As he waited for the wheel of fortune to turn in his favor, he profited as a gifted voice impersonator. Emilio marveled at his ability to disrupt and confuse the Celestino family members by pretending to be either Octavio or Saltire.

Emilio sauntered into the bungalow and took inventory of his merchandise. All at once, an argument ensued between Chargo and Emilio.

Chargo boasting said, "She's lean and mean just as you requested."

Cloaked in semi-darkness, Emilio responded violently, "I never said, starve my sister to death, you idiot!"

"Please, by all means, Emilio, be my guest!"

"She needs all her vital energy to shape-shift; what you're doing could kill her!"

"What I'm doing? Let's not be putting the blame where it doesn't belong." Chargo fired back.

Rosita shouted, "That's enough! Just give him his money so we can get the hell out of here!"

Chargo crossed the floor of his marijuana-infested bungalow, grabbed a stack of hundred dollar bills from Emilio's hand, and immediately stuck them in his shirt pocket. Emilio and Rosita left Chargo's bungalow without further incident. Chargo returned to the were-cougar and tossed her a heart ripped from a live goat. "Here, Kitty, chew on this!"

Rosita's green 1984 Mercedes-Benz 280SE was winding its way down a dirt road when three standing were-jaguars, tawny-yellow with large black rosettes, lunged in front of her car. Instinctually, she swerved to avoid hitting them and ended up with her rear-end tires entrenched in a thicket.

Appearing not the least bit concerned, Emilio said, "Hold on there, Tiger."

Wincing, Rosita cried, "This is why I didn't want to come. You can't see a damn thing out here!"

"Here move over; I'll drive!" Emilio insisted.

Rosita Maria Celestino Jakobi, age forty-eight, climbed overtop Emilio, but as Emilio was sliding into the driver's seat, his small black leather moneybag snagged on the gear shift. Emilio glared at Rosita and accused her of trying to pinch his money. Rosita shook her head in disgust and looked away.

Close by a black male were-jaguar lay camouflaged in a Parota tree. Yellow eyes were glistening as the sun began to set; he watched the three other were-jaguars with keen interest before shape-shifting into the Toltec Deity Tezcatlipoca, Smoking Mirror.

The sun was hovering right above where the horizon meets the sea. Octavio was out back in his barren-looking horse stable; he was thoughtfully placing objects into a ceremonial basket. In the meantime, the were-eagle known as the Presence of Paloma had successfully picked the lock on a large hand-tooled, walnut-colored Mexican leather trunk. As she flipped the lid, the chest revealed an immense stash of Nagual Spirit Masks and costumes propped up on a wooden hand-drawn car.

Octavio sweetly talked to the bird, "What's that, Sis? Ah, the Toltec Atlantean Warrior, interesting choice."

The were-eagle then hopped off the trunk and flew over to Reynaldo and Sergio, who were loading Octavio's pick-up truck for an evening's early start southbound to Puerto Vallarta.

As Americanized as Octavio seemed, he was still very much informed by his Mayan-Toltec ideology—sacred rites and practices. Octavio's *Seminal Being* Soul had been the Elder Eagle Knight, Kumku Ixbalanque Celestino, who presided over the Toltec Secret Eagle Knight Council located in the Santa Monica Mountains in Alta, CA. from (1879 -1905), as well as the Mayan Eagle Knight, known as, "B'en Skywalker" (Acatl/Reed/Pillar/13)—the one who embodies Silent Knowledge and infinite wisdom. He spearheaded a group of Mayan Eagle Knights that protected the trade routes from Chichen Itza on the Yucatan Peninsula to the Toltec City at Tollan/Tula, Mexico in the 10th century BC. B'en, with the aid of Quetzal Hunahpu, secretly set about rescuing the Toltec King-Priest Ce Acatl Topiltzin-Quetzalcoatl from the rival "Black Jaguar Cult" of Tezcatlipoca at Tollan in the year 987 AD. Together they plotted a safe course to Chichen Itza on the Yucatan Peninsula, where the Mayan/Toltec culture would flourish.

CHAPTER SIX

Mirrors of the Gods

The sky was cobalt blue, and the clouds beneath Flight #437 looked like spun white cotton candy. On the plane ride to Puerto Vallarta, Mexico, Noelle and Octavio sat together talking, while Cheryl was absorbed in the book "A Course in Miracles." Noelle commented dreamily on the animal shapes she saw in the clouds while Octavio joked that perhaps his founding fathers, the Mayan "Hero-Twins," were sending her coded messages. Noelle was lost in the cloud formations and did not react to Octavio's inference; instead, she asked about Octavio's family, the people she would be staying with. He was warm and open with Noelle, sharing intimate personal memories.

"It was a golden time for my family during the 50s and 60s," Octavio said proudly. "My father, Lucius Antonio Celestino, was a famous artist and Libro Gencologico, a Stud Book owner of Andalusian horses. His closest friend in those days was an American costume designer."

Octavio was thoroughly enjoying Noelle giving him her undivided attention. It was a trait that he knew would serve her well in the days ahead.

Leaning into Noelle's right shoulder, Octavio whispered, "One year on Halloween, Powell dropped off a huge box filled with colorful Nagual Spirit Masks with complementary costumes. He had made them just for us. I was bursting at the seams to know which one was mine."

Cheryl noticed that Octavio was paying a lot of attention to Noelle and interrupted their conversation.

"Would either of you like my breakfast? I simply don't do leftovers," Cheryl said disdainfully.

Octavio nudged Noelle and shouted past the aisle, "Sure ya do Cheryl, you just don't call 'em leftovers."

Cheryl put on her "having game" face.

"Where was I going with all this?" Octavio asked Noelle.

"How old were you when this happened?" Noelle inquired.

"I was eight years old when I was introduced to my half-brother, Saltire. It was Halloween. My father saw fit to put aside tradition and let us wear one of those Spirit Masks. I was "Green-Plumed Quetzal Bird," and Saltire was Blood-Jeweled Fowl, Long-Nose Turkey. Our connection was immediate.

"What does your brother do anyway?" Noelle's curiosity was aroused.

"Saltire is a mechanic by day and a magician by night. The three years spent in the Middle East and Africa, plus the four years traveling throughout Asia was a great—"

"What was he doing there?" Noelle interrupted.

"He was being trained in the High Art of Magic—Theurgy."

With a puzzled expression, Noelle took another bite of her scrambled eggs and said, "Is that the same as Alchemy?"

"Theurgy literally means "divine working," Octavio explained. "It is performing white magic to evoke Deities who aid in reuniting one's soul with their Higher Self."

Cheryl was noticeably annoyed. She never envisioned herself flying coach anywhere, least of all to Mexico. The woman next to her was unmistakably Latino: thick straight black hair, soft golden-brown skin, and a voluptuous figure that had her fit to be tied. Young attractive exotic women had always threatened her ever since high school.

Cheryl turned to her competition, all prim and proper like, and asked, "Would you mind if I placed my breakfast tray on yours? My friends didn't appear to be interested. This way, when the flight attendant comes by, she can scoop them up together."

The Latino Lady acquiesced with a tilt of the head as Cheryl proceeded to deposit her breakfast tray on top of hers.

"Gracias!" Cheryl said through pursed lips, and then returned her retractable tray table back into its slot.

Across the aisle and three rows back, Octavio continued to explore Noelle's capacity to stay present to a whole new world of possibility. He examined Noelle's kinetic energy from out of the corner of his eye, proceeding thoughtfully so as not to distract her.

"My brother has successfully shape-shifted from human being to deity, deity to deity, then deity back to human on many an occasion," Octavio said.

"Forgive me, but why on earth would anyone want to do that?" asked Noelle.

Octavio was moving his body into an unusual configuration. He continued, "Shape-shifting allows the person to access the power and knowledge of the very thing they've chosen to inhabit. By doing so, they go beyond mimicking their appearance; they also think and act as they might."

"This sounds a little dangerous to me. What if you're unable to return back to yourself?"

"Then you're weak in spirit, and you've unwittingly caused your soul to be vulnerable to attack. In any case, you'll require a Spiritual Master to restore the integrity of your soul."

"Is your brother such a Master?"

"Yes, as a matter-of-fact, he is."

Octavio realized he had just identified one of Noelle's most sensitive issues—shape-shifting. He let it be for now and decided to expound on Noelle's question from his point-of-view.

"Close your eyes, my dear, and Cheryl will think you're sleeping; I'll keep it to a whisper, so if she turns around, she'll think we're praying."

Noelle lowered her head, folded her hands, and placed them on her lap. Octavio presented Saltire's life as a retrospective: rich in color, texture, beauty, and value.

"The ancient indigenous peoples of Mesoamerica believed that a name carried with it magical properties; when you changed your name, you changed your destiny or at the very least the trajectory of your life," Octavio said under his breath. "Saltire Daghda McKenna Celestino "Sacred Cross, X, Protector of the Tribe, Ardent Love, Secret of Heaven" has Royal blood coursing through his veins. The name

Saltire represents the Saint Andrew's cross in Christianity and signifies resolution. Coincidently, its pictogram, an X, is the Toltec symbol for the essential nature—right posture—of humankind in relation to the Milky Way."

Noelle shifted her body position from rigidly forward to relaxed-sideways. She was starting to feel comfortable with the conversation.

"Saltire's beginnings are noteworthy," Octavio said with pride. "I was told he was conceived in the throes of passion in the midst of a meteorite shower. His mother, Rebecca Saltire McKenna, of Welsh/Irish/English descent, had an affair with my father, Lucius Antonio Celestino. They met at Uncle Victor's horse stables while Rebecca was visiting her aunt and uncle—WWII refugees residing in Puerto Vallarta, Mexico."

Noelle opened her eyes slightly, nodded her head "Yes," and relaxed even more.

Octavio's linear discourse was designed to have Noelle to go deeper into her subconscious. It was there, in the recesses of her mind—the divine sepulture—that he intended for her to find the truth about her "Soul's Intended Future."

"Rebecca withheld her pregnancy from both my father and her husband, Benjamin B. McKenna," Octavio continued. "She raised Saltire in Connemara within the County of Galway, Ireland. He grew up knowing nothing about Lucius until his mother deemed him a hazard to her marriage. Saltire was highly intelligent and inquisitive when he was young, and required constant stimulus. When he was not attending elementary school, he spent the majority of his weekends at his family's Stationary Horse-back Riding Vacation Inn. Saltire's favorite pastime, he told me, was to get all the horses in a circle, then coax them into high-hoofing line dancing."

"I've seen the white Lipizzaner stallions before, they were amazing!" Noelle interjected, wanting to be part of the conversation.

Octavio, slightly amused, smiled, cleared his throat with a glass of ginger ale, and then proceeded with the brief history of Saltire's unconventional childhood.

"By the age of eight, Rebecca had grown wearisome of my brother's overactive imagination and the length and means by which he entertained his grade school friends. Exasperated, she contacted Lucius in October in 1956 with the implicit desire to have him share in Saltire's upbringing. With his mother and newly appointed stepfather in tow, they met my father at his B&B overlooking Banderas Bay."

"Is this where we're headed, to your parent's place?" Noelle asked.

"It now belongs to Saltire," Octavio clarified. "May I continue?"

"Yes, of course. Sorry, I didn't mean to interrupt!" Noelle said, eyes wide-open.

I remember my father telling Benjamin explicitly not to interfere with the special All Hallows' Eve Party. Saltire and I were to meet at the top of the cement steps leading to and from the beachhead. I was the first to show up as "Feathered Serpent"—the red-breasted, green-tailed Quetzal Bird Deity. A few minutes later, Saltire, disguised as Blood-Jeweled Fowl, Long-Nose Turkey started his climbed up the steps from the beach. As soon as I spotted my brother, I ran toward him. Our father waited until we reached each other, and then shouted down to us from the second-story veranda.

"You are both aspects of the Toltec Deity Quetzalcoatl. Do you know what that makes you?"

"Soul-mates!" I yelled back.

"Brother's from a different mother!" Saltire confirmed.

Noelle's eyes opened slowly; she glanced up at Octavio, then looked back over her left shoulder. Returning to the animal clouds, she asked, "So, what's the age difference between you two?"

"Two months and a day," Octavio chuckled.

"You're practically twins."

"One better, we're Toltec Eagle Knights!"

Noelle's eyes were fixated on two clouds passing through one another; the one on the right was shaped like Mayan Hero Twin Hunahpu, while the one on the left resembled Ixbalanque.

The motioning clouds instigated the first in what would be a Series of Recapitulations—existential time travel. As Noelle settled back into her seat, she closed her eyes and let images in her subconscious penetrate her consciousness. The images were of events that until now had gone unexamined from a Seminal Being's vantage point. I distinctly remembered thinking.

Noelle's 1994 recapitulation landed her back in the year 1990. It was a serene and comfortable evening in the Common Historic District of Salem, MA. High above the neighboring buildings, a twelve hundred square foot studio in a four-story, 19th-century brick building was quieting down for the night. Benoit Dante Delacroix, a muscularly built artist extraordinaire, was sitting on a stool, painting life-sized cartoon cutouts from a three-inch thick sheet of Styrofoam. A massive steel reinforced double-door embellished in Halloween decorations was ajar.

Noelle knocked then entered. She asked Benoit if a fellow by the name of Avery was around. He pointed to a man sleeping soundly on a divan. Noelle located Avery sprawled out on a rose-colored "French Revival" chaise lounge and stood quietly over him as he slept.

Avery Emmett Millstone, "Magical Counselor, One of Strength, Male Domesticated Donkey," age twenty-seven, was the pampered son amongst three sisters. His mother, Ruth O'Reilly Millstone, age fifty-two, figured mainly in his life. His father, Emmett Lee Millstone, mid-fifties, had worked at the Marina in Salem, MA, since he was fifteen; he was the fellow in charge of all the comings n' goings at the marina. Avery resisted his father's control but no denying he was cut from the same cloth.

A historically tragic figure, Avery was a man with no conviction or higher purpose; he seemed indifferent to the commitments and aspirations of others. A somewhat successful entrepreneur, he enjoyed rubbing elbows with esteemed antique dealers and designers from Boston to Maine. With his sharp business sensibilities, Avery acquired a loyal clientele, and made a decent living buying, restoring, and selling antiques.

In contrast to his professional etiquette and standards, it was rumored that he supplemented his income by stealing people's property after placing them under duress. Avery took great pride in his skill in the "Black Arts" causing concern and fear in those who loved him most. What had served his interests, aside from his good looks, was his uncanny ability to fascinate and bewitch his family and friends.

Benoit, imitating the call of a loon in flight, beckoned Noelle's company. Noelle strolled over to the studio's center, where he had positioned his solid oak desk and cartoon cutouts.

"These are unbelievable. How'd you ever learn to do this?" Noelle asked in amazement.

Benoit handed Noelle a thick "artist book" resting against a portable easel. His book was filled with the cartoon character "Heart-Fate Wolf," in futuristic urban environments, sometimes spouting funny phrases.

"My father's an illustrator; I think I was born with a pencil in my hand," Benoit replied.

Noelle, thrilled with Benoit's life-size cartoon cutouts, asked, "Could you make one of me?"

"Sure, why not. These four just sold for two hundred and fifty each? If you can swing it, I'll do it for ya."

"Could I stop by next week and pay you? What do you need from me, a Polaroid?" Noelle asked enthusiastically, as she cupped her hands and curled her shoulders forward.

Benoit quickly scanned Noelle's figure and made a mental note: athletic built, black spandex bike shorts with red 'n green checkered trim, white tee, and dark hair cropped to above the shoulders.

"This get-up will do, any objections to a little 'artistic license'?" Benoit said teasingly.

From across the expansive open space, a loud groan accompanied by outstretched arms interfered with the finality of their business transaction.

Avery propped his head up with a pillow and addressed Noelle, "How'd ya find the place?"

Noelle closed the artist book, handed it back to Benoit, and looked in Avery's direction.

"Last week you gave me directions to this loft; you told me to stop by today around five."

Avery now on his feet sauntered over to Benoit.

"This is the girl I told you about; I met her at the Farmers' Market. What's your name again?"

"Noelle" Benoit answered.

"Weren't you the one who was being loud and obnoxious?" Avery said while joshing Noelle.

Noelle denied any wrongdoing. She directed her next comment to Benoit, "You'll never guess what thought ran through my head when I first saw Avery."

Benoit gestured as if to say, "You got me!"

"Oh my God, don't you recognize me?"

Avery interrupted Noelle by asking Benoit if he wanted to join them for dinner. Benoit said, "Yes," and the three headed for the exit.

Just before leaving, Avery pointed to a black outline drawing high up on the studio wall, to the left of the front entrance. Noelle glanced up and saw the drawing—it was of a figure falling out a window, with onlookers screaming from below. She stopped dead in her tracks.

"You did this?" Noelle asked incredulously.

Avery smirked at her as he waltzed past the Halloween decorations and disappeared behind the studio double-door. Noelle followed Benoit and the two marched after him.

Unfazed by Noelle's flashback memory I watched with amazement as Octavio sedated his disciple, then meticulously shifted the point inside her left shoulder where her perception resided. This ignited in Noelle an exploration into her traumatic past relationship.

Octavio had gone to the lavatory and spoken to Cheryl briefly before returning to his seat. He leaned into Noelle again and continued where he had left off.

"Saltire so enjoyed the introduction that he insisted on spending every summer vacation with us at the B&B. It was during that time that we became the best of friends. I taught him abstract thought and how to be in rapport with the spirit of things; he shared English horse riding skills; dressage, stadium jumping, steeplechase."

All this talk of horseback riding reminded Noelle of her summers spent at camp. Her uncle had gone to the Taylor Statten Summer Camp for Boys, Ahmek "Great Beaver," back in the 1930s. The camp was located on Canoe Lake in Algonquin Park Ontario, Canada. Noelle had a great love for horses, the water, and all things natural. She participated in the Camp Wapomeo for Girls, "Birds of Sunshine and Laughter" from 1969 to 1973 and loved it.

While at the camp, Noelle had been singled out as a hero. She had been credited with saving the life of a fellow camper, her best friend Debbie S., when the petite teenager slipped off the designated path right into a muddy swamp. Up to her chest in the muck, the young girl cried out to her friend for help. Noelle looked around frantically and saw no means of assistance.

"Don't move! And stop kicking. You're making it worse." Noelle yelled. "I'm going to go get the guide. I'll be right back. DON'T MOVE!"

Noelle kept her composure and ran back in the direction where the guide had last been seen. Within a few hundred yards, the path split in two and she had to make a decision: straight ahead or up and to the left? On impulse, she was able to picture herself walking on the path. It was then that Noelle knew where she had come from. Up and to the left, she took off like the wind. The guide was up ahead, Noelle screamed, "Help!" He dropped the canoe and ran toward her.

"You'll find Debbie on the right behind a huge tree. Hurry! She's sinking fast!" Noelle yelled.

The tall, lanky guide, in his mid-twenties, disappeared around the bend heading southeast.

When Noelle returned, the guide was about to pull Debbie clear of the swamp with the aid of a long fallen branch. She stood on the path as he crawled out on the limb, freed Debbie's right arm, and proceeded to drag her, backpack and all, to solid ground.

This would prove to be a defining moment in Noelle's life. She would never forget the look in Debbie's eyes as the leech-infested muck covered her mouth and nose in a matter of minutes. Noelle would call upon her intrinsic nature on several occasions, never recognizing nor acknowledging its source—the Seminal Being Soul *of Amrit Sandhu of which we were both a part of.*

Noelle woke up to the "FASTEN YOUR SEAT BELTS" sign in red. She buckled up, clenched her eyes shut, and withheld her breath as the plane landed safely on the tarmac. Octavio glanced at his watch; it read: 11:38 a.m. He helped Noelle to her feet, removed her WWII Marine Corps olive-colored garment bag from the overhead bin, and together they accompanied Cheryl to the hatch.

CHAPTER SEVEN

Burned Out Beach House

The Celestino's three-story Spanish-style B&B Mar Casa De La Concha "House of Seashells" in Puerto Vallarta, Jalisco, Mexico, was positioned on a terraced hillside high above Banderas Bay. The white stucco exterior supported by six twelve-foot high pilasters with its natural pumpkin Cantera Stone moldings glistened in the daylight. Rosita's primary residence and place of business as the manager, Octavio's home away from Malibu, had recently become one of Saltire's many properties. While Rosita managed the business, her daughter Dahlia oversaw dining and housekeeping affairs.

Half-shell rainbows seen directly above the property's terra-cotta roof tiles spoke to the belief that the house was blessed. When entering the B&B from the street, one drove onto an L-shaped parking lot. To the far left of the residence, a Saltillo floor tile staircase crowned with wrought-iron railings led the family to the hand-carved mesquite front doors. A carport to the right of the main entrance shared support from an adjoining motorcycle ramp. And there were four additional parking slots in front of the property. What looked like garages were four separate storage units. This meant the guests could only enter their suites from the rear of the B&B during hours of operation 8:00 a.m. to 9:00 p.m.

The clicking of sandals shuffling across waterproofed wooden floorboards on the second story veranda signaled mealtime. The eight guests' comings-and-goings made for light entertainment, as they filtered out onto the ground-floor covered patio at the rear of the building. Four large rectangular suites, each furbished with matt finish hand-painted Talavera tiles; complemented a Colonial queen-size bed and matching armoire with raised panels, handcrafted Zapotec wool rugs, tin sconces and mirrors. It was obvious no expense had been spared in last year's remodels. The patio faced a small kidney-shaped pool with a Jacuzzi and complimentary bar and grill. An informal seating arrangement with gas lighting encouraged comfortable and neighborly social exchanges, and the uninterrupted 180-degree view of the Pacific Ocean was spectacular.

Saltire arrived on his customized Triumph Trophy 1200 motorcycle and parked it alongside the exterior staircase. While walking up the exterior wrought iron staircase with his daughter Xochitl, they were graciously welcomed by his niece, Dahlia. She had anticipated their arrival and was waiting for them on the landing above.

Dahlia Concepcion Valdez, known as "Dahlia" Flower, Conception, Boldness" age twenty-nine, was an only child. A kind-hearted, natural beauty, she was very comfortable in her own skin. Loved by all her family members for her thoughtfulness and loyalty, she always could be trusted with people and matters of great importance. Dahlia was greatly influenced by her grandparents' Mayan-Toltec principles and values and took family matters somewhat seriously. As one of the most highly evolved members of the Toltec Secret Eagle Knight Council, Dahlia could shape-shift into both a were-jaguar and a were-eagle whenever a family member was presumed under psychological attack or physical threat.

After a warm reception, Saltire asked Dahlia to go find her mother, Rosita, and have her locate the basket filled with Paloma's destination letters.

"Paloma believes she has located the tenth member," Saltire confided in Dahlia. "Octavio is bringing her here for the long-anticipated final initiation."

Dahlia left and returned swiftly with Rosita carrying the basket of letters. The reunion between Saltire and Rosita was a bit icy. As Saltire examined Paloma's dispatch letters, Rosita made a snide remark intended to provoke.

"Who's our brother entertaining this time with his liberal point-of-view?"

"Why you, my dear, it's my understanding he lets you have the run of this place."

Rosita's fifth wedding anniversary was marked by being served divorce papers from her estranged second husband, Mr. Jakobi. Within a month, she had to sell the B&B to her brother Octavio to remove it from her bankruptcy filing. Rosita squirmed uncomfortably while Saltire located the letter with the Butterfly wings insignia. Letter in hand, Saltire leaned down and told his daughter to stay with Dahlia and plan the Halloween party.

"I'll be back before long 'little deer,' then we'll skip on down to the beach and back again, costumes and all. Sound like a plan?"

Xochitl smiled with joy. Eyes twinkling, she led Dahlia and Rosita back inside.

Once the taxi pulled up in front of a pharmacy in the historical Old Town of Puerto Vallarta, Octavio got out and went inside the corner store. Noelle and Cheryl dashed over to the boardwalk to grab a snack and browse the street vendor carts carrying local merchandise. By noon, the Banderas Bay beachfront promenade was a hub for tourist activity. Cheryl headed directly over to a leather goods store and started haggling with the salesman. Noelle chose to stand in line for grilled shrimp on a skewer. She was there for only a minute or two when a woman started shaking her finger at her. Noelle did not understand what the lady meant, yet the woman persisted in singling her out. Frustrated by the whole situation, Noelle went back to the taxi. Empty-handed and with a downturned smile, she waited for Cheryl and Octavio to join her.

A few minutes later, Octavio returned with a brown paper bag in his hand. He had been diagnosed seven weeks back with a rare illness that required him to drink a molasses-like herbal remedy formulated and distributed by the state of Jalisco.

"Okay, Cheryl, time's up!" Octavio hollered.

On her way back to the taxi, Cheryl said to Noelle, "Here I got you a pair of leather sandals; you can thank me later."

Octavio politely instructed the women back into the taxi.

As the taxi pulled away slowly, Noelle turned her head just in time to see three Huichol Indians at the entrance of Parish of Guadeloupe, catching a quick glimpse of her looking at them. Octavio was in the front passenger seat, sprinkling the refined herbal powder into a small glass bottle neatly tucked away inside the paper bag.

Noelle leaning forward and looking over his shoulder, asked politely, "What is that you're making? Is it some sort of special concoction?"

"It's a remedy."

"Mm-hmm."

Octavio smirked and then said, "Noelle, do me a big favor and bring it to my attention if ever you see me on the road without this bag. Will you do that for me?"

Noelle agreed to his request. Cheryl, on the other hand, said she was glad she was not asked.

"You knew better than to ask me, Sally," Cheryl chirped. "When I'm on vacation—"

Octavio cut Cheryl off mid-sentence with a grin, "Cheryl, when have you ever not been on vacation? Your life's just one big whirlwind."

From outside the taxi, Noelle's giggling streamed along as the cabby drove onward. Cheryl ignored them both and sat quietly, admiring her bargains.

Seconds later, Saltire came leaping up the front steps of the Parish of Guadeloupe and was greeted by the three Huichol Indians, ages ranging from the early forties to late sixties. Saltire handed over Paloma's letter with the Butterfly wings insignia. The eldest Huichol Indian opened the letter written in Roman Capital Letters and Mayan/Toltec Poetic Verse. He read it out loud.

"Tonight, Sower of Discord on Both Sides,
Lures lost souls to the burned-out house.
Rejecting sacred laws and provisions,
Smoking Mirror descries a host.

'Tiger Spirit' acts on our Intentions;
Staging a hostile take of her.
'Falling Waters' as the point of ambush,
Demands swift action on your part."

The eldest Huichol Indian seemed to understand the private invitation and demonstrated his approval by presenting a leather bag filled with copal incense. Saltire accepted the offering and graciously left, intermingling with the street merchants below.

The taxi deposited Octavio, Noelle, and Cheryl at Mar Casa De La Concha. The three approached the front doors by way of the stilted staircase. Upon entry, the women were told to wait in the living room until he returned. Octavio yelled for Rosita. She hollered back from the upstairs hallway; he pursued her accordingly.

Noelle and Cheryl were in a traditional Mexican-style living room: white skip-trowel plaster ceiling with hand-carved wooden beams; warm colored surrounding walls with white-lemon Cantera Stone moldings, twin Equipale Pigskin chairs with matching sofa, four iron lock plate sconces, and an antique solid teakwood bench overlooking the bay. The two women virtually ignored the beautiful handcrafted Zapotec wool area rugs, the Folk Art, and complimentary portrait paintings of Grandmother Celestino lining the plastered walls in favor of the seashore.

Cheryl was tapping her foot repeatedly on the Saltillo floor tiles, complaining, "Had I known we'd be this far from the beach, I'd of elected not to come at all!"

By contrast, Noelle was thrilled by the prospect of photographing the shoreline, and couldn't wait for Octavio to return. When Octavio reentered the room, he took Noelle and Cheryl to the second story veranda overlooking the bay and pointed to the cement stairs that lead to the beach. Once it was clear that they had their bearings, he escorted them to their designated bedrooms.

Standing on the third-floor landing, Octavio said to the women, "Cheryl, you'll be staying in Xoch's bedroom. Noelle, Saltire has agreed to let you stay in his chambers."

Noelle expressed concern over the sleeping arrangements. Octavio told Noelle not to worry; they would be spending the night at his boathouse on the beach. Before ducking into the bedroom, Noelle asked Octavio if it was safe going to the beach alone to take a few photos while the sun was setting.

"It's not the beach folk you should be concerned about, but rather the violent storm approaching," Octavio told Noelle. "This cyclone is similar to another you're familiar with. It's come once more for 'Lost Souls'."

Entering Saltire's bedroom suite together, Noelle could not help but admire the Sabino, "Mexican Cypress," antique queen-size bed, and matching armoire. The hand-painted matte finish Talavera bathroom tiles in the adjoining room to the right literally took her breath away.

"This room is so beautiful," Noelle said softly.

Octavio headed to an opened window. Pointing in the direction of "Caballito"—the bronze statue of a naked boy, toting a sombrero, mounted on a Seahorse—he warned, "I'd recommend you don't become like the identical twin of the naked boy; the one who rides the Seahorse."

"Why, what happened to him?" Noelle asked.

"He kept getting washed out to sea, until the sea tired of his folly and spit him out, once and for all."

"Mm-hmm, maybe it would be best if I waited till tomorrow."

"Nope! I've got other plans for us tomorrow. Keep to the berms and stay clear of the wind and the tide, and I'll see you back here within the hour."

"Keep to the berms and stay clear of the wind and the tide," Noelle repeated.

"Strange happenings have occurred on nights such as these. You can lose yourself in the fog and never be seen again!" He emphasized.

Octavio backed away from the window and removed a papier-mâché Toltec Atlantean Warrior spirit facemask and costume from a cherry-red Mexican Colonial armoire. The upper section of the costume comprised two adjustable panels: an eight-pointed Mayan Hunab Ku Butterfly breastplate, with a complimentary shoulder blade backplate, with a black obsidian scrying mirror. When Octavio held up the bottom portion, they could see it was easily four sizes too small. Handing the top part to Noelle, he instructed her to put it on, the mirror to the rear, convincing her that it was in her best interest.

"It will confound the dirty dog, and he won't attack," Octavio said in all seriousness.

"This is crazy! I'm now to watch out for stray dogs?" Noelle said half kidding.

Octavio hid his amused expression and left abruptly.

Octavio chuckled as he walked over to Cheryl's bedroom door. Cheryl was making a ruckus; she was desperately trying to contact her daughter, Lisa, but seemed unable to reach an operator. Octavio stopped to listen, then changed direction, and headed back down the front staircase.

Noelle took off the clothes she wore on the plane and put on a self-designed paisley denim sleeveless shirt along with a pair of cropped spandex leggings. She left her room with the Butterfly breastplate tied around her neck and waist facing forward, mirror to the rear. The Toltec Atlantean Warrior facemask was flipped up on her head as she bounced barefoot down the front staircase.

Gathered on the second-story veranda shaded by a lattice covering draped in purple-colored Bougainvilleas were Rosita, Dahlia, and Dahlia's fiancé Emilio.

Rosita Maria Celestino Jakobi, known as "Rose, Lady of the Sea, Secret of Heaven, Supplanting," age forty-eight, was the second oldest of four siblings and was considered the black sheep in the family. Rosita had been married and divorced twice and had only one daughter, Dahlia, from her first marriage to an American (USA) entrepreneur. Her sense of fulfillment came from stirring up people's emotions and then watching their defenses melt. Envious and jealous of everyone in her family, Rosita sabotaged herself with her reckless and destructive behavior: her obsession with being with her daughter's fiancé Emilio at every opportunity, her preoccupation with losing the B&B to another family member.

Lucius had purchased the B&B in the early fifties for his two girls Paloma and Rosita. It was intended to be an additional source of steady income for them when they entered adulthood. Paloma expressed no interest in managing the property alongside her sister and sold it to Rosita for a pittance. In due course, Rosita would run the beautiful property into the ground by squandering the profits on lavish parties and trips to the United States. Octavio intervened and purchased Mar Casa De La Concha at the going rate, in honor of his father's initial intention. Since 1994, Rosita had become utterly obsessed with schemes of how to reclaim the beachfront property. It would appear her ethical and moral fiber was frayed and on the fringe of collapse.

Looking out at Banderas Bay, Rosita caught sight of Noelle as she approached Saltire and Xochitl on the cement steps leading to and from the beach. Rosita asked Emilio if he thought Noelle was aware that they are family and would he consider stopping and introducing herself. Emilio declined to answer her and instead told Dahlia to fetch him a Quetzal bird feather from Rosita's bedroom.

Octavio passed Dahlia by the front door and headed outside. Gazing upon the setting sun, Octavio used *The Spirit of the Voice*—the word of the Holy Spirit—to shift the point of his perception and cried out, "INTENT!"

Noelle walked carefully down the flight of steps leading up from the beach, taking photos of the sun touching the horizon. The sand-covered boardwalk was teaming with locals and tourists. Xochitl, disguised as "Magical Deer," skipped about in front of her father. Saltire, dressed up as the Blood-Jeweled Fowl, Long-Nose Turkey Toltec Deity, had stopped and was taking in the sunset as well. Xochitl saw Noelle's Butterfly breastplate with mirror accompaniment and went rushing over to her father.

"Papi, I just saw a Toltec Atlantean Warrior!" Xochitl exclaimed.

Saltire quickly flung the elephant-like striped trunk over his right shoulder and snatched Xochitl up in his arms. Crouching down, they hid amongst tree fronds embellishing the cement steps. "Shhh! Be still!" Saltire instructed.

Noelle, preoccupied with the fiery purple 'n red sunset, walked directly underneath a palm tree, unaware she was being watched. Xochitl got a good look at Noelle's face from below, peering out from within her Magical Deer facemask.

Noelle strolled over to a narrow shoreline. Waves were crashing, parents and children screaming and laughing, as the sky was readying itself for a storm. She readjusted the obsidian mirror backplate and continued down the beach, photographing the swimmers quickly and candidly.

Looking out across the bay from the second-story veranda, Rosita commented to Emilio that Noelle would never find her way back once the fog bank has set in. Her assessment did not go unappreciated.

Octavio returned to the second-story veranda, propped himself up against the doorjamb, and insisted that Emilio go and find Noelle. Emilio left Rosita's side and took a few steps in Octavio's direction. Left hand extended, Emilio agreed to bring Noelle back home on one condition—that he would be allowed to wear Octavio's green-plumed Quetzal bird facemask. Octavio reached into the lining of his jacket and gave the facemask to Emilio.

"No shenanigans, she's family!" Octavio said, grinning on one side.

Rosita and Emilio remained silent until Octavio left the veranda and was out of sight. Rosita turned to Emilio. She insisted he does something about Noelle.

"She's in no way going to be part of this family." Rosita insisted. "I can't stand the sight of her. You know who she reminds me of?"

"Gee, let me guess."

"She reminds me of my ex."

Eyes rolling, Emilio turned his head away from Rosita.

"I'd still own this place if he hadn't been such an ass-hole." Rosita gasped. She knew right then and there that Emilio would not let that remark slide. Some secrets were left better unsaid.

Emilio placed his arm around Rosita and inquired, "I thought you were the owner?"

Rosita turned away from Emilio's affections and cast her eyes in the direction of Caballito.

"It's mine in that I can do anything I want with it," Rosita uttered.

"Well, that will get a doughnut and a cup of coffee," Emilio said sarcastically.

Rosita turned and faced Emilio and shot him an evil eye. He responded in kind.

"Rosita, what else are you ashamed of?" Emilio said as he stared her down.

Rosita, clearly covering-up for misdeeds and misleading her admirer, bowed her head and insisted they not get into it.

Emilio peeled back a smile and said affirmatively, "Chill-out! There's not going to be any search and rescue. I'll terrify the bitch once the fog hits the shore."

Rosita, in frightful anticipation, spouted, "I know, and she'll get all disoriented."

"You watch, I'll have her on the next flight out of here!" Emilio whispered.

Rosita's expression shifted from one of angst to one of sheer delight.

Dahlia entered the second-story veranda and quickly handed-off the oversized Quetzal bird feather to Emilio. Emilio walked over to the back wall, shimmied down an olive tree, and jetted on down to the beach, flaunting the feather in the air.

The storm was turning the sky from red to purple to black. A thick fog bank had enveloped Banderas Bay. It seemed to hover a few feet above the ground cover.

This had always been a magical place where fog often preempted rain. The indigenous peoples of the Americas saw the encroaching fog rolling off the waters as the pantheon—all their Deities—at hand. This was an omen of the highest Order. I thought to myself.

Swimmers sprinted onto the shore as lightning struck nearby. Noelle hid under a pier, concerned about the ominous change in weather. A man crouched down next to Noelle advised her to remove her feet from the water. She ran onto the white sandy beach, which was sprinkled with raindrops, moving in the direction of the bronze seahorse statue. Through the thick fog, Noelle could make out "Big Cat" paw prints. They were Mela's, the were-cougar. The paw prints lead to an abandoned burned-out beach house illuminated in white miniature lights. Noelle thought she saw a Mexican family milling about inside the ruins and followed the paw prints to a side entrance. Upon arrival, there was no one to be found, and the paw prints were no longer visible.

Emilio, wearing the papier-mâché green-plumed Quetzal bird facemask and holding the over-sized Quetzal bird feather, watched Noelle from the jetty situated in the bay. He had come to this location to meet Mela. When Emilio last saw his sister, she was tied to a wooden stake, taking a long-needed catnap. As Emilio walked to the end of the jetty, it was apparent Mela had escaped from her collar. A rope was placed on the ground neatly arranged in a figure eight. The other clue was a set of paw prints in the "direct registering" fashion was visible in the sand. Mela, as a were-cougar, was on the prowl in search of a good meal; the local hospitality would suffice. Emilio left his private lookout for a more intimate introduction to Noelle.

From inside the burned-out beach house, Noelle tried to see past the large picture window to the children and adults fleeing the beach. The opaque quality of the fog made everything look flat and two-dimensional. Her sight was limited to a few yards in front of her.

"Show me your mirror." A smooth, silky voice instructed.

Noelle nervously asked who was there as she placed her head through the picture window. Out from under the fog bank, she saw a huge Quetzal bird feather bobbing and weaving in her direction. Emilio, hiding behind the Quetzal bird facemask, pressed through the gypsum-grey mist and stood directly beneath her.

Noelle took two steps back and asked nervously, "Octavio is that you?"

There was no reply, so she turned to run but smacked her head on a window frame, mistaking it for the doorjamb. Noelle was thrown back and landed violently on the concrete floor. She had cracked the back of her head and passed out. The Quetzal bird facemask and feather withdrew.

Standing back and to the left of Noelle, perched on a collector beam attached to the retaining wall, was Saltire. Xochitl sat below her father curled up, holding his long-nose Turkey facemask and costume. Wearing just a black leotard, Saltire morphed into the shape of the Toltec God "Tlaloc"—the Deity of Rain, Thunder, Lightning, and Transformation. For a brief stay, a vibrant blue-faced man with goggle-shaped eyes, a long turned up nose, and two curling fangs danced in the wind. Within moments, Tlaloc's twisted ropes of hair converged, forming the green-plumed feathered serpent "Quetzalcoatl"—the Deity of self-reflection and wisdom. The Creator Sky-God tipped his snake-scaled face to the stars and called out, "INTENT!"

Paloma had surmised that Saltire was cut from a different cloth than the rest of us. Upon entering a room, he can alter the perception of people, as well as what they can expect to experience. A Master of Intent, he uses his intuition and impeccable listening as a mood-altering instrument for the benefit of all concerned. It was said Saltire had been taught how to manipulate time and space by the divine messenger Dancing Movement.

A previous aspect of Saltire's Seminal Being *Soul was believed to have been Immokalee's father, Jared Ekchuah Chisholm, named after the Mayan Deity of Traveling Merchants. One part Arawak Indian and one part African slave from the West Indies, his shamanic knowledge was well-known.*

Tragically on August 20, 1887, the cyclone that devastated North Carolina's coastline ravaged his cousin's fishing schooner when it was struck by lightning and caught fire. Jared was presumed dead at the age of thirty-six, and his body was never recovered. More astounding still was the belief that Saltire carried within him the aspect of Ce Acatl Topiltzin-Quetzalcoatl, the 10th-century Toltec King-Priest of Tollan, Mexico.

Crashing waves were muffled by offshore coastguard cursors with their sirens blaring. The all-encompassing fog bank spared nothing and distorted everything.

Suddenly, Quetzalcoatl shape-shifted into his twin aspect, Black Tezcatlipoca "Smoking Mirror." Frequently depicted in black, with two broad yellow stripes painted across his face he operates from a slight advantage—his right foot had been replaced with a black scrying mirror. As Smoking Mirror, he was the Lord of the North ruling the nocturnal sky, the God of Time, ancestral memory, and the embodiment of change through conflict.

Slithering down the collector beam that supports the house, Saltire as Smoking Mirror maneuvered himself within inches of Noelle's body. Lifting his right-mirrored foot at a forty-five-degree angle, he set the stage for possessing the images reflected within Noelle's obsidian mirror back plate—images of her personal memories of two prior incarnations. The first image to appear was the head and torso of Noelle's Great Aunt Immokalee Awinita Chisholm Intaglio in the year 1913. After a brief moment, another face graced the mirror. The Toltec Atlantean Warrior/ High Priestess, Quetzal Hunahpu, moved slowly, from left to right, across the surface of Noelle's black obsidian scrying mirror. As Quetzal was reflected against Smoking Mirror's black scrying mirrored foot, he lowered his head.

With a menacing growl, Black Tezcatlipoca proclaimed, "If I block your memory, you will be blinded to the future you've created."

At the mere sight of Quetzal, Saltire as Tezcatlipoca instanta-neously underwent the "Ideomotor Effect"— he made motions, reflexive responses, unconsciously without attributing free will or choice—and morphed into Chalchiuhtotolin Blood-Jeweled Fowl, Long-Nose Turkey. At the very moment Saltire shape-shifted into the Toltec Deity, he ignited the process of Karmic Debt Removal-soul retrieval—a mystical transformation that accelerated the healing of Noelle's *Seminal Being* Soul—that of Amrit Sandhu. Through the lens of spiritual discernment, Noelle was, from that moment forward, able to perceive the past, present, and future from "God's Perspective."

CHAPTER EIGHT

Halloween Night

Noelle's 1994 recapitulation returned to October of 1990. As Noelle remained in a deep sleep, she revisited her relationship with Avery and Mr. and Mrs. Thorndike. It was mid-morning in Salem, MA, and Sergeant Jordon Scolley, who was known as "To Serve, Down Flowing, Independent Person," age twenty-five, was spinning in slow-motion circles just under Noelle's nose. Sergeant, who was a great admirer of the 1920s silent film star Harold Lloyd, never left home without wearing a boaters' straw hat and a pair of black-rimmed glasses. What made his clowning around particularly funny was Sergeant's cherub-like face and round-bellied body. Avery, sporting torn jeans and his father's Lon Chaney were-wolf T-shirt, was juggling muffins in one hand while sipping coffee with the other. Jimmy Cliff's song "The Harder They Come" blasting from a parked car, and Noelle began singing to it. As the three treaded down a steep embankment, they laughed it up while miserably attempting to sing the song in their best Reggae voices.

All of a sudden, Sergeant picked up speed and took off down the road.

"Six o'clock my place!" he hollered.

Off the main thoroughfare in Lexington, MA, Noelle and Avery came rambling up a long gravel driveway in her 1984 Grand Cherokee Wagoneer. Noelle drove under an arched portico, past a large horse stable to the left and to the rear of a two-story historical federal-style brick manor. She parked the Jeep in front of a large riding ring, just under a Halloween sign marked: Caution Skeleton Crossing.

Avery was rummaging around the back seat in search of Noelle's paintbrush kit and drop cloth when he said, "I know someone who hired you last year to paint some murals."

"I painted a lot of murals last year," Noelle replied. "Got a name for me?"

"Painting murals is a pretty lucrative business for you, isn't it? Maybe I should take it up."

Noelle, not wanting to challenge her boyfriend's statement, waited for Avery to find what he was after and then got out of the Jeep. The two quickly descended on the manor of Mr. and Mrs. Thorndike.

Prosper Ira Thorndike "Fortune, Wind-God, Ditch," was adopted by Jean and Isabella Thorndike when he was fifteen years of age. Mr. and Mrs. Thorndike procured the teenager from a Jewish orphanage in Boston, MA, soon after their only son, Michael John Thorndike, was killed in WWII. A senior Professor of Theology at Harvard Graduate School, Prosper was a wise and unassuming gentleman who often knew more about others than they did about themselves. A nature enthusiast, he preferred to ride his bicycle along the Minute Man Bike Way to and from Cambridge, MA, to his manor in Lexington. Two years her senior, Prosper married his best friend, Sophie Caroline St. Ours, and kept the Old English surname alive with his three sons, Michael Jean, Cheval Pascal, and Lambert Benjamin. The family had made a name for themselves as one of the finest breeders of Clydesdale horses east of the Mississippi.

With a paintbrush kit in hand and a drop cloth around his neck, Avery was busy kicking leaves about when they approached the Thorndike Manor side entrance. As Noelle admired all the Halloween decorations, Avery adjusted a life-size skeleton costume attached to the arched portico and freed its legs and arms. Situated in the center of the vaulted drive-through was the relief of the Roman God Janus; he was keeping an eye on the whole situation. Noelle promptly removed the paintbrush kit from Avery's grasp as she walked under the arched portico and entered the manor through the left-wing side door entrance.

Avery walked directly in the opposite direction. He headed over to the backyard patio area; his intentions were not clear. A series of French glass doors stirred his interest; he went over and peered through one of the panes.

Noelle was kneeling down in a far corner of the living room. She was mixing and stirring paint in small, half a gallon, white plastic buckets.

Noelle called out, "Avery! Avery! Mr. Millstone?"

Avery cleverly stepped away from the doors undetected. He then entered the living room where Noelle had set up her paint shop.

"Where do you want me to put this?" Avery asked, referring to the drop cloth draped over his shoulders.

"Just through that door and to your left is the dining room. Could you go ahead and spread it out in there, starting with the left side?" Noelle instructed.

Avery left Noelle's side, dumped the drop cloth off in the dining room, and then headed back outside and over to Noelle's Jeep.

Noelle heard a car motor running from the living room. She leaped up, rushed down the hallway, and through the side door entrance to investigate. Avery was pulling away when Noelle caught up to his window.

"Where are you going?" Noelle asked, looking alarmed.

"Well, you're not going to finish today," Avery said with a laugh.

"What are you talking about? The dining room fresco was signed off two days ago. All that's left are the pantry doors!"

Avery gave her an ultimatum, "You want my help or not?"

Noelle replied in a panic. "Of course, I want your help. I need your help!"

"Okay then, all I'm saying is that I need more coffee. You know of a place nearby?"

"We passed it on the way here. It's just down the street and to the left."

Noelle offered to pay for the coffee and food. She gave Avery directions to the Bagel Café and reassured him that the job would flyby and be fun. Avery accepted the money and rolled down the driveway and onto the main thoroughfare.

Noelle was left standing in the driveway with the life-size Halloween skeleton blowing about in the background. Prosper walked over to the skeleton and reattached it to the ivy vines clinging to the exterior façade of the portico.

"Is your friend one costume short this evening?" Prosper asked.

Noelle shook her head and replied, "I've no idea; I'm sorry."

Noelle and Prosper entered the manor together through the side door. Prosper offered to put on some music and traveled down the hallway and into the living room. Taking a sharp right, he went directly over to a built-in stereo system. Albums from the 40s—80s filled the shelves.

"Beethoven's 'Erotica.' Do you like classical music?" Prosper inquired as he scanned through his collection. "Bet you've never heard them played like this before? This old gal's wired for surround sound."

Noelle waited in the hallway until she was invited to accompany Prosper into the parlor for tea 'n cookies. She sat down at a café-style table and fiddled with the white crochet tablecloth. After a moment, Prosper joined her with a pot of steeping hot tea, accompanied by two teacups 'n saucers.

Gesturing to a rattan tray sporting an assortment of cookies, Prosper said, "Please help yourself. My wife Sophia made them last night. Dang if they ain't good!"

"Thank you, Mr. Thorndike. These look delicious," Noelle replied as she placed three small sugar cookies on her saucer.

As Prosper poured the tea, he offered Noelle a bit of advice regarding her and Avery's relationship.

"Don't be so overly concerned about your friend. It's you that you ought to be mindful of."

Noelle glanced around the parlor taking in the family photos preserved under glass supported by antique picture frames.

"How did you know your wife was 'the one'?" Noelle asked.

"She stayed with me until I could match her commitment, then we both made the choice to get married."

Noelle was touched by his words and lowered her head. Noelle said modestly, "I just can't imagine why he'd want to be with me. I'm much older than him and not nearly as attractive as his other girlfriends."

Prosper set the teapot down clumsily on the tablecloth. Noelle raised her head and caught Mr. Thorndike glaring at her.

"Thoughts of that caliber will get you into trouble."

"What? What do you mean by trouble?" Noelle asked unabashedly.

Prosper, with a slight smile in the corner of his mouth, said, "Have you not heard, 'true love' retreats in the presence of self-doubt."

Noelle's face softened, but her eyes looked sad, "Too late, I wonder what he's doing with me all the time."

Just as Noelle was sipping her last bit of tea, she thought she heard Avery approaching. Noelle stood up, thanked Prosper, and returned to the dining room.

Avery had beaten Noelle to it. He was tapping on one of the dining room windowpane's from outside. She opened the window and took two large coffees and a bag filled with muffins off his hands. Avery asked where the owner was, and Noelle informed him Mr. Thorndike was in the parlor having his tea.

Prosper rose and strolled back down the hallway, teacup in hand, past the dining room, and into the living room. Avery waited until he saw Mr. Thorndike turn to the right, then he proceeded down the hallway until he arrived at the dining room. Many turn-of-the-century homes had these long hallways that carried folks from one end to the other, depositing them at their destination.

Avery was standing in the doorway to the dining room, facing Noelle. She had her back to him and was carefully flattening out the folds in the drop cloth. Avery slid across the hardwood floors, dragging with him the right edges of the drop cloth, and grabbed Noelle in front of the pantry door.

"Gotcha!" Avery whispered on the back of her neck.

A tingling sensation spread from Noelle's cervical to her shoulders, then through her fingertips, as her knees buckled, causing her to relax entirely into Avery's embrace.

For a brief moment, Noelle's recapitulation returned to October 31, 1994. She was still unconscious at the abandoned burned-out beach house on the beach in Puerto Vallarta. Her head was oscillating in the wind as raindrops splashed down upon her face. Loud thunderclaps and lightning bolt streaked across the night sky, while below in Banderas Bay, the remains of an 1887 three masted fishing schooner bobbed about, immersed in smoke and fire.

There was no sign of the Blood-Jeweled Fowl, Long-Nose Turkey Toltec Deity. He had accomplished his mission. He lifted the veil for the emerald-green spirit Dancing Movement, to shape-shift into another aspect of the Toltec Deity Quetzalcoatl. The aspect was known as "Ehecatl," the Deity of wind and movement. He was the divine visitation of a Toltec Warrior, wearing a tall cone-shaped crown made of ocelot (spotted cat) skin and a pendant fashioned in the shape of a conch shell known as the "wind jewel."

Ehecatl reached down and lifted up Noelle's left hand. While holding her palm open, the Deity released a drop of his own saliva into the center of her palm. At that very moment, Noelle's eyes opened as Ehecatl leaned directly over her body.

"Don't hurt me," Noelle pleaded.

In contrast to her fears, Noelle received a spoken mandate from Ehecatl,

"Movement is your access,
Movement comes from within,
I AM where Movement is."

Noelle closed her eyes and began to levitate off the cement floor. A flash of white light encapsulated Noelle in a hermetically sealed enclosure in a Bell Jar shape. Noelle was entering the 5th Dimension and activating *The Spirit of the Voice*, known to mystics as "the Living Word of God," the Intent.

Noelle began to rotate on a horizontal plane, much like a spool of yarn guided by a weaver's shuttle; she was in the process of metamorphosis. From this stage, Noelle was reformed and integrated her prior soul aspect—that of her Great Aunt Immokalee. Rotation upon rotation, the shape of Immokalee then harmonized with the female Toltec Atlantean Warrior, Quetzal Hunahpu. The final rotations had Quetzal shape-shift into a were-quetzal bird and then disappear into a chrysalis mass of becoming. Ehecatl then entered the enclosure, and together, they witnessed a synergistic fractal dance of free-floating inverted triangles forming a "Fibonacci Sequence" inside a hermetically sealed enclosure—"Imaginal-Vignettes®."

This was Noelle's means of embracing the three intrinsic natures within her Seminal Being: the animal soul, the human soul, and the spirit soul.

Returning to her flashback memories at the Thorndike Manor, a ghost fluttered in front of the life-size Halloween skeleton and landed at its feet. At the front of the manor, Noelle's Jeep was being prepared for a speedy departure. She had completed the month-long job for Prosper and was double-checking that her painting materials and supplies were all accounted for.

Avery popped his head through the dining room window and yelled at the top of his lungs, "Have we got everything?"

"Wait Up!" Noelle said in a hurried tone.

Noelle and Avery met in the dining room and saw that nothing had been left behind. Crossing the hallway, they entered the living room and took their last look around.

"I've been watching you all day, and never once did I see your 'wheels' turning," Avery said in a provocative tone,

"What's that supposed to mean?" Noelle winced.

Avery doesn't respond.

Noelle's kneejerk reaction is to leave immediately.

"You heard him, the pantry doors came out beautifully. Let's go! What are you doing?"

Avery was circling a billiard table in the far left corner of the living room the way a hyena does before its first strike at a dimwitted wildebeest. Nip at the hoofs then the belly. Take it down and keep her down.

"How do you know if a person really loves you?" Avery asked Noelle.

"I don't know. How do you know?"

Avery, changing tactics, blurted out, "I don't think I've ever been in love!"

Noelle recoiled and then shamefully fired back, "What? What are you talking about? You told me you loved me just yesterday. Why'd you say it if you didn't mean it?"

Avery ignored Noelle and began playing billiards.

"Please stop, Avery. Mr. Thorndike wouldn't appreciate you touching his things."

Avery kept playing, and his approach was becoming wild and reckless, sending billiard balls off the table and onto the hardwood floor. Noelle informed him she was leaving and headed for the exit. Avery stopped all play and put the billiard cue back in its rack. Noelle turned around to confront him.

"Is this a test of some sort?" Noelle asked.

Avery leaning up against the built-in bookshelves nodded his head "No" then "Yes."

Noelle argued with Avery, sitting that it was mean-spirited to go around messing with people's heads.

"I don't think this bull-shit is funny," Noelle shouted. "Come on; I'm leaving!"

Prosper was standing behind by the living room pocket-door handle, twirling the brass ring, when Noelle, exasperated by Avery's antics, turned around to leave.

"Hold on a second; I have something for you, Noelle. Something I think you might appreciate." Prosper said as he crossed the living room on his way to the bookshelves.

Mr. Thorndike stood six feet two-inches high in his favorite pair of brown leather cowboy boots. Standing on his toes, he reached for the handmade "artist book" entitled *The Spirit of the Voice*, written by Nicholas Renato Intaglio III and Immokalee Awinita Chisholm, published in 1913.

"I'd bet my last penny that you can't tell me what's in this book," Prosper said as he peered down at Avery.

"Got me there?" Avery snickered.

"Noelle's Great Aunt Immokalee co-authored this rare and rather exceptional book," Prosper answered coolly as he waved the book over Avery's head.

"Are you serious?" Avery fired back. "I think that's highly unlikely; her family comes from North Carolina, and I'm sure back then they didn't have but an eighth-grade education." Go ahead, Noelle, tell him, tell the Professor where your family comes from!"

Noelle walked over to Prosper and asked to see the artist book, "Do you mind if I see it?"

Prosper opened the book and showed Noelle a watercolor landscape painting of a lighthouse at Cape Hatteras, North Carolina. Noelle instantly recognized the painting and shared what she knew about her Great Aunt Immokalee,

"This is how my mother tells it," Noelle began. "When my Grandmother Chantal was just twelve years old, she was orphaned and left to raise her younger sister Immokalee in the Smokey Mountains, on the North Carolina side. It took weeks before anyone could confirm what had happened to their parents. When the news got out, no one could believe it. On August 20, 1887, a cyclone raked the coast of North Carolina, sinking their cousin's fishing schooner. The following morning a "search 'n rescue" was issued by the Cape Hatteras Coast Guard, but no bodies were ever found."

"So you're telling us that their education improved after that?"

"Just because they were orphaned, half-Cherokee Indians, doesn't imply they were uneducated savages. To the contrary, they both proved to be very talented and resourceful!"

Prosper watched and waited as Noelle and Avery left the living room before he placed the artist book on top of the 17th-century burl oak writer's desk in the hallway.

It was close to six o'clock when Noelle, Avery, and Mr. Thorndike strolled over to the Jeep Grand Cherokee Wagoneer. Prosper gave Noelle a hug, a check for $4,000 dollars, and thanked her for the beautiful artwork she had produced in his home.

Noelle hesitated then asked, "My Great "Auntie Lee's" book; I was wondering if I could buy it from you. I know my mom would love to have it!"

"You may have it, my dear. It's yours as of this moment!" Prosper said, smiling. "Why don't the two of you stop by later for cider and homemade boysenberry pie à la mode? I can gift it to you, then Noelle."

"Hold up! I've got to make a quick phone call." Avery said to Noelle.

Prosper showed no objection. Avery headed back over to the arched portico and disappeared through the side entrance.

When Avery was out of earshot, Prosper said to Noelle, "See if later on, you can free yourself from your friend. My son, Michael Jean, will be at the house tonight, and I'd like the two of you to meet."

Noelle, still bruised by Avery's earlier remarks agreed, "I'll leave the party early, I'll take the Commuter Rail into North Station then transfer to 'the T,' and get off at David Square. From there, I'll—"

"Prosper knew where she was going and interrupted Noelle, "When you come up from the station, turn left; you'll find two bicycles chained to a bike rack."

Noelle nodded as she watched Prosper remove a set of keys from his pants pocket. "In a blink-of-an-eye," he unlatched one of the keys to a bike lock and slipped it in her hand.

"This key unlocks the ten-speed bike. You'll have an easier time getting here than if you try to catch the T on Halloween."

Prosper bid Noelle goodbye and jogged around the horse stable to where a three-car garage was located.

Avery deposited a slice of boysenberry pie onto a paper towel in the kitchen while he made a last-minute phone call to his best friend, Blake.

"Blake, pick up! Pick up, asshole!"

"Hey, everybody's getting ready. Where are you at?" Blake said sounding annoyed.

"I'm on my way," Avery replied.

Avery reemerged from the Thorndike Manor, eating a slice of boysenberry pie in one hand while securing Prosper's copy of the artist book, *The Spirit of the Voice* between his T-shirt and jeans.

Avery had no idea Immokalee's copy was the only record still in existence substantiating my very existence. It was in pristine condition. The secrets it held, if deciphered with precision, contained my destiny as I had willfully intended.

Avery looked around to see if Mr. Thorndike could see him. When he saw Prosper's 1987 Green Range Rover taillights turn right onto the thoroughfare, he quickly stole the life-size Halloween skeleton costume from the portico.

Holding the skeleton up to his shoulders, Avery said, "Come with Meeeee."

Noelle caught sight of Avery imitating a "dead man walking" and slinked into her car seat.

CHAPTER NINE

Karmic Debt Removal

L ayered clouds interrupted a deep blue sky. It was twilight in Puerto Vallarta, and Noelle had been missing for over two hours. The waves crashing on the sand berms acted as cymbals and reawakened Noelle to her surroundings. Lying next to Noelle was a small beaded leather pouch filled with copal incense. Noelle picked up the pouch, made an unsuccessful attempt to open its drawstrings, and opted for Plan B. She slipped her right wrist through the opening and clutched it in her fist. Rising to her feet, Noelle found her way out of the abandoned burned-out beach house by following a path of pepita seeds, which led her to the shoreline. From there, she proceeded in the southerly direction toward Mar Casa De La Concha. Children and their parents had returned to the waters' edge. The storm had passed, and they resumed running up and down the shoreline, buck jumping, and screaming as traditional Mexican masks nipped at their heels.

"There's the Atlantean," Xochitl said.

Noelle squinted and placed her right hand under her chin as the small eight-year-old child in a papier-mâché Magical Deer facemask and costume approached her.

"Atlantean, there you are!"

"And who might you be?" Noelle asked wearily.

"I'm Magical Deer. Come on, you're late!"

Xochitl initiating the climb back to the B&B took hold of Noelle's hand. Xochitl's hands were well hidden inside of her costume, Noelle had no way of knowing her hands were misshaped—*"Lobster Claw Syndrome."* Saltire discretely followed close behind his daughter in his Blood-Jeweled Fowl, Long-Nose Turkey facemask and costume.

The sky had cleared, and stars were twinkling by the time the threesome made it back to Mar Casa De La Concha, situated high on a cliff overlooking Banderas Bay. Four of the six family members were hanging out on the second-story veranda: Octavio the "Quetzal Bird" which stood for a sacred messenger, Rosita the "Turtle Rabbit" which was an animal totem for the devil, Dahlia the "Tawny Spotted Jaguar" was a symbol for the Chilam Balam, and Emilio the "Black Jaguar" was the animal totem of Smoking Mirror. They had gathered around the teakwood dining table and were finishing their dinner when they heard a rustling at the front door.

Noelle the "Toltec Atlantean Warrior," which was the Guardian of the Lord of Dawn, and Xochitl the Magical Deer, which served as a spiritual guide, entered the foyer and went their separate ways. Saltire, the "Blood-Jeweled Fowl, Long-Nose Turkey," the Toltec Deity of Karmic Debt Removal soul-retrieval, closed the front door behind them. He then descended the front staircase and snuck around to the first-floor guest patio undetected. The purple Bougainvilleas from the lattice covering and the Saltillo floor tile throughout the home acted as a sound barrier.

Noelle went upstairs to change into dry clothes. She headed directly into the bathroom, removed her facemask and costume, then jumped into the shower stall to clean up. The hot water combined with her soapy hands burned the back of her head. She felt the sting behind her right ear and hesitated before removing her hand. Blood was dripping down from her fingertips.

Noelle determining it was only a flesh wound, rinsed off and wrapped herself in a pink terrycloth robe. She then walked over to the mirror and was taken aback by what she saw—a sizeable egg-shaped bump had flared-up on her forehead.

"You idiot! Now they're all going to want to know what happened." Noelle said to herself.

Xochitl ran over to Octavio on the veranda and announced she had found his "Atlantean."

"Thank you, Xochitl, for returning my guardian friend safely to me," Octavio replied.

"When I found her, she was lost. I think she'd been trying to flee from Turtle Rabbit the Devil!"

"No, my little doe, from the 'tiger' that saw fit to borrow my mask."

Emilio was offended by the accusation. He got up and left the veranda in favor of investigating Noelle's whereabouts.

Noelle's mood had improved. She was happily singing "Humpty Dumpty," and her voice could easily be heard from the third-floor hallway. Emilio stopped to listen, pushed his way through the bedroom door, and gently tossed an object into the room. Bouncing across the fabric of Noelle's WWII Marine Corps olive-green garment bag was a smooth clay figurine of a were-cougar.

Cheryl Bekenkol, known as the "Box Turtle," a symbol for inner wisdom, waddled onto the step leading to the veranda. She had somehow managed to wrap a yellow telephone cord, like a fourteen-foot long python, tightly around her neck.

"Can someone kindly get me the hell out of this chokehold?" Cheryl motioned with her head.

Emilio reentering the veranda, flicked his tail, leaned in, and whispered in Cheryl's ear, "Don't worry, I'm not going to let you die in the Tropics."

"Step off!" Cheryl said harshly.

Emilio stepped down and slinked over to his fiancé Dahlia.

"What's with the phones around here?" Cheryl questioned the group. "Upstairs, downstairs, it really doesn't seem to make any difference."

Rosita squirmed in her seat.

"I've just spent my entire afternoon trying to reach my daughter. Her baby is due any day now! Sally, can you get a hold of the operator?" Cheryl requested.

Octavio got up from the dining table and asked Cheryl if she would like to sit next to him. Cheryl, a sucker for male attention, placed the phone on a hat rack and wiggled out from under the 'mile-long' cord independent of any helping hands.

Noelle entered the veranda wearing a matching cocoa brown T-shirt and yoga pants. She held her Toltec Atlantean Warrior breastplate against her chest as she took a seat next to Cheryl. Cheryl popped off a few Polaroids of everyone in their spirit masks and costumes. Noelle, aghast at her image, attempted to scoop up the photo of herself without her face.

Octavio objected, snatched it from her hand, and placed the Polaroid inside his costume.

"Your soul's mine now," Octavio laughed under his facemask.

The last time her photo was taken on Halloween, it didn't go so well. Spells were cast, and she almost died.

Octavio rose to his feet, stepped away from the women, and walked over to a long folding table propped up against the balcony. There he prepared an authentic Mexican dinner: grilled fish, local vegetables, corn tortillas, beans, and rice. While Octavio delivered the plates of food to his American guests, Rosita got up from the dining table and began to gather up the dirty dishes.

"Please sit back down, Rosita; I'll take those, thank you," Octavio said.

Octavio reached across the table and removed the plates from his sister's delicate fingers. Rosita sat back down between Dahlia and Emilio and glanced over at Noelle then at Cheryl.

Rosita lifting her Mexican three-banded Armadillo facemask and directed her comments to Cheryl, "I'm sorry, had I known you were trying to reach your daughter, I would have let you use the phone in my bedroom. It's the only one that's reliable in this godforsaken place."

Cheryl shot a look over at Rosita, acknowledging the offer, and said, "After dinner then?"

Noelle was feverishly polishing off her plate when Rosita lowered her Armadillo facemask.

"Oh, for God's sake, where's the rest of your costume?" Rosita asked Noelle.

"It's a long-standing tradition around here, no costume, no dessert!" Emilio chimed in.

"It's upstairs. Should I go get it?" Noelle asked Rosita.

"How about it, Noelle? Feel like messing with a little tradition?" Octavio said, while glaring at Rosita.

Saltire nestled in the branches of an olive tree, partially sheltered by the second-story floorboards, was within earshot. He was keenly listening to what was NOT being said.

"How'd you get that nasty bump on your head?" Rosita initiated. "We were all worried sick with anticipation that something dreadful had happened to you."

Octavio, sipping on his molasses-like remedy, jumped in and answered for Noelle, "May I?"

Noelle encouraged him to speak on her behalf.

"She bumped her head in a flight of fancy. To quote my brother, 'all is, as intended.' "

Rosita shielded by her armadillo facemask, raised her hand and took a long drag on a menthol cigarette. Signally, dinner was officially over.

Xochitl looking around the veranda, asked, "Where's Papi?"

Octavio informed his niece her father would be joining them any minute.

Saltire dropped down from the olive tree, jogged past the carport, climbed the elevated exterior staircase, and entered the pistachio-green study to the right of the front entrance. Rosita and Cheryl had left the veranda and were ascending the second-story staircase on their way to Rosita's bedroom. Octavio and Xochitl were in the kitchen, off and to the left of the veranda, busily rinsing and drying dishes. Dahlia and Emilio were at the long folding table preparing fried ice-cream with sticks of chocolate in dessert bowls for dessert.

Noelle excused herself and was on her way to the powder room when a portrait in the living room grabbed her attention. Alone in the ochre-colored living room, she thoughtfully gazed upon a series of images: paintings of a single woman at different stages of her life. Saltire remained in the study to allow her ample time to examine the artwork.

After a few minutes into her exploration, Saltire disturbed Noelle's solitude by walking directly over to her.

Noelle, facing away from the intruder, asked, "Who are these paintings of?"

Before Saltire could reply, Magical Deer appeared from around the corner.

"Papi! Where were you?" asked Xochitl.

Saltire leaned down and scooped his daughter up in his arms. He spoke to Xochitl privately and then very gingerly lowered her down onto the hardwood floor. Xochitl peeled off in the direction of the veranda.

Saltire, still hidden under his Blood-Jeweled Fowl, Long-Nose Turkey facemask and costume, turned and faced Noelle before answering, "My grandmother on my father's side, Cab-Coh "Honey-Puma.""

Noelle slowly looked over her shoulder then turned around to listen to whatever else Saltire might have to say on the matter.

"If she were here this evening, she'd insist that I introduce myself in verse," he added.

Saltire crossed his chest with his left forearm and bowed sharply, fanning out his arm and fingers before continuing: ("But I, being poor have only my dreams, I have spread my dreams under your feet, tread softly because you tread on my dreams."—Yeats)

With a ting of trepidation in her voice, Noelle asked, "Yours?"

"Yeats." Noelle stood corrected.

Noelle heard her name being called from the veranda. She hastened to leave but was blocked by Saltire. He then positioned his bare hand a few inches in front of the egg-shaped bump on her forehead. Noelle stood still as if momentarily paralyzed.

Saltire, in a commanding voice, prescribed a treatment, "HEAL!"

After a two-second count, Saltire removed his hand and politely gestured for Noelle to leave. Noelle stopped in the vestibule and checked out her forehead in a sun-shaped rattan mirror; the shiny egg-shaped bump protruding from her forehead had vanished.

Everyone but Cheryl and Saltire had returned to the veranda for a serving of fried ice-cream garnished with thin stalks of chocolate from the Celestino Cocoa Bean Plantation in Veracruz.

The dining table and chairs lining the perimeter formed a protective circle intended to highlight the individual receiving a Toltec Oracle card reading from Dahlia. How the game was played: The Oracle upon reading the cards conveyed his or her interpretation. If the card reading had a positive conclusion, then the recipient was offered a follow-up Scrying Mirror reading with which to see various aspects of their *Seminal Being* Soul.

Noelle was seated in the center directly across from Dahlia and waited in anticipation of her first oracle reading. Ten Toltec Oracle cards, out of a fifty-two card deck, were placed face up in front of her. Dahlia appeared confused with the first two cards; *Lust* crossed by Sorrow, and concerned with the seventh and eight cards, but comforted by the prospects of the outcome of the tenth and final card the *Universe*.

Cheryl remained upstairs, on the third floor, in Rosita's bedroom, talking on the phone with her daughter, Lisa. Faint giggling from Cheryl could be heard downstairs by the front entrance. Saltire intentionally stayed away from the festivities. He was reclining on the living room sofa, snacking on his personal stash of pepita seeds.

Dahlia was just finishing up Noelle's reading when a loud crack interrupted her. Rosita, eager to hear Dahlia's final prediction on the fate of the young American, insisted that Emilio handle the situation.

"Emilio, go and see who's out there?"

Emilio rose to his feet and begrudgingly shuffled over to the front door.

Dahlia, after much consideration, stated the final outcome that was most likely to occur over the course of the next three days for Noelle.

Dahlia, in a low sweet voice, spoke a prophetic Toltec verse:

> *"The serpent has outlived its usefulness,*
> *In the face of Baile Movimiento.*
> *Soon you'll see the world as it truly is,*
> *A place of bright imaginings."*

Emilio opened the front door, caught sight of two guys and one girl attempting to vandalize Saltire's Triumph Trophy 1200 motorcycle.

"I suggest you politely ask your friends to leave my bike alone." Saltire said.

Emilio pretended not to know the vandals and began threatening "his friends." He leaned down and picked up the grapefruit-size rock they had flung at the front door and threw it back in their general direction, hitting the front tire of Saltire's motorcycle.

"Ah, there's my boy," Saltire said nonchalantly. "Once a criminal always a liability."

Emilio slammed the front door.

Emilio, a known-to-be juvenile delinquent, was seventeen years old when he stole a motorcycle from a gang member outside of the discothèque "Christine." Three days later, he was able to divert suspicion by anonymously contacting the gang members and disclosing the motorcycle's location at a rival Mafia hangout. Soon after that, he learned from a local merchant that two of the rival gang members were killed over the incident. It was rumored in the *Otherworld,* that Emilio was a double agent for a Mexican Mafia family. They apparently were in cahoots with the diabolical Toltec Deity Tezcatlipoca Smoking Mirror back in the nineties.

"Dahlia!" Emilio yelled from the vestibule, "Get your ass over here; we're leaving!"

Saltire was disrobing when he walked over to an impatient Emilio. He delivered his Blood-Jeweled Fowl, Long-Nose Turkey mask and costume to Emilio with two simple instructions.

"Here, Black Marauder, give these to Rosita, then tell Xochitl to meet me out front."

Emilio took the mask and costume off Saltire's hands and headed back toward Rosita. Saltire, sporting a black V-neck T-shirt and cobalt blue swim shorts, started to leave, then spun back around and glared at Emilio. Emilio felt Saltire's eyes burning a hole in the back of his head and whipped his head around. The front door was left wide-open, and Saltire was nowhere in sight.

The second-story veranda appeared a bit disheveled. The group was disbanding by the time Emilio arrived. Visibly fired-up, his next outburst was directed at Xochitl.

"Xochitl, your dad wants you out front!"

Xochitl, as Magical Deer, started to skip past Emilio when he put his leg out to stop her. Crouching down, he reached into his black leather moneybag and showed her a clay feline figurine in flight.

Xochitl playing along, inquired into the cat's nature, "Are you a good kitty or a bad kitty?" She then hopped over Emilio's leg and dashed through the front door.

Dahlia made several attempts to placate Emilio. He, however, was totally unmanageable and was having no part of her. The group agreed it was in everyone's best interest to call it a night.

Meanwhile, Xochitl was curled up on Saltire's Triumph Trophy 1200 motorcycle seat with her Magical Deer facemask cuddled in her arms. Saltire was inspecting his motorcycle for any damage as he freed a 1950s half-belt brown leather motorcycle jacket from a saddlebag.

Octavio descended the elevated staircase, leading from Mar Casa De La Concha to the private driveway, and strolled over to talk to Saltire.

Noelle pushed through the front door and waited for Octavio at the front door landing.

Emilio approached Noelle from behind and accosted her, "I'd watch your step if I were you. I've seen the future, and you're not in it." Immobilized by his threatening remark, Noelle does not respond.

"You don't know what this is all about, do you?" Emilio continued. "No matter, far be it from me to be the one to spoil the surprise."

Octavio, fully aware that Noelle was under some sort of psychic attack from Emilio, left Saltire's side, ascended the staircase, and confronted Emilio at the top of the landing.

"Don't be tampering with things you know nothing about." Octavio insisted.

Noelle looking painfully unsure of the situation, bowed her head to dodge any verbal blows.

Rosita and Dahlia approached the landing from the vestibule. Octavio, sensitive to Noelle's feelings, requested that the matter of Emilio be resolved by those of the greater persuasion. He raised his hand as if to say, "will you please." Rosita and Dahlia snagged Emilio and yanked him away from Noelle and back inside.

"Don't go anywhere; I'll be back in a flash," Octavio told Noelle.

Octavio quickly walked back over to Saltire and Xochitl. After a brief visual assessment of Noelle, he voiced his concerns, "She's a difficult read," Octavio said to his brother in all seriousness.

"As it stands, her whole demeanor spells disaster." Saltire replied.

"Paloma seems to think she's suffering from a systemic loss that has been dominating her *Seminal Being* Soul for centuries. We may want to consider looking there first for answers."

Changing the subject, Saltire interjected, "And what's up with Emilio?"

"You've spent more time with him than I have. You tell me." Octavio insisted.

Before answering, Saltire walked Octavio over to a flickering streetlamp, pretending to be interested in its malfunction. Xochitl was still curled up on her father's motorcycle seat, Magical Deer facemask in arms, sound asleep.

Saltire standing under the streetlamp, declared, "We will subject him to the trials that tour tradition dictates, and see how he fares when pitted against his own inadequacies. And I intend to maximize his sister."

"Mela?" Octavio questioned. "I thought you kicked her out of the Council months ago."

"She asked to be reinstated and put an end to her brother's debauchery. Besides, we can't get Noelle to where she needs to be without her."

"Alright then, how do you want to do this?"

"Tomorrow morning Noelle and Xochitl will take the boat taxi to Yelapa. Mela will instigate a mock attack at the waterfall. I can assure you, the thrust of her intention will be tempered by our friends the indians!"

"Yes, but how will Xochitl respond?" Octavio asked, sounding concerned.

"We've played "The Stalking Game"—Baby Eagle to Big Cat— many times before. She'll catch on straightaway and counter the "virtual" attack."

"Noelle in this situation is going to be at quite the disadvantage." Octavio pointed out.

Saltire, upon reflection, agreed. "Point well taken, Noelle's become far too homogenized to be effective."

"Somehow we've got to get her to—"

"—acknowledge Immokalee," Saltire said. Then, the *Seminal Being* Soul will be free to utilize the Silent Knowledge retained in that indian's soul, and dormant forces will spontaneously influence Noelle's behavior."

As I stood on the landing with and inside of Noelle, I saw the holographic 3-D image of Saltire and Octavio when they were both young men. The year Saltire turned twenty-one, he changed his surname from McKenna to Celestino. He felt that by changing his name, he would change his future. Almost immediately, he began to access "Silent Knowledge" from deep within his Seminal Being Soul—the place where perception is assembled, stored, and accessible. It was at this time that both

Octavio and Saltire were initiated into the ancient "Quetzalcoatl Cult" of their forefathers, which in turn led to their graduation into the Toltec Secret Eagle Knight Council. By becoming Masters of Intent, they were able to reactivate the Chamber of Mirrors and the Original Intent of their Seminal Being *Souls and their combined Intended Future.*

Octavio knew all too well the inherent dangers during the early stages of initiation into the Toltec Secret Eagle Knight Council and asked Saltire if Xochitl's involvement was really required.

Taking into account Octavio's question, Saltire turned and proceeded toward his daughter. Xochitl had changed her position; her head was resting peacefully on his motorcycle handlebars.

Octavio walked close behind Saltire and inquired into their mother's current status, "Melita. Is she still in the picture?"

"Oh yeah, I'll make sure the "Blonde Lady" knows her shtick," Saltire reassured his brother.

"Afterwards, PARVULO X'S BIKE SHOP 'N REPAIR will do," Octavio stated.

"It's the perfect environment for Noelle's Karmic Debt Removal-soul retrieval."

Octavio caught up to Saltire and, looking forlorn, said wistfully, "Hey, do you remember when we were teenagers, we traded in the bay for the Hills of Tonala."

Saltire's eyes swelled with tears as he stopped short of his bike, "Victor got us to train his horses to dance around that ring of fire."

As the brothers recalled their summers spent at Cousin Victor's Hacienda, I gained insight into their journey into mysticism. Saltire expressed his interest in being educated in the ancient Art of Karmic Debt Removal-soul retrieval—"The Self-Correcting Principle." While Octavio voiced how he had wanted to know everything there was to learn about animal shape-shifting.

Under the tutelage of Cousin Victor, it would appear they had been generously indoctrinated into the long-forgotten Magical Arts of Mesoamerica. At age twenty, the audacious young men had expanded their spiritual development to include teachings from the "Chilam Balam"—four Huichol Indians/Toltec Shamans were-jaguars, residing in Old Town Puerto Vallarta, Mexico. Under their instruction, they had learned how to listen for, have access to, and assimilate "Silent Knowledge"— Universal wisdom that was transferred from the Milky Way (the generator) to Mother

Earth's Sun (the receptacle/transistor). The knowledge was and still is, released through sun flares whose trajectories co-mingle with the Earth's magnetic field. This allowed Saltire and Octavio to perceive the 4th Dimension and the Universal Laws of causality and creation, furnishing them with the tools to commune with Prime Mover/God directly.

"I'm just sorry I won't be there when she remembers the Intent that is at the source of her very Being!" Octavio added just before Saltire's departure.

Saltire push-started his motorcycle down the road before disappearing around a bend. Xochitl was tucked inside his leather jacket; her little claw-like hands were clasped in her lap.

Noelle was still standing on the landing when Octavio joined her. With a look of trepidation in her eyes, Noelle said cautiously, "Mind if I tell you something?"

Octavio interrupted Noelle sharply, "It will have to wait until tomorrow."

"But it can't wait," Noelle exclaimed. "I feel someone's been following me!"

Without warning, a gust of wind rushed at Noelle and threw her inside the front door.

"Yes, something, as in plural, is at your heels," Octavio agreed. "I suggest you become friends with them first 'n foremost because life ain't going to get any better until you do."

Octavio was thinking along the lines of the *Seminal Being* Soul's perspective. The aspect that was the individualized soul-particle of her Great Aunt Immokalee—as well as that of the Toltec Atlantean Warrior, Quetzal Hunahpu—had to be recognized and embraced in order to dispel the nature of her suffering. Without this advanced perception and understanding of her "Soul's Journey," Noelle would remain affected by her prior conditioning.

Mexican glass sconces flickered three times from the third-floor hallway announcing to everyone it was time to "call it a night." Rosita and Cheryl retired to their bedrooms while Dahlia and Emilio quietly closed and bolted their bedroom door. Octavio accompanied Noelle to Saltire's bedroom.

"Puerto Vallarta is a magical place. It's where the past and future coexist. Only a thin line separates them . . . your dreams," Octavio explained.

"That's odd that you'd bring that up. Ever since I met you, my dreams have been conjuring up my past," Noelle revealed.

Octavio, closing the window overlooking the beach, said smiling, "I know, it's all part of the Bigger Picture."

On his way out, Octavio noticed the small clay figurine of a were-cougar flopped on top of Noelle's WWII Marine Corps olive-colored garment bag. He reached down and pinched it. Showing Noelle the clay figurine, Octavio challenged her level of spiritual discernment.

"See this? What's it doing here?" he asked harshly.

After inspecting the clay were-cougar, Noelle glanced up at Octavio. "I've no idea what it is, I've never seen it before, so I can't tell you how it got there."

Octavio glared straight into Noelle's eyes, which sent a shiver down her spine.

"Someone is attempting to compromise your position."

"My position?" Noelle asked.

"Black Magicians use these clay figurines to put spells on people, places, and things. More to the point, Black Magicians place spells in the place where a person gathers perception."

Noelle looking up and down her body, asked, "Where's that on me?"

Octavio focused on Noelle's garment bag and inquired about its contents, "What's in the bag?"

Noelle glanced over at the beaded leather pouch filled with copal incense peeking out from her garment bag.

"I suppose I should have told you about this too?" Noelle said.

Octavio points to the corner of a book barely visible inside her garment bag.

"You're fine. The book Noelle, show me the book!"

Noelle walked cautiously over to the garment bag, bent down, and dislodged the handmade artist book *The Spirit of the Voice* by Nicholas Renato Intaglio III and Immokalee Awinita Chisholm, published in 1913.

"May I see your book?" Octavio politely insisted.

Noelle delivered the artist book to him and backed away. Placing his finger randomly inside the book, Octavio flipped it wide open.

"I will make your first entry into Dreamtime as painless as possible. May I borrow your book tonight? You'll have it back in the morning. Any objections?" Octavio asked.

Noelle shook her head "No." Octavio left quietly, artist book under his green feathered costume. He sauntered down the hallway and entered his bedroom located directly across from Cheryl's room.

Dahlia and Emilio were getting ready to go to sleep. Emilio remembered he had to call Chargo, and excused himself. Emilio went to knock on Rosita's bedroom door. Rosita appeared with two marijuana cigarettes dangling from her mouth. She presented herself as a tramp—scantily dressed—with more slits to her nightdress than a fish has for gills. It was obvious Emilio had elicited these late-night rendezvous with her before.

"Well, that didn't take long, what did ya do, knock her upside the head?" Rosita said while pulling back the bedcovers.

Emilio put Rosita off and got right to his phone call with Chargo. "Okay, so we're cool for tomorrow? . . . What? . . . Stop worrying . . . She'll be there . . . We're all going . . . Sounds good!"

Rosita started undressing in an attempt to get Emilio's attention.

"Hey man, I got to boogie, my naked lady friend here, she's a wee bit distracting."

Emilio handed the phone off to Rosita, kissed her neck, and then headed back over to the bedroom door. When closing the door behind him, he looked over his right shoulder and said to Rosita, "Don't be reading into what's not there!"

Just before entering his bedroom, Emilio looked under Saltire's bedroom door and saw that Noelle had the light on. "What are you doing?" He snarled. "Lights out bitch!"

Dahlia overheard Emilio's verbal attack. She had been standing in the doorjamb, looking perturbed. When Emilio raised his head and gave her a come-hither glance, she complied. The two went back to her bedroom and closed the door.

Noelle, dressed in a white T-shirt and striped underwear, was brushing her teeth in the bathroom when she noticed the facemask and costume of Black Tezcatlipoca, as Smoking Mirror, hooked to the back of the bathroom door. Curious, she reached down and grabbed hold of the black obsidian scrying mirrored foot and lifted it to her face. There was no reflection of Noelle in the mirror, only a smoky-gray, four-dimensional non-descript mist leading nowhere. Fixated on the obsidian-mirrored foot, Noelle stared deeper into it—as if waiting for someone or something to appear. Out from behind the mist, Saltire emerged as the Blood-Jeweled Fowl, Long-Nose Turkey Deity and hypnotized Noelle. She remained motionless as the Toltec Deity of Karmic Debt Removal—also known as soul retrieval—engaged in the shamanic act of Facial Imprinting, the overlaying of an identity's features onto your own. This noninvasive technique was used to access Noelle's thoughts, feelings, and emotions regarding particular people, experiences, and significant events throughout her Recapitulation.

CHAPTER TEN

A Soul's Perspective

"It's nineteen ninety, October thirty-first; you're Greta Garbo at a big Halloween Party. May I view it from your soul's perspective, so that I may see the source of your affliction?" Blood-Jeweled Fowl, Long-Nose Turkey whispered.

Noelle returned to Halloween night in 1990. She was inside Sergeant's "turn-of-the-century" row house. Sergeant and his friends were having an electrifying Halloween costume party. Sergeant was Harold Lloyd, the silent film star, and his girlfriend Lucy, half Japanese, was the spitting image of "Betty Boop." Avery's best friend Blake came knocking at the front door of Sergeant's modest city dwelling. He was spearheading a rogue-gallery of frightful witches; they were all looking particularly ghoulish that evening in their black robes, white greasepaint faces with smoky charcoal eyes and blood-red dripping lips.

Blake Samuel Parris, also known as "Son of Lake, God Has Heard, Son of Priam," age twenty-eight, boasted he was related to the main instigator and minister at the Salem Witch Trials, Samuel Parris. Disconnected from his parents and sister Mary Ann Parris, he had lived at the Millstone shoebox-style house in Salem, MA, since he was fourteen years old. An overt homosexual, Blake put on the pretense that he was not interested in Avery, and instead befriended his "flavor" of the season. This allowed him to remain close to Avery without arousing suspicions. An avid reader of the occult, Blake seriously dabbled in magical spells . . . spells that involved poisonous spiders from New England. Although he could afford a flat of his own, he preferred to share the 1,200 sq. ft. studio with his best friend and secret obsession.

Sergeant and the group of early arrivals were all arranged like sardines in his front galley kitchen, preparing a turkey dinner at the tune of "racy" humor.

Over in the far corner, near the staircase leading to the second story bedrooms, Avery and Noelle were fidgeting with each other's costumes. Avery wore the Thorndike Manor's skeleton costume; his garb was underneath a long black 1920s vintage overcoat that had been his grandfather's. On this evening, he was the spitting image of the twenty-seven-year-old John Gilbert, the silent romantic film star of the 1920s. In a cap and gown with impeccable make-up and hair, Noelle was masquerading as John Gilbert's true love interest, Greta Garbo. Avery was pretending he was being filmed—no words—no sounds—only emoting.

The relatively large living room was arranged like a small local pub; a billiard table in the center surrounded by eight card tables set for four players each, and an eating section adjoining the kitchen. Blake had snatched up a pool cue and was practicing while waiting for his entourage to follow suit. Out of the corner of his eye, he spied Noelle and Blake kissing on the stairs.

Noelle, catching sight of Blake leering at her, joshed around for his benefit.

"Is there anything better than to be longing for something when you know it is within reach?" Noelle spouted the first of three Garbo quotes in her repertoire.

Avery stepped back and smiled; Blake pretended to enjoy her performance.

Sergeant noticed Blake scoping Avery's new love interest and defused a potentially awkward situation by leaving the kitchen and walking Blake over to where the two were standing. With no prior indication, Sergeant whipped out his Polaroid camera and took several snapshots of Avery, Noelle, and Blake "Vogueing" for the camera.

"Payback's a bitch ain't it?" Sergeant needled Blake. He presented him with a contrived photo of Avery, Noelle, and Blake mock laughing.

Showing no emotion, Blake leaned down and proceeded to gather the rest of the Polaroids scattered on the floor.

Avery confidently introduced Blake to Noelle, "So isn't she incredible?"

Blake smiled at Noelle and said to Avery, "Love you, man."

Noelle leaned backward and whispered in Avery's ear, "I don't think your friend likes me very much."

"That's just his way. He'll come around." Avery assured Noelle.

Feeling uncomfortable, Noelle left Avery's side and joined the other Halloween guests milling about the kitchen. She stood where she would not infringe upon anyone seated and ate her meal in silence, avoiding any further contact with Blake.

Kitty-corner to Sergeant's turn-of-the-century row house was the Charter Street Cemetery "Old Burring Point," the second oldest cemetery in the nation, established in 1637. A procession of children in Halloween facemasks and costumes were entering the graveyard with their older teenage siblings. Shrills of screams and laughter came from a rowdy gang of high school kids dressed in black and white; they were racing toward the children. A brief push, snatch, and run ensued. The high school thugs came out the victors, taking four out of the seven Halloween laundry bags filled with assorted candy and "Cracker Jack" trinkets.

One of the siblings, a mini Clint Eastwood "Spaghetti Westerns" cowboy, yelled after the thieves. "You're going to look pretty silly with that knife sticking out of your ass." The quote was from the movie "High Plains Drifter."

The children looked frightened; some were crying while others were looking up at their older siblings with expressions of sadness.

Noelle was outside the front door of Sergeant's house doling out Halloween candy from an orange plastic jack o' lantern container when she witnessed the entire incident from across the street. Noelle was on red alert!

Inside Sergeant's Halloween party were shoulder-to-shoulder friends decked out in Halloween costumes. Various interactive-type games were captivating the guests. Billiard competitions with a five dollar per head, entry fee established the amount of money given to the winner of the midnight playoff round. Apple dunking races for silly prizes and slight-of-hand card tricks for free shots of tequila added to the frivolity and gaiety as the evening carried on. Most notably, the "Best of the Night Costume" granted the winner a dinner, for four, at a seafood restaurant.

Noelle reentered Sergeant's flat and was looking around for Avery. Truth be told, she had lost interest in the party and wanted to leave. Blake swung out from behind the front door and took hold of Noelle's hand. Dodging and weaving, he maneuvered her body effortlessly across the living room floor. At the foot of the staircase leading to the second story, he grabbed Noelle around the waist and pulled her upstairs, all the while saying, "Avery has got something he wants to show you. Come now be a 'sport,' don't be afraid."

Noelle resisted going any further when she reached the top of the stairs. Blake intentionally prodded Noelle from behind, forcing her to enter Sergeant's bedroom against her will. Sergeant wanted no part of Avery and Blake's diabolical plan. He passed Noelle as she entered and proceeded to dance back down the hallway, toward the staircase, in a comedic fashion.

Sergeant's bedroom was odd at best. Thick maroon-colored drapes covered a bay window with classical architectural detail. Orange bare bulbs screwed into a standing candelabra highlighted a six-foot-wide circular drawing of "The Pentacle of Protection" in the center of the room. Placed inside the five points that made up the Pentacle were numerous Polaroids taken earlier that evening of Avery, Noelle, and Blake. Confronted by The Pentacle of Protection outlined in red paint, Noelle felt uneasy. Her eyes registered eleven Polaroids; her memory recorded only five. How strange the expression on Blake's face, not to mention the seven-foot-long mustard-colored leather couch pressed up against a closet to the right of the doorjamb.

Avery entered the bedroom wiping his hands on his black overcoat. "Who's first?" He asked plainly.

Blake standing over by the window immediately took charge. "Let's have Noelle be part of our covenant."

Noelle deposited her tiny pearl threaded evening bag in the corner of the couch while she offered up another Greta Garbo quote, "There seems to be a law that governs all our actions, so I never make plans." She knew the quote didn't fit the situation, but she was stalling for time.

"Come now, you know what this is, quit holding out on us." Blake implored.

Noelle faced Blake and insisted she was not familiar with the symbolic drawing. "I've no idea what this is. What is it?"

With a broad, toothy smile, Blake argued in favor of Noelle initiating the Black Magic Ceremony that would bind her soul to theirs. After another disclaimer, Noelle excused herself.

Feigning tiredness, Noelle hid her feelings of trepidation. "Avery, where's the upstairs bathroom?"

Avery stared at Noelle and did not respond. Noelle resorted to her third and final Garbo quote, as a last attempt, one she had just memorized earlier that day. The statement was directed at Blake.

"Anyone who has a continuous smile on his face conceals a toughness that is almost frightening," Noelle said as she backed away from Avery and scuttled out of the bedroom.

Noelle left her creepy-crawly chucos—the gang bangers—and skipped to the end of the hallway and turned right into the bathroom.

Blake entered the center of the Pentacle of Protection from an inverted/retrospective position. By doing so, he reversed the original Intent of the symbol and manipulated a much different outcome: base matter over will. He then lowered a stainless steel handcrafted dagger from his ruffled black shirtsleeve. Avery, admiring Blake's devilish demeanor, joined him inside the Pentacle of Protection. Blake was an experienced Black Magic Master and had been preoccupied with the Black Arts since his early teens. He owned quite an impressive collection of hunting knives and spider traps that he kept locked up in the upstairs linen closet. Sergeant had given Blake the key to the closet years ago and never even bothered to ask what he needed the space for.

Locking the door behind her, Noelle immediately investigated an old-fashioned, wall-mounted pull chain water closet. She reached up above her head and pulled the chain to flush away the remains of used toilet paper. The chain's pull down disturbed one of Blake's brown recluse spider webs situated on the back of the tank and out of view.

Noelle then moved over to the sink and removed her great aunt's artist book "The Spirit of the Voice" from around her waist and placed it on the edge of the sink. Avery had given the family heirloom to Noelle earlier that evening when they were getting dressed in their Halloween costumes. She was appalled that he had stolen it from Mr. Thorndike and intended to return the book later that night.

Noelle returned to the toilette, gracefully raised her Greta Gearbox costume above her waist, and lowered herself down over the toilet seat. With skill and dexterity, the brown recluse spider dropped down from its web and landed on the back of her neck. Noelle took a backhanded swipe at the spider with dismal results.

"Gotcha," the spider whispered.

Noelle leaped to her feet, rushed over to the sink, splashed water all over her neck, and then attempted to see the spider bite in the wall mirror. She tried to calm herself. "Okay! Okay! Everything's fine, I'll be alright."

Noelle accidentally knocked the "artist book" to the black 'n white checkerboard floor, scattering a handful of loosely compiled parchment sheets. Each sheet of paper was identified with a logo illustration— an emerald green androgynous humanoid. Kneeling down, Noelle gathered up the sheets of paper that were most easily accessible and flew from out of the bathroom. In her state of fright, she had overlooked her Great Aunt Immokalee's artist book hidden underneath and behind the wastebasket.

Blake was finishing his invocations when Noelle rushed back into the bedroom in search of her evening bag; it was sitting undisturbed on the god-awful mustard colored leather couch.

"Something just bit me in there!" Noelle said, half-winded. "I've got to go, in case I have an allergic reaction of some sort."

Avery and Blake attempted to reassure Noelle that nothing would come of the bite, siting it was improbable that whatever bit her was poisonous.

"You're fine!" Avery insisted.

"Come on, you don't have to leave. Let's go downstairs and get something to eat." Blake cajoled her, knowing all too well her well-being had been compromised.

Noelle did not appreciate their lack of concern; she sensed "foul play" on their part and wanted to leave the premise immediately. On her way out of the bedroom, Noelle attempted to snatch up all the Polaroids inside The Pentacle of Protection. She failed miserably yet was able to escape with the picture capturing the three of them imitating belly laughter. The Polaroid had ample time to process, and in the background, the faint image of a face in black with two broad yellow stripes was now visible.

Black Tezcatlipoca, Smoking Mirror, had been waiting a millennium to strike. It appeared he had known for some time where Quetzal Hunahpu's *Seminal Being* Soul resided. Shape-shifting into the spider allowed for this stealth attack to happen under the assumption of an accident. Even Blake and Avery were oblivious to the Toltec Deity's presence.

Noelle managed the staircase two steps at a time, grabbing hold of the railing all the way down. Eyes fixed on the front door she left the Halloween party without thanking Sergeant or acknowledging anyone on her way out.

Upstairs, Avery and Blake had yanked open the set of maroon colored drapes. Their faces were pressed up against the windows to watch Noelle as she passed Avery's vehicle.

"Yep! She's leaving." Blake said without a bit of regret.

"What should I do?" Avery asked with a grimace.

"Nothing! I'll call her in a day or two."

Running down the main street in Salem, Noelle was looking about frantically for the entrance to the Commuter Rail into Boston's North Station. From there, she was planning to take the underground "T" to David Square in Somerville, MA, and then ride one of Mr. Thorndike's bicycles the rest of the way to his manor in Lexington.

Noelle flagged down a red sedan driving toward her and asked the lady driver where the Commuter Rail was. The woman told her it was on the outskirts of town and offered to give her a lift. Eyeing a space in the backseat, Noelle accepted and got in. Inside the car, three small children in Halloween facemasks and costumes offered to share their Halloween candy with her. First, she secured the loose sheets of illustrated parchment inside her Greta Garbo costume and then partook of the candy from each child. As Noelle turned to look out the window, she noticed the brown recluse spider bite had become inflamed. It was on the lower part of her neck, the size of a pinky nail, with two noticeable fang bites.

In what seemed only a few minutes, the lady driver announced they had arrived at her destination. Noelle hopped out of the car, thanked the woman, waved to the kids, and then jogged up a fleet of steps to the Commuter Rail. Noelle's adrenalin had kicked in and suppressed her nausea and dizziness, for the time being.

Avery and Blake were downstairs watching their good friend Sergeant doing a little sleight of hand with a deck of playing cards.

"You know if you want to find out about your girlfriend's true character, do something totally unexpected and see how she reacts. At least that way you can gage her psychological makeup and see if you want to take the relationship any further." This was Blake's less than sound advice to his "dear friend" Avery.

"Okay, as long as you tell me what to do."

Blake glanced over at the Billiard Competition about to commence and said under his breath, "I'll tell you later. Let's get our team together. There's got to be at least two hundred dollars we can take from these bastards."

The Commuter Rail was packed with Halloweneers of all ages and sizes. Noelle was seated with her eyes closed and her head pressed up against a window. The sound of the railcar added a sense of urgency to her situation. In a "waking dream" state, Noelle pictured herself finding Mr. Thorndike's bikes. She saw herself unlocking the bicycle he had recommended earlier and riding it swiftly, with her evening gown wrapped tightly around her hips.

As the stroke of midnight approached, the Thorndike Manor took on the illusion of an earlier time; a time when streetlights defined one's status in the community. Noelle arrived at the manor, reeling in pain. She had just enough stamina to ride the bicycle over to the far right of the front entrance, then collapsed on the ground.

Just prior to Noelle's arrival, the wrought iron gate to the main entrance was still open for Halloweners, who were mostly teenagers now. Those who ventured down the driveway were accosted by life-size skeletons attached to an arched portico that led to a four-car garage with an adjacent carriage house. In front of the carriage house was the "Grim Reaper" stationed upon a Clydesdale mare. Michael Jean Thorndike, age twenty-eight, had stuffed homemade cookies and candies inside the saddlebags, and whoever approached him, without upsetting his horse, could grab a handful of goodies. If the mare took a step backward, however, then the kid was out of luck and faced the scythe. And, for tricksters hell-bent on vandalizing the skeletons, they were chased off the property in a no-holds-bar medieval fashion. This was a tradition at the Thorndike Manor. All the kids in face masks and costumes lived in the neighborhood and were friends of Michael's. He was head of the Swimming Program at one of the public schools during summer vacation, and he made a point of inviting them.

Everyone that night was in full Halloween attire. Noelle was camouflaged to look like Greta Garbo in a cap and shimmering gown, and the Thorndikes were dressed to resemble the famous poet William Blake and his adoring wife, Catherine Sophia. A great, great, grandfather clock standing proud just inside the parlor door chimed once for 11:30 a.m. The parlor décor, Cajun-influenced, had several statues of "The Assumption of Mary into Heaven" poised gently against the white on blue fleurs-de-lis velvet wallpaper. The request for Noelle's return to the Thorndike Manor on Halloween night had been initiated by Prosper; his wife Sophie had no prior knowledge of the invite.

Sophie Caroline St. Ours Thorndike, known as "Wise, Full-Grown, Holy, Ditch," age sixty-one, was the eldest of seven children, four girls, and three boys. Her lineage went back to the 17th century when French Protestants came to Louisiana in search of religious freedom. A mixture of French Huguenot, Chitimacha Indian, and African slave, Sophie learned the Art of Healing from her grandmother, a Traiteurs-Cajun "Faith Healer."

Sophie's parents, Francis Marius St. Ours and Charlotte Louisa Duplechien, were of French Acadian descendants and both born in South Louisiana in 1915. After Sophie's birth in 1933, her parents moved the family to South Carolina, where they were hired to manage the kitchen for the horseshoe crab harvester, Mr. Baptiste. Sophie's interest in marine life peaked as a child; for several years she helped the fishermen with the capture of the horseshoe crabs for biomedicine purposes. Combined with her mother's skill as a Traiteurs and her father's knowledge as a forensic anthropologist, Sophie had a fruitful childhood mastering earth magic.

Valedictorian of her high school, she was a shoo-in for Radcliff College, in Massachusetts, where she majored in Theater with a minor in Linguistics. She spoke five languages fluently. Sophie met her future husband, Prosper Ira Thorndike, at a coffee shop after starring in a musical in the French Quarter; he was smitten during Sophie's solo performance that evening. Soon thereafter they hung-out on a regular basis, fell in love, married two years later, and then raised three boys out at the Thorndike Manor. Sophie was a very attentive and harmonizing wife, mother, and friend. The entire family lived and loved with a passion and no regrets.

When her three sons were old enough to be at school all day, Sophie attended the Graduate School Program at M.I.T. Her major was in Bio-Chemistry with a minor in Infectious Diseases. Within six years, she received both her Master's and Doctorate degrees in Infectious Diseases. During the 80s and 90s, Sophie spearheaded a U.S. Government Nonprofit Program specializing in identifying and preventing infectious diseases. Afterward, the United States Infectious Disease Department hired her, and there she worked closely with the Military's Special Operation Forces.

The first floor of the two-story manor was divided into wings and those wings into designated areas. The left wing included: the portico side entrance, mudroom, hallway to the back and front entrances, dining room, and half of the living room with a billiard table. The right wing included: The other half of the living room with an adjoining study, kitchen, laundry room, and the parlor with its own private side entrance. Each of these rooms was comparatively large, given the 7,000 sq. ft. total living space.

In the adjoining kitchen, Sophie and Prosper were cleaning up after a late dinner. Clunk! Clunk! Clunk! The sound of a pair of riding boots laden down with extra weight compromised the peace and tranquility of the homestead. Upon hearing their son, Prosper and Sophie left the kitchen to investigate. Michael Jean walked into the parlor carrying the lifeless body of Noelle in his arms.

"Quick, bring her over here!" Sophie said as she pointed to a footstool in the parlor. "I'll get my medical bag." He ran to the linen closet to grab the kit.

Michael Jean carried Noelle across the hardwood floor and gently lowered her limp body down till it sat on the footstool. In the meantime, Prosper was removing additional sheets, blankets, and pillowcases from the nearby linen closet. Sophie returned to the parlor carrying a black leather doctor's bag and a plateful of white candles. The light emanating from the flickering wicks shed light on Noelle's condition; she was hunched over, hands to her knees, and drenched in sweat.

"Come let's get her over to the bed. We certainly don't want her to wind up face first on the floor!" Sophie raised her concern to Prosper.

Michael Jean escorted Noelle over to a cast iron canopy bed. She had immediately fallen victim to the bacterial infection, ragging havoc on her body, mind, and soul. When he placed Noelle on the queen-size bed, Sophie had a clear view of the infected spider bite and knew immediately of its origin.

"She's been bitten by a brown recluse. Michael Jean stop what you're doing—get me my IV system from the pantry and the "blue blood" that's in the small freezer in the tack room. Go right quick!" Sophie said with a southern accent. "This girl's spirit is leavin' us!"

On the precipice between life and death, Noelle was in a semi-paralyzed and catatonic state. Until this very moment, neither woman knew of the spiritual importance of their first meeting.

A close-up view of the bluish colored blood being pumped into her left forearm was enough to return Noelle's awareness of Saltire's bedroom in Puerto Vallarta, if only for a few minutes. Saltire, as the Blood-Jeweled Fowl, Long-Nose Turkey Deity, had completed his facial imprinting when Baile Movimiento, known as Dancing Movement, reappeared as the Toltec Deity Ehecatl. The creator, Deity, activated a cloister of inverted pyramids from inside the Deity's obsidian-mirrored foot. The Karmic Debt Removal-soul retrieval-Deity recognized he was no longer needed and shape-shifted back to being Saltire.

In the far corner of the bedroom, Saltire watched as Noelle was assisted by a sacred Fractal Pattern of a sound currency. The cluster of inverted pyramids moved through the obsidian-mirrored foot and circled Noelle. Then, one of the inverted pyramids disengaged from the cluster and transformed into the idealized androgynous humanoid Dancing Movement. The humanoid's color immediately turned from off-white to emerald-green as he/she defined and redefined its form. Dancing Movement then placed his/her hands above Noelle's head, causing her to continue with her recapitulation and healing treatment. Noelle Intaglio Leandre's 1994 *Flashback Sequence* continued. It was still the year 1990.

Peering out from the dimly lit room was Sophie managing an IV drip mixed with the blue blood from the Horseshoe Crab. As soon as the candles began flickering wildly, Sophie lowered herself onto a green plaid armchair stationed next to Noelle's upper body and removed a handful of loosely compiled parchments from inside her Halloween costume. Each sheet of paper was identified with a logo illustration of an emerald-green androgynous divine messenger. While Sophie was rifling through the illustrations, a playful looking Polaroid of Blake, Avery, and Noelle laughing fell onto her lap.

Sophie looked at the photo and said, "I know these boys. I see them at the Farmers' Market every Saturday getting handouts. Don't tell me she's gotten herself mixed-up with those two!"

With no time to spare, Sophie initiated a time-honored treatment intended to identify Noelle's spiritual affiliation and her attacker. To accomplish this, Sophie first evoked "Silent Knowledge."

"Silent Knowledge reveal her affliction,
Rise in spirit God-Loving Souls.
Unleash the Denizen at twelve tonight,
Dispel the presence of this bite."

Prosper was standing in the farthest corner of the parlor, diagonal to where Sophie was seated. His image was reflected in a mahogany English Country cheval mirror. Sophie waved Prosper away from the mirror and stared intensely into its reflecting surface. There before her, disclosed only in the mirror, was Noelle's face covered in the markings of a were-jaguar. In reality, Noelle stirred as the black rosettes on her face became more pronounced.

Prosper was alarmed by what he saw. He asked his wife, "What do you make of those spots?"

Sophie responded as if hearing a voice inside her head; she recited out loud her interpretation of the events that transpired earlier that evening.

"Casting doubts born from false testimony,
The witches, Millstone and Parris,
Conjured up the spider that locks down speech,
Adding insult to injury."

The clock on top of the Mexican antique nightstand pointed precisely to 3:00 a.m. Noelle's subconscious had shifted to the point where perception was gathered, and she was sound asleep in bed. Saltire and Dancing Movement were nowhere in sight.

Without provocation, a were-cougar squeezed through the black obsidian scrying mirrored foot on Saltire's Blood-Jeweled Fowl, Long-Nose Turkey costume. The half-man, half-creature was Mela, attempting to steal some of Noelle's vital energy to empower her shape-shifting feats-of-wonder for tomorrow. Mela was acting purely at the solicitation of her brother Emilio, and therefore could not be held responsible for her actions when in this altered state. Yet much to her chagrin, Mela was unable to penetrate the positive ions deposited by Ehecatl and sauntered out of the bedroom, shutting the door behind her with a swat of her tail.

Mela lumbered down the back stairs then through the Talavera tiled kitchen; the were-cougar wound up on the second-story veranda. In one leap, she cleared the balcony. A blur of tawny yellow slashed the starry night, lighting up the sky.

CHAPTER ELEVEN

Four Bleeding Hearts

It was crystal clear on the morning following Rosita's All Hallows' Eve get-together. The sun was dressing the tropical rainforest in Puerto Vallarta in a ray of vividly contrasting colors. Three Huichol Indians in tandem trail-blazed their way through the terrain, which led to Yelapa. Each toted a blowgun; they were on a hunting expedition, tracking a were-cougar. As the were-cougar stalked a mother deer, so too, the indians stalked the were-cougar—Mela.

Noelle awakened from her *Flashback Sequence* to Mexican instrumental music pouring through the B&B surround-sound speakers. As she rolled over, Noelle noticed her Great Aunt Immokalee's artist book, *The Spirit of the Voice*, wedged underneath the bedroom door. Octavio had kept his word. She leaped to her feet and retrieved her treasured heirloom. While doing so, a letter from inside the front cover slid out and fell on the floor. Noelle flipped the letter into her palm, then sat at the edge of the bed and read it out loud:

"Noelle, I've taken Cheryl to the airport. Lisa went into labor last night. Please look after Xochitl. I'll see you upon your return, Octavio."

Noelle no sooner put the letter down when she heard tapping at the bedroom door.

"Who is it?" she asked.

"Put your suit on; we're going swimming!" shouted Xochitl.

Octavio was at the Mexicana Airlines ticket counter in Puerto Vallarta with Cheryl; he was purchasing a first-class ticket for her. Cheryl was in no shape to handle her affairs—news of her grandchild's premature delivery had her in tears.

"I promised Lisa I'd be there when her baby arrived. I should have known better than to come on this trip!" Cheryl grumbled.

Octavio told Cheryl to keep her chin up. "When I spoke to Lisa, she said, 'Please tell mom we're doing just great!'"

Then changing the subject, Octavio encouraged her to "keep the faith," and not to worry about Noelle.

"Noelle's the least of my concerns," Cheryl jeered.

The two remain side by side till Cheryl was cleared to board the plane.

Unbeknownst to Cheryl, she was being taken out of the equation to make room for Noelle's spiritual awakening. And, it was clear to Octavio that it had never occurred to Cheryl that her unfulfilled life was at the effect of an unexamined life from her soul's perspective. Cheryl's Seminal Being *Soul and Noelle's* Seminal Being *Soul had a karmic debt connection—there was an aspect of Cheryl's* Seminal Being *Soul that had once been Immokalee's older sister, Chantal Salali Chisholm. When Chantal was just twelve years old, she was orphaned and left to raise Immokalee, age eight, after their parents were proclaimed dead on August 20, 1887. A cyclone had ravished the coast of North Carolina, sinking the fishing schooner they were aboard. Determined to survive, Chantal contacted her closest relative, Mrs. Kilakina, and the girls were invited to live with their aunt and her family. The three-bedroom cabin, in a remote indian village, nestled in the Great Smoky Mountain Range would be their home for the next ten years.*

Octavio hurried out of the airport and over to Rosita's luxury Mercedes.

"Ah, a moment to myself," Octavio said in a scratchy voice.

No sooner did Octavio begin to relax back into the passenger side seat when a coughing fit ensued. He opened the glove compartment and removed a brown bag, exposing the bottleneck of a dark molasses-like remedy. Octavio took a big gulp and then capped the bottle. Holding the bag to his chest, he leaned back, extended his body the full length of the seat, and took a short nap.

Out on the second-story veranda, Xochitl and Rosita were eating mangos 'n cream and admiring the ocean view as endless whitecap waves washed ashore. Noelle entered the veranda wearing a blue and white striped Speedo partially covered by her purple and yellow floral sarong. She plunked herself down across from Rosita and slipped into the sandals Cheryl had given her the day before. Noelle informed Rosita of Cheryl's sudden and unexpected departure.

"Does this mean you'll be leaving us soon? Rosita asked.

"I don't have any plans on going just yet. I guess we'll know more when Octavio returns." Noelle said, doubtful of her situation.

"Oh! He'll want you to stay." Rosita said.

Glancing up at Rosita then over to Noelle, Xochitl smiled as she twirled her sundried starfish.

"Twinkle!" Twinkle that was very good!" Xochitl praised."Keep up with your cartwheels; Papi says they'll help you learn how to balance."

Noelle asked Rosita if they could have something to eat. Rosita told her they had ten minutes to find something in the kitchen. Xochitl hopped down from her father's hand-honed chair and ran into the kitchen.

"Better eat and run, you two. We've got the 8 o'clock water taxi to Yelapa yet to catch!" Rosita reminded them.

Noelle stepped into the kitchen and saw Xochitl preparing a bowl of mangos 'n cream for her. Noelle expressed her thanks and turned to head back out to the veranda.

Suddenly, Xochitl stopped her with a swift tug at the side of her swimsuit.

"Did you bring a pet?" asked Xochitl

"I don't own a pet." Noelle replied.

Xochitl left the kitchen shaking her head and returned moments later, dragging a basket full of seashells.

"Go ahead, pick one." Xochitl nodded.

Noelle looked through the seashells and chose a Tiger Cowrie shell.

"This shell reminds me of my late Great Aunt Immokalee. She was part Cherokee Indian from North Carolina and used to make jewelry out of all sorts of shells."

Meanwhile, the Pacific Ocean just off the coast of Puerto Vallarta was still roiling from the storm. A sizeable wooden ocean canoe cut through four-foot waves as it headed its way to a deep-sea fishing boat.

The Captain, a middle-aged fisherman, and his crew were playing poker, smoking cigarettes, and drinking espresso coffee. An athletic-looking man, sporting just cutoffs and a straw hat, boarded the fishing boat named "Xquic"—Mother of the Hero Twins.

"Saltire, you Old Bird," The Captain of the ship shouted, "Pay up boys, told ya he'd be on time."

The crew forked over whatever change they had in their pockets. It was all in fun, not a serious wager by any means. The Captain walked over to a cast-iron hatch and looked down into the hull of the ship.

"We got her on ice. Go on down, she's been ready since yesterday," The Captain spouted.

Saltire went below the cargo hold and examined a 150 lb. swordfish. He smiled broadly and gave a nod of approval to the crew.

"She's magnificent!" Saltire said.

The crew descended upon the swordfish that was packed in bags of ice, and secured the locks on the wooden crate. One of the younger mates unlatched the hatch, and the container was lifted onto the ship's deck. The Captain raised his mug and toasted Saltire. Saltire laughed and offered to sit in on a game of poker. The crew was overjoyed and pulled him up a chair. The cards were dealt, and Saltire seemed to be posturing himself for a big win against the better player, The Captain.

One by one, each crewmember was eliminated. Saltire, glancing up at the sun, called and raised the "action player" beyond what he had been willing to part with. The Captain folded, and Saltire showed he had been bluffing with a 7-2 (off-suit). The crew went berserk and pretended they were going to throw him overboard.

The water taxi skimmed across the Pacific Ocean at maximum capacity. Rosita was sitting between Dahlia and Emilio as they rummaged through a picnic basket. Rosita spoke softly; she expressed her opinion of Noelle while she examined her from afar.

"Will you take a look at her; is she not the worst of 'em yet?"

Noelle and Xochitl were at the bow of the water taxi; the wind was blowing their hair every-which-way. Xochitl looked up at Noelle and clamped down on her left wrist. Noelle immediately shuddered—she had never felt a sensation quite like that. Xochitl's hands were bifurcated and resembled the shape of a tiny lobster claw.

"Surprise!" Xochitl said smiling.

Noelle responded with a hug, then turned her head and observed the ocean spray.

The were-cougar, from earlier in the morning, had made her way to Yelapa, a coastal village south of Puerto Vallarta. Shrouded in the tropical rainforest, the were-cougar was following the river that led to a waterfall basin. The mother deer, which the were-cougar had been so keen on having for breakfast, had caught wind of her scent and was scampering away up a sheer cliff. As the were-cougar neared the edge of the waterfall basin, three Huichol Indians positioned themselves behind corpulent trees surrounding the area. All three Huichol Indians gazed into the waterfall basin at a forty-five-degree angle. They were preparing to shift their perception so they could successfully shape-shift into were-jaguars.

The three Huichol Indians spoke of themselves as "Mirrors of the Gods" (Reflections of a Sacred Vision) from Aztlan. Father Hunahpu and the sacred "Hero Twins," Hunahpu and Ixbalanque, (who were from the ancient times following the Great Flood), influenced their evolution. Their ancestors were friends and neighbors to the Toltec Indians that founded the city of Tollan around the year 754 AD; during that same time period, Teotihuacán was collapsing from within. The Huichol "Wixáritari" was an indigenous ethnic tribe living in the Sierra Madre Occidental range in Nayarit, Jalisco, Zacatecas, and Durango, Mexico.

These civilizations were disrupted when Cortez invaded Mesoamerica in 1519. The Celestino family—who were residents at Ek Balam on the Yucatan Peninsula—broke all ties with their indian comrades in Puerto Vallarta. Word of the attack on the Aztecs caused all those of Toltec ancestry to return to their volcanic sustainable cave dwellings. It took three hundred and twenty-seven years until the Mexican-American War (1846—1848) for sixteen Huichol Indians to reunite with the Celestino family for a brief stint.

Then in 1990, three Huichol Indians residing in the mountains surrounding Puerto Vallarta were invited to join the Toltec Secret Eagle Knight Council located on Lake Patzcuaro. In a short period of time, they became very powerful shamans capable of shape-shifting into were-jaguars. These shamans have given their word to assist in the spiritual development of an initiative seeking to fulfill their *Seminal Being* Soul's intended future.

A boat paddle dripped water from its blade as it reached around to the front of the ocean canoe. Saltire paddled in a steady rhythmic beat as his canoe glided toward the shore. It lay lower in the water than usual, heavy with the weight of the magnificent swordfish. In the distance, a smattering of white stucco estates terraced the shoreline, giving Banderas Bay a look of sophistication.

The beach had once again begun to percolate with eager swimmers, sun worshipers, and hopeful merchants. Reynaldo and Sergio were sleeping next to the were-eagle cage, inside Octavio's pick-up truck bed located on the flip side of the jetty. A stray dog came sniffing around in search of something fresh to eat. He was frightened away when the were-eagle—Paloma's ethereal body double—stepped out of its cage unassisted.

Saltire ran his canoe ashore, threw a rock at Octavio's pick-up truck, which startled the two "sleeping beauties." Reynaldo and Sergio hustled on down to assist Saltire.

"Tio! What'd ya catch?" Sergio asked.

"The Spirit of the Sea," Saltire said with a grin.

Reynaldo and Sergio lifted the wooden crate free from the bow of the ocean canoe and set it aside. Saltire raised the canoe to his chest, flipped it above his head and shoulders, and carried it over to the pick-up truck. He laid the canoe down to one side and jogged back to help Reynaldo and Sergio get the crate. It was a tight squeeze; the crate just cleared the were-eagle's cage. Saltire then placed his canoe on top of the crate and secured it firmly with rope.

"How's my brother doing lately?" Saltire asked his nephews.

Reynaldo and Sergio, with expressions of grave concern, told Saltire they have asked their father how he's been feeling, but he has refused to tell them anything.

"Well, I think it's best if we don't say anything at this time." Saltire said. "He's not giving up, and neither are we."

While Octavio was in the B&B kitchen preparing a cup of tea, a green-plumed were-quetzal bird feather floated down from the oak kitchen cabinets to the kitchen counter. After brushing softly on top of Octavio's remedy bottle, positioned gingerly in the sink, it retook flight and landed on his shoulder. Octavio coughed a few times and then reached earnestly for his medication. Popping the lid, he took a swig of the molasses-like remedy then bowed his head. The were-quetzal bird feather tumbled down lightly and ended up cradling Octavio's brown bag.

"Ah, Quetzal, your feather just confirmed what I always knew," Octavio said wistfully. "Noelle's *Seminal Being* Soul is the one that can liberate all *Seminal Being* Souls."

The three Huichol Indians were removing their white shirts and placing them under groundcover. With blowguns in hand, each indian wrapped himself around a tree to make himself invisible to the naked eye. Even their white cotton pants were no cause for suspicion; they took on the appearance of misplaced laundry spewed about as a result of the previous rainstorm.

Noelle and Xochitl were weaving their way between the colorful stucco houses. Noelle's sandals were making a clattering sound as she ran along a footpath leading to the waterfall basin. Protected by a forty-foot waterfall, sheer rock cliffs, and a lush tropical rainforest, it was an ideal place for swimming.

Xochitl was out in front and the first to reach the pool of spring water. She waited for Noelle at the top of a rock formation to the far left of the path. Exhausted and out of breath, Noelle flopped herself down next to Xochitl. Xochitl took Noelle's Tiger Cowrie shell from her hand and placed it next to her starfish Twinkle.

"What's its name?" Xochitl asked.

"It hasn't got a name," Noelle replied.

Xochitl picked up the Tiger Cowrie shell, turned it over, and noticed its sharp ridges. Xochitl informed Noelle that her pet shell's name was Sharky. Growling, Xochitl put Sharky down near Twinkle and jumped into the waterfall basin. Noelle leaped in after Xochitl and followed her over to the tall standing waterfall. Xochitl swam behind the cascading waters and crawled up on a small ledge. Noelle looked through the waterfall, feigning she could not see the little girl. They played hide-and-seek for few minutes; each one took their turn behind the waterfall.

Emilio came strolling over to Rosita and Dahlia, who were resting on canvas lounge chairs. Clenching three Corona beers within his fingers and a handful of limes in the other, he pretended to sound pissed-off.

"No music! Not till the CAT is caught." Emilio said.

"What's this?" Rosita inquired.

"The Navy Patrol has taken control of the airwaves. They're telling everyone to look out for a cougar."

"Where's it now?" Dahlia asked.

"Mogul says he saw a strange looking cougar chasing a deer earlier this morning."

Emilio snickered.

Dahlia voiced her opinion over the safety of Xochitl and Noelle. Rosita acted like she was hearing this news for the first time; like she was not in on the whole were-cougar let's kill Xochitl from the get-go.

"Oh, Please! There's nothing to worry about," Rosita said in objection to her daughter's fearful reaction. "Besides, it seems to me, 'Miss America' has taken quite a liking to the locals."

The conversation deteriorated into an argument.

"I'm not about to sit here any longer. I think we should go find them," Dahlia insisted.

"So go!" Emilio said nonchalantly.

"What! You've got to be kidding? You're not planning on staying here with my mother, are you?"

"Yeah, I am; why should I go. I'm not on duty!"

Dahlia grabbed her sandals and leaped to her feet, "All right, you two, see if I care!"

Rosita, amused by their bickering, was smiling the whole time in Emilio's general direction.

Dahlia wasted no time; she slipped on her sandals and jogged up the beach toward the path leading to the waterfall basin. When Dahlia neared the pool of water, she calmly approached the three Huichol Indians, each curled unperceivable around the base of a tree. Their message was clear; all of a sudden, she lowered herself till her stomach touched the groundcover and then shape-shifted into a tawny yellow were-jaguar with black rosettes.

On her fifteenth birthday, "Quinceanera" Dahlia surprised everyone at her uncle Saltire's annual *Days of the Dead* celebration. She did so by first shape-shifting into a were-jaguar, then a were-eagle. By integrating her animal and bird-like intrinsic natures with her authentic human nature, she anticipated the behavior of others through spiritual discernment.

The half-woman half-cougar, Mela, was lying hidden underneath the rock formation. Dahlia, as the were-jaguar, and the three Huichol Indians were keen to the were-cougar's whereabouts and intention.

Xochitl was holding onto Noelle's right arm, pretending to be a baby dolphin riding alongside its mother. "Wait!" Xochitl said, "Let's get Twinkle and Sharky; maybe they want to play baby dolphin too."

Noelle swam over to the rock formation; Xochitl climbed up and snatched Twinkle and Sharky, then while twirling around, she flung them into the swimming hole.

"Stay there," Noelle yelled as she dived for the sinking Tiger Cowrie shell.

Xochitl applauded the starfish Twinkle as it floated over to the waterfall.

The were-cougar crouched below the boulder Xochitl was standing on, flipped its tail, and prepared to attack. But just that moment, Noelle resurfaced with Sharky in hand; Xochitl screamed with joy and leaped back into the water. Xochitl asked to see Sharky and then placed it in her swimsuit for safekeeping. Releasing Twinkle to Noelle's care, Xochitl told her she had something to show her and swam to the other side. Climbing on stone-cut steps, Xochitl left the waterfall basin for an upper ridge that resembled a diving board. Noelle watched, Twinkle, in hand, as Xochitl made her way up the cliffside. Scampering up a series of steps, Xochitl made it to the upper shelf.

"Papi showed me how to dive from here," Xochitl shouted.

Noelle pleaded with her to come back down and not to jump from there.

Xochitl raised her arms over her head, exposing her claw-like hands and let out a loud cry, "Kee! Kee! Kee!"

In one fell swoop, the were-cougar made her threat known. The menace before them was ravenous, ill-tempered were-cougar—Mela. Having been mistreated by her brother Emilio for weeks, she no longer could control her natural animal instincts—violating the vows she had made with the Toltec Secret Eagle Knight Council many years ago. Mela had gone rogue.

The were-cougar leaped fifteen feet and landed on the rim of the basin. With Xochitl clearly in her sights, she moved assuredly in her direction.

"No! No! No!" yelled Noelle. She swam frantically toward the girl.

The were-cougar lunged at Xochitl.

"Jump now!"Noelle commanded Xochitl.

Xochitl was not buying into this whole "cat-and-mouse" game. She adamantly stood her ground.

Noelle began ripping shards of rock from the edge of the waterfall basin, slinging them at the were-cougar with all her might. The pieces either missed the animal entirely or ricocheted off the basin and sunk below the surface. Xochitl was now within a paws reach and started to quiver and cry. The were-cougar swatted at Xochitl and grazed the top of her head.

Noelle, desperate to prevent the molestation, shape-shifted into her previous life as her Great Aunt Immokalee when she was thirty-five years of age. Immokalee grabbed Twinkle by one of its arms and flung it at the were-cougar's head. Twinkle hit the animal in her eye, and for a fleeting moment, the starfish appeared to come alive. Staring intently at the were-cougar's injured eye, Immokalee watched as the arm of Twinkle reached in and tore at the were-cougar's cornea. The big cat lost its balance, pivoted, and lurched backward. Simultaneously, Xochitl leaped into the waterfall basin and was met by Immokalee's protective embrace. The were-cougar quickly recovered and plodded back down the cliffside. Turning in the direction of Immokalee and Xochitl, the were-cougar looked terrified by what it saw.

Four tawny-yellow were-jaguars covered in black rosettes, all walking on their hind legs, crossed the riverbed and sprung on top of the massive rock formation. Each were-jaguar held in their front paws a freshly cut bleeding heart. After a few moments, the four were-jaguars put the hearts down and retreated into the tropical rainforest. The were-cougar descended upon the hearts—bringing the scent of a fresh kill, strung together by a twisted vine. The animal bit into one of the organs, dragging the other three beneath its belly. She slinked off down the river and disappeared into the dense forest.

The "Four Bleeding Hearts" were a metaphor for the four main compartments that made up the natural cave channel underneath the Pyramid of the Sun, located at Teotihuacán near Mexico City. I knew it well. It had been a critical location for the pilgrimages I spearheaded after being elevated from Toltec Atlantean Warrior to High Priestess.

Immokalee quickly withdrew back into Noelle's psyche and dissolved her physical properties and facial features. From this moment forward, Noelle will reemerge with a greater understanding of her power, accessing her Silent Knowledge at will.

Noelle gently lifted Xochitl up and out of the waterfall basin and then rescued Twinkle from the pool. The tips of Noelle's fingers on her left hand were chafed and bloodied from grabbing onto Twinkle too tightly.

"Are you alright?" Noelle asked Xochitl.

"Yes! I'm alright."

Come on, sweetie, let's go."

Just then, the were-quetzal bird feather that was last seen drifting back into Octavio's brown bag dropped out of the sky and into the waterfall basin.

Hidden deep within the tropical rainforest, Dahlia transformed from the were-jaguar back into her human form. Entering the footpath just below where Noelle and Xochitl were walking, Dahlia waved in recognition. The girls ran toward her. Overjoyed, Dahlia reached out to Xochitl, picked her up, and then carried the small child the rest of the way in her arms.

Emilio was the first to spot Dahlia, Xochitl, and Noelle walking back down the beach.

Nudging Rosita on her shoulder, he said, "Not one word!"

Then signaling to his friend Mogul, Emilio scribbled a message for Chargo on the receipt for the Corona beers. Note Read: FIND MY SISTER!

Rosita, seemingly confused, walked over to the water taxi while Emilio jogged over to greet Dahlia, Xochitl, and Noelle. Xochitl leaped down, grabbed Noelle's wrist, and took her running along the shoreline to the water taxi. When they arrived, Xochitl got onboard first. The driver of the boat walked over to Noelle and offered her a clean rag dipped in saltwater. She took the cloth graciously, and immediately, the bleeding fingertips congealed. Following Noelle's medical attention, Dahlia, Emilio, and Rosita boarded the water taxi, which moments later motored away from the shoreline. Xochitl clearly tuckered out from the whole ordeal, moved from her aunt and cuddled up in Noelle's lap.

Octavio was putting bottles of water, avocado sandwiches, and freshly cut fruit in the oversized cooler into his truck. Xochitl and Noelle had arrived at Octavio's white pick-up truck a few minutes ago and were both sitting patiently on the passenger side. Noelle's eyes were shut, and her head was resting against the side window. Xochitl pulled out from underneath her swimsuit the Tiger Cowrie shell, Sharky, and placed it on Noelle's lap. Noelle opened her eyes and patted the seashell; the bloody rag was still wrapped around her fingertips.

"So, looks to me like you took a tumble too," Noelle said in a whisper.

Noelle undid the bloody rag from her fingers. She placed it in her overnight bag, which was securely situated in the extra cab. Xochitl started giggling while tugging at Octavio's shirt.

Looking up at Octavio, Xochitl said, "Sharky almost died, and Twinkle saved my life!"

"Sounds like you two had quite the morning; care to tell me about it?"

Eyes popping, Xochitl and Noelle looked at each other and shook their heads. No!

"Nothing to report?" Octavio questioned, looking a bit doubtful.

Octavio reached down and gently held Noelle's damaged fingers.

"Leave this wrapped until I remove it," Octavio said. He poured some of his molasses-like remedies onto a yellow bandana then bandaged her fingertips with it.

Leaving the driver's seat, Octavio walked around to the passenger side, opened the door, and began rummaging through the glove compartment to take stock of the items.

"You know," Octavio continued. "The radio said four were-jaguars were spotted leaving the falls; I guess you just missed them."

"Suppose we had seen them, what then?" Noelle asked.

"What then precisely?" You'd have been bitten and turned into were-jaguars at the stroke of midnight on the next full moon. No! I take it back, you both would have been bitten in the head, nibbled on around the ears, then left for dead."

His remark transformed the grimaces on Noelle and Xochitl into smiles.

"Do you have were-wolves here?" Noelle asked.

Octavio suddenly found what he was looking for: a 1960s cartridge for an antique mutoscope hand-cranked circular flipbook. He placed it inside his leather jacket pocket. Leaning against the passenger-side rearview mirror, Octavio answered Noelle in all seriousness.

"Not anymore! They've all migrated north. I've heard of sightings as far north as Alberta, Canada. And, the were-jaguars keep their cousins the were-cougars in check. It's the way it's been for thousands of years."

Noelle, confronted by the idea of a half-human, half-cat crushing Xochitl's skull, confessed.

"We had an incident this morning with one of your cat-creatures, and it didn't look like any cougar I'd seen at the Zoo. It looked more like a cougar with human-like features."

Octavio removed from his jean's pocket the smooth clay figurine of the were-cougar he had pinched the night before and handed it to Noelle.

"Look something like this?"

Noelle inspected the clay figurine and confirmed his suspicions.

"Here, take it. You've earned it," Octavio insisted.

Catching sight of the change in Xochitl's expression, Octavio quickly turned his attention to her.

"Xochitl, are you and Papi visiting Ruben later?"

Xochitl closed her eyes and envisioned her baby brother. She remembered, all too well, the day her twin brother, Ruben, died of *"sudden infant death syndrome."* She was lying next to him in their crib when he gasped for air then suddenly stopped breathing. Xochitl observed Ruben's soul leave his body. It looked much like a facet dislodging from a quartz crystal; only it was invisible.

The fact that Xochitl could see the unseen was due to her enlightened state. The right eye, which is the "Watchdog of the Soul," sees only what the mind is prepared to comprehend. Xochitl was enlightened from inception, and for this reason, she was able to perceive this reality in real-time and in actual space. This also meant that, for the most part, she operated from the perspective of her Seminal Being Soul—*which was her larger consciousness beyond time and space*—*a manifestation of Virtue, spoken of as Intent.*

With Ruben's image still present, Xochitl returned to the question proposed by her uncle.

"I'm not sure if I'm riding with you or Papi. I think he said he wanted to show Noelle the cemetery."

"Well now, Noelle, that ought to be another auspicious adventure," Octavio said cheerfully.

It was close to 11:00 a.m. before everyone was ready to move on from Mar Casa De La Concha. Rosita, Dahlia, and Emilio were the first to leave; Rosita drove them in her brand-new Mercedes to Saltire's estate on Lake Pátzcuaro.

Saltire arrived shortly after they had left on his Triumph Trophy 1200 motorcycle. Xochitl hopped down from Octavio's pick-up truck to greet her father. Saltire lifted Xochitl up and gave her a big hug. He then carried her back over to the truck and lowered his head to speak to Noelle, who was still seated on the passenger side.

"I'm so pleased you chose to stay and attend my party. Be sure to take in all the sights."

Saltire's comforting voice and quiet manner dismantled Noelle's awkward silence and put her immediately at ease. This was the first time Noelle had gotten a close-up look at Saltire, and she noticed something unusual concerning his features. They seemed to have changed from when she saw him under the streetlamp the night before. He also appeared leaner and a few inches taller. Maybe it was all in her imagination; it had been quite an unusual evening after all.

"Twinkle and Sharky are fraternal twins, and where one goes, the other must follow," Xochitl said as she flung her starfish next to the Tiger Cowrie shell.

Noelle, while looking up at Xochitl, was disturbed by what she heard next. It was the unsettling sound of a man wracked with dry, hacking coughs. Noelle spun her head around and saw Octavio through the rear window.

Octavio was standing over by the motorcycle ramp, nursing his molasses-like remedy in vain. This whole time, Octavio and the were-eagle—Paloma's ethereal body double—had been observing Noelle in relationship to Saltire and Xochitl with great interest. Noelle's eyes then followed Saltire as he headed toward the back of Octavio's pick-up truck. Saltire put Xochitl down on the stamped concrete, walked over to the first storage unit, and removed two large bags of ice. Returning to the truck, he proceeded to add additional ice blocks around the surface of his magnificent swordfish. Octavio joined Saltire and placed the were-eagle inside its cage, fastening it down firmly for the long haul.

"I'm going to stop by and see Melita before heading over to Parvulo X's Bicicleta Tienda and Reparar. Are you sure you're up for it? If you want me to call it off, I will," Saltire said.

Octavio opened his brown paper bag and showed Saltire the quetzal-bird feather.

Saltire was taken-a-back and said, "I never thought we'd live to see the day, at least not in this lifetime. My Lord! It seems she has come back to us."

It was high noon, and Rosita was barreling down the highway, slicing her way through the Colonial Heartland of Mexico. She was on her car phone talking to Edmundo Jose Basilio, also known as "Fortune, God Shall Add, Kingly," age fifty-nine; Edmundo was Saltire's Head Chef and Paloma's love interest. Rosita was arguing with him about what was being served for dinner and said she should have been consulted. Bent over in the passenger seat, Emilio listened to loud music on his CD player while manipulating balls of clay into figurines that resembled Noelle, Saltire, and Xochitl. Dahlia, lying down in the back seat asleep, had learned how to block them out entirely.

Local townspeople were setting up Buffet tables on the back terrace at Saltire's Mayan-Toltec Estate in Pátzcuaro, Mexico. Gathered near the horse stables, a team of seven dancing horses was being fitted for traditional *Days of the Dead* masks and adornments. The mood was light and pleasant. Edmundo was in the backyard serving the musicians a late lunch—grilled meats and raw vegetables rolled tightly in corn tortillas, along with a healthy supply of cold Corona beers with limes. Everyone appeared to be enjoying themselves.

Saltire and Xochitl had stopped for refreshments and to refuel his motorcycle. Xochitl was chasing her father around the convenience store, attempting to be the first to catch a Monarch butterfly that was trapped inside the store. Another little girl, around Xochitl's age, saw what they were doing and tried to capture the butterfly, too. Saltire slipped outside through the rear screen door and released the butterfly cupped in his hands. The two girls caught up to Saltire, then watched the Monarch butterfly flutter away toward a grove of trees.

"Back to Tollan, my little friend, tell them she is coming," Saltire said under his breath.

Xochitl and the little girl break out in giggles.

Octavio had veered off the freeway to visit with his second cousin Victor. His cousin was much loved and admired for his guitar playing and his ability to breed the Azteca-the national horse of Mexico.

Octavio's sons, Reynaldo and Sergio, were inside Victor's remodeled Mexican-style hacienda. Each had gone to the restroom, and now they were polishing off cold brews in the classic oak kitchen.

Octavio, Noelle, and Victor were strolling through his rock garden when Victor reached into his shoulder bag and retrieved a buckskin leather bag filled with quartz crystals.

"I'll trade two of yours for one of mine," Victor said teasingly to Noelle, pointing at her pouch.

Octavio told Victor to hold up a minute. He then walked back over to his pick-up truck and freed the were-eagle. The were-eagle glided over to where Noelle was standing and landed, facing her, on a gathering of quartz crystals embedded in an enormous geode. With a flick of his hand, Victor said to Noelle, "No one is going anywhere until you make up your mind."

Noelle glanced over at Octavio and nervously gestured for him to help her. Octavio offered her no such thing. Directing her attention toward the were-eagle, Noelle proceeded cautiously, inching closer with each step to the crystallized geode. Gracefully and with minimal fuss, the were-eagle loosened several large quartz crystals from the geode with its enormous talons. Noelle reached down to grab hold of a long slender crystal when the were-eagle suddenly attacked her. The huge bird had sprung onto Noelle's bare shoulders.

"No sudden movements," Victor instructed her. "I'm afraid you forgot your manners!"

"What should I do?" Noelle's thought telepathically reached Victor.

Understanding her question, Victor was going to give it to her "good and proper."

"Must you always rely on others to tell you what's appropriate?" Victor asked, point-blank.

Trying to right her perceived wrong, Noelle placed the freed crystal back with the others.

"Nope! That won't do," Victor pointed out. "Once you've chosen a crystal, you can never give it back, nor can you give it away for that matter."

Frustrated, Noelle snatched up the quartz crystal from before and backed away slowly. The were-eagle countered her body movements by letting go of Noelle's shoulders. While eyeing Noelle, the creature dislodged two smaller quartz crystals from the geode with its talons. Precious gems in tow, the were-eagle soared back over to Octavio's pick-up truck bed and reentered its cage on its own accord.

Paloma, as the were-eagle, had given her sign of approval. At that moment, Octavio knew unequivocally that Noelle was a "complimentary soul aspect" of the female Toltec Atlantean Warrior, Quetzal Hunahpu "Sacred Bird, One Marksman Lord, Eternal." This meant they shared the same *Seminal Being* Soul from its very inception.

Victor walked Noelle back to Octavio's pick-up truck and waited for her to settle down in the passenger seat.

"The crystal you chose looks familiar?" Victor inquired.

Noelle re-examined the diamond pointed quartz crystal wand. "Yes, it reminds me of another time."

"How's that?"

"I don't know, I can't explain it."

Octavio, keys in hand, was getting ready to leave. Victor rifled through his pants pockets and pulled out a blank strip of paper. He showed both sides of it to Noelle, then crinkled it up in his right hand.

Noelle was amused by Victor's sleight-of-hand." Are you a magician?" she asked.

Victor blew three times on his closed fist and then released the strip of paper into the air. A handwritten proclamation was legible on one side of the paper. As the strip of paper slowly fluttered back into Victor's right hand, Noelle read the declaration out loud:

"I AM THAT WHO YOU ARE,
IS A MESSENGER AWAKENING PEOPLE
TO THEIR SOUL'S INTENDED FUTURE."

"More to the point, yes, I am a magician," Victor continued. "Just not in the way you mean it!"

Victor Ruis Celestino, also known as "Conqueror, Renown, Secret of Heaven," age sixty-six, was the first cousin to Lucius Antonio Celestino—which made him the second cousin to Paloma, Rosita, Octavio, and Saltire. A highly respected horse breeder of the American Quarter Horse, Victor expanded his stable by purchasing Lucius' (Stud Book) of twelve Andalusia horses. A few years back, he acquired a third breed, the Azteca, the national horse of Mexico, and sold them to highly respectable individuals in the Americas.

They all lived in the hills of Tonala, Mexico; his horse breeding business was a very successful family affair. The profits had afforded Victor the opportunity to dabble in his first love, harvesting quartz crystals and obsidian rocks used in the restoration of the Toltec Secret Eagle Knight Council's *Chamber of Mirrors*. The Council members said Victor's *Seminal Being* Soul was infinite and that it had existed before time itself.

Victor had been married to Tamar "Date Palm" for forty-one years. He had two daughters Tototl, and Tlalli, also known as "Bird," and "Earth" respectively, plus a son Sol, who was known as "Sun."

Dust flying, Reynaldo and Sergio came running over to Octavio's vehicle. They flung themselves on top of the truck bed in a race to see who could claim the open spot next to the were-eagle's cage. Victor walked around the pick-up truck and over to Octavio. Noelle was pretending not to pay attention as she listened in on their conversation.

"Yes, we're still going ahead as planned. Saltire has agreed to take her the rest of the way," Octavio whispered.

Victor reached into his shirt pocket and pulled out a pouch filled with sacred herbs. Handing the pouch over to Octavio, he said, "Sprinkle this on top of the fish; it will assist in the synchronization of souls."

Victor then moved away from Octavio's pick-up truck and gave a nod as they drove away.

Saltire was crisscrossing his way through the city streets of Guadalajara, Mexico. Thousands of Mexicans and foreigners were parading about in traditional *Days of the Dead* facemasks and flamboyant costumes. There was a stir underneath Saltire's motorcycle jacket.

"Where are we?" Xochitl asked as she popped her head out from under her father's jacket.

"Guadalajara, and it's almost time for another pit stop."

"I love you, Papi!"

"Back-at-ya!" Saltire said.

Saltire maneuvered his motorcycle over to the curb just long enough to speak to a beautiful Blonde Lady who appeared to be in her mid-thirties. The lady seemed to be flirting; in truth, she was Saltire's youthful-looking stepmother putting on a terrific impersonation of her daughter, Rosita.

Mrs. Eztli "Melita" Modesto Celestino, alias "Blonde Lady," age seventy-two, was the widow of Lucius Antonio Celestino. The mother to three of the Celestino children: Paloma, Rosita, and Octavio, and stepmother to Saltire, lived at Saltire's four-bedroom condominium in Guadalajara, Mexico. An intelligent and multifaceted individual, she managed her stepson's multimillion-luxury car and motorcycle company, founded in 1978, with an air of confidence. Melita was a part-time actress and stage performer. As a young adult, she taught herself to impersonate her family members for shits' and giggles, never intending to lead to a profession with financial benefits. Melita participated in many Celestino family's clandestine activities and took great pride as a voice impersonator.

Saltire whispered in Melita's ear, "Give me a sampling would ya Ma?"

Melita, as the Blonde Lady, pulled back, spun around, and did an impeccable job of sounding exactly like Rosita. "Don't just stand there, Mister, show me you care!"

Saltire feigned being interested in the Blonde Lady for a pedestrian passerby and then told in Melita where she would be able to find Emilio after dark.

"You're sure Noelle's worth all this trouble?" Blonde Lady implied. "I just don't understand why your ailing brother is so hell-bent on rescuing some halfwit from herself. I feel we have our priorities all wrong. We need to be focused on family matters right now!"

Looking amused, Saltire replied, "No, that's not it at all. We believe Noelle is the other soul aspect of the same *Seminal Being* Soul—the same all-knowing, larger than life consciousness—that Toltec Atlantean Warrior Quetzal Hunahpu once inhabited. And, it is happening just as Quetzal prophesized over one thousand years ago.

Saltire push-started his motorcycle as Blonde Lady apologized. "Please accept my apology. Thank you for telling me; I'd no idea she meant that much to us. I'll be on my way shortly."

Saltire turned down a narrow side road heading in a southerly direction. The motorcycle bounced over the cobblestone streets on its way to a local bakery. Xochitl was showing a sign of approval; both hands were exposed to taking in the breeze.

Octavio pulled into Tlaquepaque, Mexico, and stopped to break for lunch in a park. Noelle was in a trance, curled up with her back against the passenger side window. In the right hand, she clutched her Great Aunt Immokalee's artist book *The Spirit of the Voice,* while in the left hand, she cupped the cartridge for Octavio's antique Mutoscope.

Octavio leaned to the right and whispered, "Noelle, are you with me?"

Noelle had consciously returned to the *Flashback Sequence* of 1990. No amount of feelings of awkwardness and isolation were going to deter her. Seven days had passed since Noelle's incident with the brown recluse spider. She was wrapped in a down comforter, lying half asleep on her queen-sized antique mahogany bed positioned in the corner of her five hundred square foot, third-story loft apartment. The apartment was in the attic of a late 1800s Victorian House in the center of Lexington, MA. Furnished by the owner Mrs. Agatha Winton Morgenstern, alias "Kind, Friend, Morning Star," the loft was filled with WWII paraphernalia. Noelle's favorite item was a Marine Corps olive-colored garment bag with folding tree trimming tools neatly stashed inside. In the same vicinity was the eggshell-colored kitchenette with walnut cabinets, porcelain Farmhouse sink, and lime-green Sears' refrigerator, late 70s model. Throughout the apartment, hardwood floors were interrupted only by the bathroom's multicolored mosaic tiles arranged in a patchwork pattern. The loft had plenty of sunlight, which allowed Noelle to paint murals that transferred well into other environments.

Noelle woke up and called after Avery, "Where are you? I can't see a thing," she grumbled.

Out of the darkness, Avery moved to the side of the bed.

"Oh! How funny, I didn't even see you. What time do you think it is?"

Avery slipped back into bed and said, "Does it matter?" He then rolled on top of Noelle and kissed her passionately. Taking her face in his hands, he looked deep into her eyes.

Noelle said, "Hey, you!"

Avery interrupted the mood with "Shhh!"

An endless stream of silver light flowed out from Noelle's pupils as her face took on the appearance of her Great Aunt Immokalee when she was thirty-five.

Avery, not able to perceive the shift in Noelle's physicality, asked, "Do you have anything sweet to eat in your kingdom?"

Feeling a bit strange, Noelle got out of bed, threw on one of Avery's "Fruit of the Loom" T-shirts, and then walked out of the bedroom area and into the kitchenette. Avery followed her after putting on a pair of jeans and his floppy dun sued hat.

Snatching a plastic cup out of the kitchen sink, Noelle tossed it in Avery's direction. He fumbled with the glass and caught it behind his back, upright, and on his right toe. He looked exactly like a Dr. Seuss character to Noelle, and she buckled over in hysterics. When she regained her composure, Avery sprung the "Big Question" that most women to hear.

"Will you marry me?" Avery asked doubtfully.

"Are you serious or just kidding?" Noelle asks sheepishly.

"Please! Please say, yes!"

Noelle hesitated for a few seconds and then agreed to marry Avery in two years' time. Pleasantly surprised by her response, he reached out for an embrace.

Eyes shut, Noelle had the good sense to leave the 1990 Flashback Sequence, for the time being, in favor of her Mexican odyssey of 1994. It was critical that her Recapitulation (the process of reviewing her earlier life) occurring in 2015 in "The Chamber of Mirrors" continue without any adverse effects on her spirit and soul. Being able to discern between the two different time zones, as she progressed in dismantling the overwhelming Karmic Debt she had incurred, was the only means of restoring her fragmented Seminal Being *Soul.*

Octavio had gotten out of his white pick-up truck to prompt his sons into action. He smacked the side of the truck bed; Reynaldo jabbed Sergio, and the two quickly carried the cooler containing ice water, sandwiches, and snacks over to a picnic table. Octavio remained behind just long enough to check in with Noelle. His right hand was spilling over with assorted condiments: green, pumpkin, tomato, and chili salsas.

Octavio whispered in Noelle's right ear, "We all get hooked from time to time by those we love. The challenge is to never allow yourself to get ensnared in the drama."

Noelle heard Octavio's communication but was not fully cognizant of its deeper implication. Even three carloads of teenagers whizzing past Octavio beeping their horns were not evasive enough to free her mind completely. The smell of the exhaust from the passing cars actually triggered the sense of memory of when Noelle first met Avery's parents. This was the first time she witnessed a disturbing family dynamic in place. Her 1994 Flashback began to reveal the underlining intentions and agendas of Avery, his parents, and his closest friends.

The Noelle of 2015 had gone further than she ever had in previous Recapitulations; however, she was ignorant of the influence her prior incarnations had on her current life condition. I knew this to be the case from my own experience, as Quetzal.

The roar of hundreds of vehicles devoured a leveled field. Over 200 acres were temporarily turned into an open flea market. The flea market came to the New England area biannually. Every September, Avery and his parents planned on attending the one held in November.

Noelle and Avery showed their affection openly while moseying about in search of a great find. Avery came up from behind Noelle and wrapped his arms around her shoulders. Noelle ducked and spun out from underneath his embrace. It felt awkward, as if he were putting on a show.

Pointing to a large silver cross attached to hand-carved wooden beads, Noelle commented. "Look at this cross, isn't it beautiful?"

Avery encouraged Noelle to buy it. Noelle asked the conservatively dressed lady overseeing a table covered in religious icons the cost of the Rosary Cross; she was told the monk's cross was only $25.00.

"That's all? I'll take it," Noelle shouted with excitement.

Avery and Noelle continued to wind their way through the thousands of antique dealers and hopefuls milling about. They commented on how they wished they had brought more money. Noelle scanned the flea market and thought she saw a middle-aged couple that looked like Avery's parents. No, she hadn't met them yet; she remembered seeing a picture of them with Avery at his studio. Avery confirmed Noelle's suspicion, and the two trotted over to greet them.

Mr. and Mrs. Millstone, in their fifties, were rummaging through the "Used Books Section."

Avery showed his mother Noelle's rosary cross, and Mrs. Millstone gushed over it, voicing how she wished she had come upon it first.

"If you like it, you can have it. I don't mind. Here, take it!" Noelle said.

She then took three steps toward Avery's mom and presented the monk's cross as a gift. Mrs. Millstone rejected the offer, sitting that she mustn't impose on Noelle. Noelle insisted, Mrs. Millstone declined, and then Avery took a cheap shot at religious zealots.

"Look at you two Christian martyrs still stuck to a cross!"

"What? We're not martyrs!" Noelle explained, feeling slightly ashamed.

"And I was so hoping you two would hit it off," Avery said, adding to Noelle's insecurities.

Noelle turned her back on Avery and his mother. Glancing down at the folding tables in a row, she thought she saw her Great Aunt Immokalee's handmade artist book *The Spirit of the Voice* by Nicholas

Renato Intaglio III and Immokalee Awinita Chisholm dated 1913. An elderly lady, in her mid-eighties, who was responsible for selling the used books, was nowhere in sight. Noelle rejoicing inside, reached across the table, retrieved her stolen heirloom, and hid it under Avery's brown and white flannel shirt. Avery informed his mother they were going to pass on dinner. Mr. Millstone, who has been quiet the whole time, tipped his tattered baseball cap and made a silly face directed at his son. It was meant to mock Noelle's tomboy appearance. Avery understanding his father's sense of humor ran at his dad crazy faced and swinging his arms. The communication between the two men was hardly lighthearted. Noelle found it to be somewhat creepy and disconcerting.

On his way back over to Noelle, Avery said, with an air of conceit, "If you'd like to get me something, I'll take that book you've hijacked off your hands."

"You'd die trying! Noelle spouted in defiance. "Oh, and by the way, I don't suppose you can tell me, how it arrived here?"

As Avery's parents started to distance themselves from the couple, Avery told Noelle, "Take it. I don't want this piece of shit!"

Accepting defeat, Avery stepped away from Noelle and followed behind his parents in a manner befitting a well-trained dog. Passed the "Used Books" section and the Christmas holiday baskets; they rested their weary legs at the "Hot Cider and Cookies" booth.

Noelle stayed behind and removed the artist's book very gingerly from beneath her shirt. Clutching it to her chest, she walked it over to the far corner of the display table and presented it to the white-haired old lady in charge of sales.

Flipping through the pages, she said to the saleswoman, "Excuse me. Could you tell me where you got this book?"

"My nephew brought it to me last week." The old woman said in her defense. "He's very reputable; his collectibles are very much in demand."

Stone-faced Noelle seemed unimpressed. She recognized the original copy, minus the pages she kept carefully hidden in the bottom of a dresser drawer in her loft apartment. Noelle managed to keep her composure while she calmly closed the book and then pointed to the two individuals that had published the book in 1913—Nicholas Renato Intaglio III and Immokalee Awinita Chisholm.

"See this?" Noelle said calmly, "This is my family. They mean everything to me."

"Well, of course they do, my dear. Will you be purchasing this today? I can give you a good price." The elderly lady said in a patronizing way.

So who's your nephew; what's his name?" Noelle asked, raising her voice a tad.

The old lady, fidgeting with the sales and receipt book, rudely persisted, "You want the book or not?"

"Damn straight, I want it! I'll be taking it. Noelle responded in kind. "And if you so much as hesitate, I'll yell for the police, and we can get to the bottom this right now."

Noelle only waited but for a second, then slipped the artist book into her shoulder bag. Before leaving, she asked for a receipt saying paid in full. The elderly lady wrote up a receipt registering the title, the date and scribbled frantically "Paid in full. No charge!"

Receipt in hand, Noelle turned around and located Avery. He was gesturing with his hand, "Let's go!" Noelle took flight and chased after him.

When Noelle reclaimed the artist's book, she set in motion the healing that would soon occur between her soul aspect and that of her Great Aunt Immokalee Awinita Chisholm Intaglio.

In 1994, the park at Tlaquepaque was developed with indigenous plant life. Easy to maintain, it required little effort on the part of the landscapers. A number of people enjoyed the natural habitat; families and couples, in particular, were seen returning time and again.

Noelle was interrupted by a man and woman speaking Spanish with Octavio and tilted her head in their direction. Noelle gazed into the man's eyes. His eyes were twinkling as he joked and kidded with the woman. They danced the rumba to music coming from a transistor radio. Then without warning, a sharp stabbing pain entered Noelle's right shoulder, and her fingers tightened into a cramp. Horrified that she might damage the book, still attached to her right hand, she flung the artist's book, *The Spirit of the Voice*, to the rubber mat in Octavio's pick-up truck.

CHAPTER TWELVE

Blind Ambition

Noelle continued with her demanding 1990 *Flashback Sequence.* She had jumped ahead one week. "Larry King Live" was playing in the background; the sound was turned down. Stan Getz's version of Andy Williams' song "Quiet Night of Quiet Stars Corcovado" was blasting from Noelle's third-story loft apartment. Noelle swayed back 'n forth, like a Big Cat, in front of a six-foot-high by eight-foot-wide landscape mural when Stanley, a sixty-two-year-old homosexual male, flung wide her front door. Singing and dancing to the infamous song, the rather handsome and statuesque man shuffled over to her. Stanley, a world traveler and charitable donor of the National Endowment for the Arts (NEA), knew the Bossa Nova Brazilian dance movements. Noelle did her utmost with the lyrics.

Smiling and laughing, Noelle and Stanley took turns leading each other through a series of dance steps. Noelle's moves were totally improvised, while Stanley's appeared well-rehearsed. There was much hip-swaying, shuffling of feet, and bobbing of shoulders; it was clear they were having a ball. Just as the song ended, the phone rang. Noelle rushed across the living room and into the kitchenette. Seizing the wall-mounted phone by the refrigerator, she breathlessly uttered hello.

Avery was on the other end of the phone inviting Noelle to the movies, "Meet me at the T in Harvard Square, the one nearest the theater around 4:30 p.m. A good buddy of mine is in from New York City, there's a movie playing there that Guy wants to see."

"Okay, sounds great, see ya there."

Noelle got off the phone and cha-chaed her way over to Stanley, who was checking out Noelle's life-size cartoon cutout of herself. In the artistic interpretation of Noelle, she was partially hidden by a green and fuchsia sponge painted canvas. Her body was avocado-green and her hair cobalt blue. Plastered across her face was a look of dumb surprise. The cartoon version of Noelle had her carelessly dripping yellow paint onto the canvas.

Examining the art piece, Noelle turned to Stanley and asked, "Am I this checked out?"

"Why you're no more of a ding-a-ling than I am," Stanley replied.

He then spontaneously broke into another Stan Gent's song. Noelle followed Stanley, giggling and shaking her head as he sashayed his way out of her apartment.

Noelle yelled after her dear friend, "I love you, Stanley, you're the best!"

Stanley continued singing and dancing down the partially lit staircase, flashing his silhouette on the walls.

Noelle willfully ventured deeper and deeper into the Recapitulation Process—the Self-Correcting Principle had taken hold of her subconscious and was actively shedding light on an event that would change the trajectory of her life.

Tomorrow had arrived! It was the Holiday Season, and Christmas decorations adorned Harvard Square in Cambridge, MA. The sun was slipping behind the trees causing everything to lose its luster. Noelle came galloping up the subway steps in anticipation of meeting Avery and his friend Guy. Avery and Guy Branton Cook, known as the "Guide, Brushwood, Seller of Meats," age twenty-eight, were there waiting in the crisp cold air, people watching. Avery introduced Noelle to Guy on their way to the Harvard Theater. Once inside the glass double doors, Avery purchased their movie tickets, then took their food and drink orders. Guy watched Avery skip over to the concession counter before asking Noelle how long she had been seeing Avery.

"I'm not sure, ten weeks?" Noelle said.

Guy started to walk away when Avery returned with popcorn and sodas. Avery handed off the drinks to Guy and then began to juggle three large bags of popcorns. Noelle requested that he knock-it-off; Avery proceeded to spill popcorn all over the red carpet. Noelle, looking aghast, hustled up the ramp that led to the movie theater.

Noelle sat down, and Avery and Guy followed accordingly. Noelle was positioned between them. Avery removed his floppy dun suede hat and offered it to Guy.

"Here man, you can wear it."

Looking perturbed, Guy took the suede hat from behind Noelle's neck and put it on his lap. Noelle ignored the young men and watched the black 'n white foreign film, *When I Was A Dog* in total silence. A scene from the movie depicted Noelle's actual state of mind—all gray and fuzzy. It was a bit of a drive back to Noelle's Loft in Lexington. Avery and Noelle hardly spoke to one another. Avery parked his father's 1986 tan Chevy Cargo Van, in front of the late 1800s Victorian house. After departing, he bee-lined over to a snowman decked out in a Santa's elf costume. Before toppling its head, Avery snagged the scarf from around the snowman's shoulders and proceeded to stockpile snowballs.

"That's not mine, you know!" Noelle hollered.

"I don't care; it's mine now!" Avery shouted.

Avery and Guy ran around in the snow, laughing and slinging snowballs at one another. Noelle made a feeble attempt to participate in the snowball fight; she only did this to alleviate the tension between Avery, Guy, and herself. After several minutes, the young men descended upon Noelle's third-story loft apartment in a haphazard playful manner, pushing and shoving their way up the staircase. Noelle did her best to keep up. She unlocked the front door and allowed the young men first entry into her apartment.

Once inside, Guy appraised the space making a mental note of the living room. He then nudged Avery, and the two entered the bathroom just to the left of the kitchenette and at the end of the hallway. Noelle paid no attention to their actions or to the sound of the door as it locked.

After draping her beige parka on top of a coat rack, just inside the door, Noelle scuffled across the hardwood floors to the open floor plan.

The Bohemian living room furniture merging with WWII military souvenirs evoked a sense of honor and individual style. A burnt orange 19th-century antique couch and New England Hadley chest with low relief carving of trees and ferns were beautiful additions to the room. The surrounding had a fresh coat of white satin paint, which highlighted the framed poster art. Noelle loved everything Motown, and she had her favorite Bluegrass and Country singers too: Bob Dylan, Joan Baez, Tom Petty, James Taylor, and Joni Mitchell.

Guy quickly ensnared Avery in his clandestine scheme. He told him to break up with Noelle, and to give her no explanation. Guy asserted that by doing this abruptly, Avery would determine whether or not Noelle truly loved him.

"When we're on the couch, you tell Noelle to give me a hug. I've no doubt she'll do it," Guy said gleefully. "Then say something like, see, I told you. Doesn't she hug you like my mother? This will be my cue to get up and go outside."

Avery responded enthusiastically, "Is this what Blake meant by finding out about a person's psychological make-up?"

Guy's eyes twinkled as he pulled back a crooked smile, "Yep! The workings of a genius."

When Avery was thirteen years old, he witnessed his best friend Blake getting beaten up by four classmates at a Halloween party. Blake had done nothing to provoke the attack from Avery's perspective, and he sought retaliation. Three weeks later, he helped with Blake's revenge. Avery enlisted the support of his older sister, Suzy, in a bait-and-switch scheme. Suzie, the most popular girl in her senior class, got a group of her friends to invite the boys over to a Thanksgiving party at Salem's Wharf District. When the boys arrived, they were assaulted. Blake and Avery had solicited a band of hoodlums a few days back to kidnap the four bullies for the night in exchange for a pound of weed. As agreed, the boys frightened and ruffled were taken blindfolded to another part of town and released at sunup. Needless to say, Blake was never harassed again in school. The word got out that he had connections with organized crime syndicates. The rumor, although exaggerated, proved to be very effective.

Noelle kneeling on her couch facing backward, yelled in Avery's direction, "What are you guys doing?"

Avery shouted through the bathroom door, "Be out in a second!"

Noelle shrugged her shoulders and turned back around, and headed into the living room.

Avery and Guy joined Noelle. Once again, Noelle found herself situated between Avery and Guy. Noelle cuddled up to Avery while they all discussed the movie. Avery interrupted the conversation and ordered Noelle to hug Guy; she complied.

"See what I mean, doesn't she hug you just like my mother," Avery mockingly said to Guy.

Guy lowered his arms to his sides, stood up to leave, and directed his comment at Noelle.

"I'll be outside. Avery has something he wants to say to you."

Noelle looked over at Avery as Guy closed the front door behind him.

Avery rose to his feet and then blurted out that he no longer wanted to be engaged to Noelle. Noelle asked why? Avery said he never considered them actually engaged and pointed out he never gave her a ring.

"It didn't take you very long to accept. What was it, all of three seconds?" Avery spouted in a condemning tone of voice,

Noelle hesitated momentarily and then resorted to defending her position on the whole marry-me-matter, "If you think I'm crying because you're calling off our engagement, that's not why.

I'm upset because you're not honest! Something else is going on here; I can feel it!"

Noelle gathered her composure and strutted over to the front door. Guy had left it slightly ajar. As Noelle walked through the front door, she brushed up against Guy as he headed back inside. Guy never did go for his walk; he had been standing on the landing this whole time, listening to their conversation through the crack in the door.

Guy headed over to the bay window, where Avery was monitoring Noelle's behavior.

"What's she doing? I can't see a damn thing!" Guy inquired.

Noelle walked back and forth on the sidewalk in front of the Victorian house. She was moving painfully slow, making every effort to catch her breath. Unable to breathe easily, Noelle yanked her purple and red paisley turtleneck down around her shoulders to allow more air into her lungs. Walking with her nose pointed to the night sky, Noelle felt dozens of snowflakes land on her face.

Avery and Guy were preparing to leave; they carried some of Avery's belongings over to his father's Cargo Van. Avery had a 40s-style wooden coffee table flipped upside down and above his head, while Guy was struggling to carry his friend's antique wrought iron candelabrum.

Fearing the worst outcome, Noelle walked timidly over to them.

"I think it's best if we don't see each other for awhile," Avery said to Noelle.

Noelle's countenance, void of light and her eyes of all expression, was but a mere shadow of her Seminal Being Soul's Intent. Immokalee Awinita Chisholm Intaglio, age thirty-seven, had dominion over Noelle's emotional wellbeing. Noelle, unwittingly, recited the very words her great aunt uttered after she received the State Department letter stating her husband, Nicholas Renato Intaglio III, had been shot in the head and killed in WWI.

"When you die one hundred deaths, who do you suppose covers you in cloth, friend or foe?" Noelle whispered softly to herself, just as Immokalee had done in the year 1916.

Avery looked at Noelle as if she has gone mad; the inflection in her voice and her posture were otherworldly. Noelle, as Immokalee watched from the sidewalk as Avery drove away.

During the times when Noelle took on the physical appearance of her Great Aunt Immokalee Awinita Chisholm Intaglio, she was attempting to activate Karmic Debt Removal-soul retrieval while healing the debilitating effects of personal trauma. Undeniably it was during these times when Noelle was the most vulnerable and most powerful. She reclaimed lost vital energy while shifting from the realm of duality toward wholeness. In doing so, she experienced an inkling of the actualized Seminal Being *Soul of Amrit Sandhu, an even earlier incarnation prior to Quetzal Hunahpu.*

The sun was bearing down on the picnickers at the park in Tlaquepaque. Noelle was still sitting in Octavio's white pick-up truck, half asleep. Paloma's body double, the were-eagle, lifted the latch to her cage and pulled a papier-mâché and wire skull kite in front of Octavio's truck. As Noelle awakened, she heard a faint Tap, Tap, Tap, on the passenger side window. Noelle jerked her head away and opened her eyes. The mysterious kite, crowned by an apple tree and wearing angels for ears, spun around the antenna; then flew up and out of Noelle's view. Glancing down at the driver's seat, Noelle noticed Twinkle and Sharky. Xochitl had them tied to the pull strings of Noelle's leather-beaded pouch filled with copal incense. They acted as Noelle's good luck, charms; they had been deliberately left next to her for protection.

Xochitl, insisting that Noelle take part in the picnic lunch, tapped again on the passenger side window. Noelle was aware of Xochitl's efforts, yet seemed unable to resist a fractal pattern swirling and pulsating inside the elongated quartz crystal that she clutched in her left hand. Noelle, attempting to resist its influence, reached around to the passenger side door and tried to open it. As soon as the door swung open, she lost control of her faculties and experienced a "full body convulsive wave."

Her entire body shook uncontrollably. With eyes closed, Noelle was able to perceive an eight-inch glowing white sphere emerge from her solar plexus. The convulsions lasted a good minute. At no time did she express pain, nor was she afraid. The toxic, chaotic energy surrounding Noelle's sudden and unanticipated breakup from Avery was leaving her body. The enlarged solar plexus in a fixed position, amidst the tremors, was a testimony to the will of her *Seminal Being* Soul. This phenomenon was encouraged by psychotherapists and shamans when healing the debilitating effects of a long-standing traumatic event.

For the very first time, I felt truly alive and an integral part of Noelle's Spiritual Journey and reformation. The memory played tricks on Noelle's mind when her Recapitulation Process began on November 1, 2015. She had intended to only relive the Halloween week of 1994 and advance her status within the Toltec Secret Eagle Knight Council. However, unresolved issues from two prior interconnected soul aspects of the same Seminal Being Soul were running interference.

This dynamic created unconscious habitual behaviors, which manifested instinctual thoughts and actions. Thus, Karmic Debt became the dominant force *in Noelle's life. Only by dispelling the nature of suffering through an extensive Recapitulation—*Flashback Sequences*—was Noelle even capable of living an authentic and fulfilling life.*

November 1, 1991, Noelle and Avery left at the crack of dawn from Lexington, MA. Noelle appeared tired and disheveled and Avery, still partially dressed in his Halloween skeleton leggings, looked ridiculous. It took Noelle and Avery twelve days to make the transition from East Coast to West Coast. The cross-country road trip was nothing like Noelle had imagined. Only the meals were worth remembering. At every opportunity, Avery spun off and left Noelle by herself, alone to have her own experiences of the different cities and towns. By the time they reached California, Noelle couldn't take another day with Avery.

It was coming up on 6:00 p.m., when Noelle and Avery crossed over into Los Angeles County. Avery was driving Noelle's 1984 Jeep Grand Cherokee Wagoneer through a sea of lights on the California 405 Freeway. A mini U-Haul® trailer was being towed behind the vehicle.

"Is this ever going to end? Noelle wistfully asked Avery.

"I'm sick of driving, aren't we near the turn-off?" He replied.

Noelle reviewed the roadmap and said they ought to be coming up on it soon. Out of nowhere, a large and imposing were-eagle flew straight for Noelle's Wagoneer and deposited a rock on its hood. The rock bounced off the windshield and out of sight.

"What the hell was that?" Avery yelled.

"Here, take this exit!" Noelle shouts alarmed.

Avery swerved onto the exit ramp and headed eastbound on Sunset Boulevard. Noelle kept her eyes glued to the signposts and her thumb on the Los Angeles road map. The combination she figured could get them to her destination without much fuss.

Avery pulled up in front of a 1930s Spanish-style house off Fairfax Avenue in Los Angeles, CA, just after dusk. The five-bedroom home turned boarding house of Mr. and Mrs. Lowenstein had been renting to young women for some time. The stock market growth had slowed, and it was about to get worse. Avery remained behind in the driver's seat as Noelle prepared to enter the house. An unidentified woman, mid-twenties, came walking over to Noelle and informed her that the "master of the house" was out to dinner. She was advised to go inside and get her keys from Michelle.

"Michelle's in the kitchen. I'd hurry if I were you," The unidentified woman said sharply. "I just saw her devouring your bowl of ice-cream."

Noelle entered the house and headed directly for the kitchen. There she was, greeted by a bubbly brunette in her nightwear.

"Hi, I'm Michelle! Your keys are right there on the counter. Whatever you do, don't lose 'em. It will cost you ten bucks to replace them."

Noelle spotted the keys on the kitchen island, snatched them up, and then thanked Michelle. Michelle asked Noelle for her name, as she was just about to leave the kitchen and go straight to her bedroom.

Appearing disoriented, Noelle stopped at the foot of the staircase and spoke loudly as she introduced herself, "Noelle Intaglio Leandre, I'm Native American!"

Noelle often introduced herself that way; she was brown skinned and proud of her percentage of Cherokee Indian.

Meanwhile, Avery had already begun unloading the U-Haul trailer; he was lumbering up the front walk with a large moving box in both hands when Noelle rejoined him.

"Go upstairs and check out the railroad-style compartments. I mean apartments," Noelle said sarcastically. "Mine's the first room on the right."

The move happened quickly; neither one was talking particularly. Avery finally asked Noelle where she wanted him to put the last box. She pointed to the only uncluttered space in her twelve-foot by fourteen-foot bedroom. Avery dropped off the box and headed back downstairs. Noelle scanned her bedroom: red velvet flocked wallpaper, a burnt orange shag carpet, dark wood blinds, and tacky maroon-colored floor-to-ceiling drapes.

"What is this place, a brothel?" Noelle mumbled to herself. "No wonder I wasn't allowed to see the room ahead of time."

Noelle could barely contain herself; she looked lost and frightened. Leaving quickly, she shut the door and hopped downstairs, two steps at a time. Avery was eating leftovers on the U-Haul trailer ramp. Noelle headed over to him, expressing her grief over having to say goodbye.

"I feel terrible that you're going to be leaving tomorrow, and I may never see you again."

"I'm sure we'll see each other again. I'll come out for a visit one of these days." Avery said.

Noelle invited Avery to join her upstairs for the night, as it was cold and damp outside. He declined and said he felt more comfortable sleeping in her Wagoneer. So, she gathered up the bags of leftovers, waved goodnight then re-entered the Lowenstein's modest-looking boarding house.

Avery lit up a cigarette and locked down the U-Haul before crawling into Noelle's Wagoneer for the night.

Noelle looked out her side bedroom window facing Fairfax Avenue and watched as the wind swirled and blew the fallen leaves about. Even their beauty could not alter her mood. Tired and visibly upset, Noelle collapsed on the queen size mattress flopped down on the carpet. Eyes fixed on the skip trowel ceiling pattern, Noelle's voice began to tremble. In a trance-like state, cried out to God:

"God is this all there is to life?
Is this all there is to my life?
If so, snuff me out quickly,
If not, give me something to do!"

CHAPTER THIRTEEN

Scrying Mirror Magic

Inside Octavio's white pick-up truck at the park in Tlaquepaque, Mexico, Noelle's ethereal body double was rapidly spiraling downward. It landed back in her body just as she was waking up from her 1991 *Flashback Sequence.*

The windshield of the truck was reflecting the movements of playground children. Noelle felt the tingling of seashells as they wiggled and jumped across her body. Xochitl was sitting next to Noelle, holding Twinkle and Sharky in her little crab-like hands. She had been choreographing a death and rebirth modern dance routine with her Oceanside pets.

Xochitl whispered, "Wake up! Come out from under your nightmare!"

Noelle sighed.

Xochitl shouted in fun, "It's picnic time!"

"Some picnic I'm having."

A moment later, Noelle started laughing as she wiped the tears from her cheekbones. Saltire leaned in the passenger side window and studied her intensely.

"He is tragically unforgettable—Yes!" Saltire said assuredly.

Noelle nodded in agreement.

Saltire opened the passenger side door, and Noelle stepped out, taking her Aunt Immokalee's artist book with her. Bound to her other hand, Noelle was attached to her leather-beaded pouch accompanied by Sharky and Twinkle.

Octavio had made a place setting for Noelle's packed lunch; it was clear she was to sit at one end of the picnic table. Saltire and Xochitl were at the other end of the picnic table. They were drawing with small "array sponges" on sticky-back sheets of peel away paper. Noelle had her head down and was picking at her food when Saltire got up and sat down kitty-corner to her.

"Shall we continue?" Saltire asked.

Noelle nodded her head in approval.

"It is important that you see your relationship with Avery for what it was. There's something you haven't quite been able to accept concerning yourself," Saltire further contended. "Your anguish over your unrequited love is merely a function of the very thing you are covering up."

When Saltire began to talk with Noelle, she removed three symbolic items from her pouch: the diamond-tipped crystal wand, one piece of copal incense, and the smooth clay figurine of a were-cougar. She placed them on the picnic table and examined her stash.

"I don't remember putting this cat-like creature in here!" Noelle remarked as she intuitively created a three-pointed triangular shape and charged the items.

Noelle took the initiative to arrange the diamond-tipped crystal wand *(Spirit)*, the copal incense *(Fire)*, and the smooth clay figurine of the were-cougar *(Earth)* into the sacred geometric shape of the upside-down triangle—the symbol of eternal life—"Pharaoh to be a God." She was intuitively responding to her *Seminal Being* Soul's intention to be complete and whole once again. The residence of Dancing Movement, the *"Dreaming Universe"* was in effect training Noelle to be sensitive to "Silent Knowledge"—the Wisdom of the Ages. All that was missing were two more objects, a Golden Eagle feather *(Air)* and a small vial of holy water (Water). These additional objects were to only show up when Noelle had successfully passed through a major Spiritual Threshold/ Rite of Passage.

In my era, sacred geometry was considered a belief system attributing religious and cultural values; to many of the fundamental forms of space and time. Accordingly, the basic patterns of existence were perceived as sacred because in contemplating them, I was considering the origin of all things. Thus, by studying the nature of these forms and their relationship to each other, I garnered insight into the philosophical, psychological, and mystical laws of the Universe. Over time, my inquiring mind, which took me into the recesses of my own soul, also brought me in touch with the unlimited energy of the Intent of the Seminal Being *Soul of which I Am apart. I sensed Noelle was on the precipice of her spiritual awakening. I had been instructed not to interfere, so I waited patiently and purposefully.*

Octavio, sitting to the right of Noelle, started to unravel the bandages on her fingertips. Noelle showed no signs of resistance.

"Noelle, listen to what your heart is telling you," Octavio lovingly implored.

Noelle took a moment then said, "Listen to what my heart is telling me? Sometimes I feel as though I have more than one to attest to."

Raising her head slowly, Noelle glanced over in Saltire's direction.

Saltire stood up and signaled for Xochitl to gather up her Array Sponges and sticky-back sheets of paper. After graciously thanking his brother for sharing his picnic lunch, Saltire and Xochitl galloped down a slope, across a parking lot, and out of sight.

"They've just gone to "Parvulo X's Bicicleta Tienda," Octavio told Noelle. "My boys won't be back with the ice for a while. Beat it on down, I know where to find you."

Noelle placed the items back inside her leather-beaded pouch and loosely tied the drawstrings through her belt loop. She smiled and then took off in the direction of the parking lot. Turning the corner, she looked up and saw a big wooden sign in red, yellow, white, and green. It read:

Parvulo X's Bicicleta Tienda and Reparar

Directly across the street from Xochitl's Bike Shop and Repair a "Young Boy," looking age six, hollered over to Noelle and asked in Spanish if she wouldn't mind retrieving a white T-shirt from a 300-year-old Ceiba tree.

The Ceiba tree in Mayan-Toltec mythology was believed to be "The Tree of Life." For Noelle, the Ceiba tree was symbolic of her resurrection into the Toltec Secret Eagle Knight Council.

Noelle does not acknowledge the Young Boy at first and heads on over to the front garage of Parvulo X's Bicicleta Tienda and Reparar.

Alongside Young Boy, a group of children, numbering twelve, were playing a game called "Statue." They, too, were under the old Ceiba tree, spinning and chasing after one another. The children are pretending to be human-like animal creatures: were-jaguars, were-cougars, were-wolves, were-eagles, were-lizards, were-frogs, were-butterflies, and so forth.

Noelle peeked through the garage windows and into Xochitl's bike shop. Saltire and Xochitl were removing various children's bicycles from ceiling hooks in different shapes, sizes, and colors. It looked as though they were putting them in order depending on size and attaching a personalized note to the handlebars of each bicycle. Noelle watched their production for a bit then turned around and considered retrieving the child's white T-shirt from a high branch springing forth from one of the branches. After taking a second glance at Young Boy, Noelle strolled over to the child.

"All right! I'll get it for you, not to worry," Noelle said.

Noelle proceeded to climb the old Ceiba tree carefully and methodically. The other children were standing still in silence. As Noelle climbed, the branches became getting thinner and thinner. To get to the T-shirt, Noelle had to crawl along the narrowest of limbs. Noelle stopped when she reached near the top of the tree and glanced down at the group of children gathered around its trunk. The children were shaking their heads "No," and waving at Noelle to come back down.

Without warning, Noelle was overpowered by Octavio's were-eagle—Paloma's body double. Nose-to-beak with the were-eagle, Noelle looked directly into her eyes. The were-eagle responded by spreading its wings and attaching its talons to Noelle's wrists. She remained calm as the were-eagle dragged her within inches of the T-shirt. Bobbing and swaying, Noelle reached for the T-shirt, only to realize it was not a shirt after all. What looked like a white T-shirt was nothing more than several white paper napkins sticking out from a tiny quetzal bird's nest. Noelle giggled as she tore off a piece of a napkin and watched it tumble into Young Boy's hands. The were-eagle took to the air and returned to its cage stored on Octavio's white pick-up truck.

Xochitl's bike shop was a commercial cement building built in the mid-seventies during the economic boom in and around Guadalajara, Mexico. Displayed was a beautiful mural depicting Tollan/Tula, Mexico, painted by local artists. The one-story storage facility appeared as a thriving cityscape in the 1990s. It was the home of twenty-five small bicycles and the primary storage space for Saltire's scrying mirrors made from black obsidian lava.

Saltire and Xochitl, while raising the bike shop garage door, celebrated Noelle's victory.

"Papi, look at Noelle. She did it! She did it! She faced the were-eagle, and it became her ally; Xochitl screamed in delight."

"Yes, Noelle is beginning to experience being in rapport with the spirit of things. Now she'll be equipped to embrace varying aspects of herself," Saltire said in agreement.

Xochitl eyeing the other children, yelled, "I want to go play! I want to go play!"

Saltire told Xochitl she could play the game Statue with Noelle and the other kids for fifteen minutes. Xochitl looked both ways, then zipped across the road and skipped on over to Noelle. The children were whistling and cheering as she climbed safely down from the mighty old Ceiba tree. Noelle started to laugh when she asked if she could play in their game too. They appointed her "Spin Master" and directed her to the center of the circle.

Young Boy, all smiles, came running over to Noelle, "Spin me! Spin me first!" he cried.

The children engaged in "Statue" surround Noelle. Each took their turn being spun into half-human, half-animal indigenous creatures.

"Okay, Xochitl, it's your turn," Noelle said enthusiastically.

Xochitl glanced down at her hands and froze.

"I plan on twirling you like a butterfly dancing above a flower," Noelle conveyed. "Then I'll place you down gently, right here in the same spot."

Xochitl jumped up and down with joy and clamped onto Noelle's left hand. With her right hand, she covered the little girl's claw-like hands and lifted her off the ground. Immediately Noelle began to spin in a tight circle raising Xochitl a few feet off the ground. After two spins,

Xochitl was lowered back to her original starting point and set free. She raced away, leaped like a grasshopper, and spun like a butterfly. The group of children tried to disqualify her with their touch but to no avail.

From Octavio's pick-up truck, Octavio, Reynaldo, and Sergio were enjoying watching the interaction between Noelle and the Mexican children. Octavio waited till Xochitl had taken her turn, then he called after her.

"Come on, 'Pequeno,' you're riding with me this afternoon."

Xochitl scurried over to Octavio, raised one of her crescent appendages, and asked to see her drawings on the sticky-back paper. She quickly located the one she felt resembled Noelle and ran it back over to her.

"Here, I did this drawing while you were sleeping," Xochitl confessed.

Noelle holding the picture up to her face burst out laughing.

"That's not me, although I do see an eerie resemblance to Auntie Lee. My mom says she was a great artist and a poet as well?"

"Xochitl, let's go. This train's a pull in' out!" Octavio howled.

Noelle accepted her self-portrait from Xochitl and thanked her kindly.

Xochitl ran back over to her uncle, repeating her affirmation, "I am a great artist and poet!" The front entrance to PARVULO X'S BICICLETA TIENDA AND REPARAR was crawling with children from the neighborhood. Noelle positioned off to the side, enjoyed the interactions. Happy and excited, all the children claimed their bicycles, thanked Saltire, and sped away.

Saltire calmly walked to the rear of X's BICICLETA TIENDA AND REPARAR while Noelle waited for him outside. She sat down on the curb and considered Xochitl's portrait of her as her Great Aunt Immokalee; the likeness could not be denied.

"Hmm, we do look awfully alike. What's up with that?" Noelle questioned out loud.

Saltire was in a fourteen-foot by twenty-five-foot storage space devoted to his spiritual practices. The majority of the room was sparsely lit by Mexican tin light fixtures and filled with shipping crates with packaging labels to foreign countries. A ten-foot by fourteen-foot area had been designated for scrying, and remote viewing magical practices in the back left corner. A floor-to-ceiling, semi-opaque black curtain was all that separated the crates from the sacred space. Saltire lifted aside the curtain, headed over to an intricately designed wooden altar pressed up against the back wall, and began preparing it for a "Scrying Mirror Ritual." The ritual involved: cleaning the altar with a soft golden cloth; placing a pure white cloth on the altar; positioning a circular black obsidian scrying mirror one foot above the altar; and then lighting a piece of copal incense in a small iron cauldron just off to the right.

Stepping away from the altar, Saltire moved about the room, extinguishing all light sources except two white candles mounted to the adjacent walls, casting a dim glimmer of light. Before returning to the altar, Saltire picked up an antique cypress stool and placed it directly in front of the altar. Sitting on the three-foot-high stool, Saltire reached into the front pocket of his Levi jeans and pulled out a glass vial filled with essential oils, sacred herbs, tinctures, essences, and gold. In his other pants pocket, he removed a clean white cloth from inside a silk pouch. Dabbing the "fluid condenser" onto the cloth, Saltire proceeded to anoint the black scrying mirror for magical charging and imaginary purposes. While still seated, Saltire closed his eyes and visualized a twelve-foot by twelve-foot circle drawn in white chalk on the cement floor encircling the wooden altar and his chair. Opening his eyes at a forty-five-degree angle, Saltire gazed into the black obsidian scrying mirror. Nothing happened at first. And then, the Blood-Jeweled Fowl, Long-Nose Turkey Toltec Deity of Karmic Debt Removal-soul retrieval came out from behind the darkness. Saltire solicited guidance from Blood-Jeweled Fowl, Long-Nose Turkey in preparation before he activated the black scrying mirror. This allowed him entry into the Akashic Records—"the Milky Way's archives,"—which gave him access to Silent Knowledge.

Saltire's voice crackled, shifting his assemblage point in preparation for his physical metamorphosis into Chalchiuhtotolin's Blood-Jeweled Fowl, Long-Nose Turkey. Saltire's consciousness expanded in the Toltec Deity's invocation:

> *"Virtuous dependant moving freely,*
> *Renew the bond forged by Intent.*
> *I will lift my sights to match your vision,*
> *Using the Spirit of the Voice."*

Noelle had let herself back inside Parvulo X's Bicicleta Tienda and Reparar and was slowly walking past the crates when Saltire called to her.

"Noelle, you may come in now," Saltire said in an unfamiliar voice.

Noelle followed the sound of the voice over to the semi-opaque black curtain and waved it off to one side.

Saltire was standing behind the stool. As Noelle walked over to him, Saltire turned his body to hide his face, all the while instructing Noelle to sit down on the stool.

Noelle, it would seem, was to be liberated from Immokalee's transgressions and be allowed to cleanse the link between her great aunt's fragmented soul and the majestic Seminal Being *Soul originating with Amrit Sandhu. She would accomplish this by going deeper and deeper into the Intent that was giving Noelle her Being—Advocacy.*

Noelle sat down and gazed into the black scrying mirror. Oddly enough, Noelle did not seem the least bit concerned that her face was not reflected in the mirror. She waited motionless until Saltire asked her a question.

"Noelle, do you remember saying something that may very well have brought you here?"

Noelle attempted to answer the question with a question. "Hmm, are you implying that something I said brought me here?"

Saltire, still standing out of view and directly behind Noelle, shared the prayer with the same intonation she had used one and a half years prior. Saltire's voice was coming from his solar plexus; it had a rich, resounding sound to it:

"God is this all there is to life?
Is this all there is to my life?
If so, snuff me out quickly,
If not, give me something to do!"

Noelle sat up straight on the stool and said, "That's my prayer; I said those exact words, in the same way, you just said them, about a year 'n half ago." Grasping her head with her palm, Noelle blurted out. "How can you possibly know what I said to God that day?"

"Your angels are here; they're standing right behind me." Saltire declared. "They told me what you said."

Noelle blushed, and her mouth dropped open slightly.

"Now we have to do something about it!" Saltire said unequivocally.

Noelle agreed, "Okay, so how do we change the past?"

"We don't!" Saltire explained. "Now is the time for you to move away from duality and into totality. You do this by way of the Self-Correcting Principle and clarifying process known as Karmic Debt Removal-soul retrieval.

Noelle remained seated and looked directly into the black scrying mirror.

Saltire stepped back away from the stool and shape-shifted into Chalchiuhtotolin. Through "Magical Passes," he contorted his body and became Blood-Jeweled Fowl, Long-Nose Turkey and activated the black scrying mirror that initiates the removal of Karmic Debt.

Noelle watched with great interest as the head and shoulders of some of her previous incarnations moved from left to right inside of the black scrying mirror. The faces varied in both age and ethnicity: An elderly Algonquin Indian with shoulder-length black hair, a female child dripping in gold jewelry from the Incan Empire, a middle-aged woman from Mongolia, a black man with deep scars on his face, a young male Blackfoot Indian Warrior with a Bald Eagle feather in his ponytail pointing downward were just a few that stood out at first.

Fascinated by the faces from all different nationalities, she asked Saltire, "Who are these people?"

"They're aspects of your Self," Blood-Jeweled Fowl, Long-Nose Turkey replied.

Noelle watched as several more of her previous incarnations floated by. Not once did Noelle see her reflection in the scrying mirror, yet this did not deter her from continuing. The next group to follow included: A young male Houma Indian with his black hair cropped sharply around his face, a stingray's underbelly, followed quickly by a female dancer from Indra's Court, Avalokiteshvara—the bodhisattva, who made a great vow to assist sentient beings in achieving Nirvana; Quetzal Hunahpu, Mayan/Toltec High Priestess, with grey tattoo markings across her face; and then, Immokalee, the half Cherokee Indian appeared in the scrying mirror.

Suddenly, just as Noelle recognized Immokalee, something unimaginable stirred from within the black obsidian mirror. In the center was the figure of a hairless man emerging from inside of a cave. At first, he was barely discernable, and then he moved into a cross-legged sitting position. The face had charcoal-brown retinas and similarly dark irises. The forehead mimicked a similar downturned smile on his lips. Overall the man of clay appeared angry and aggressive. He was the only three-dimensional moving image that gravitated to front and center.

Noelle's archetypal aspect of herself as a man in the process of formation, her animus, did not seem to apply here. I could not identify with her experience, so I kept still.

Noelle let out a scream!

Her scream seemed to have disrupted the frequency of the black scrying mirror; the man of clay vanished immediately. The black scrying mirror returned to its original molecular structure.

Saltire instructed Noelle to get up and leave the room. He told her to meet him outside and that he would be there in a few minutes. As Noelle rose from the stool, she saw, out of the corner of her eye, an unrecognizable creature masked in shadow. Saltire was in the initial stage of shape-shifting from the Blood-Jeweled Fowl, Long-Nose Turkey Deity back into his natural state. His metamorphosis happened quickly.

Noelle left by parting the black semi-opaque curtain; she was not disturbed by the experience and continued to walk back through X's Bike Shop stopping only once to use the bathroom facilities and splash some cold water on her face. Saltire reemerged and proceeded toward the front entrance, glancing around the interior, making sure nothing was out of place. Noelle was leaving the bathroom and heading outside when Saltire exchanged the motorcycle he rode in on for his personal favorite; a bike he had built from scratch. Swiftly and with no fuss, Saltire secured PARVULO X'S BICICLETA TIENDA AND REPARAR for the winter.

"Ever ridden one of these?" Saltire asked Noelle.

"Once in college."

"Only once? So that explains the long face; your one time was nothing more than a tease!" Saltire joshed.

Noelle cracked a smile and waited with hands claps for further instructions from Saltire.

"Keep your feet on the foot pedals, legs in, and hold on tight."

Saltire handed Noelle a black motorcycle helmet and told her to apply Xochitl's drawing on it. Noelle peeled off the backing and adhered the portrait of Immokalee on the back of the helmet.

"It's yours now. Own it!" Saltire said.

Noelle glanced at Xochitl's drawing of her Great Aunt Immokalee and grinned shyly just before putting it on. Straddling Saltire's motorcycle, Noelle wrapped her arms around his waist. Saltire patted Noelle's hand three times and spoke in a very definite tone.

"I built this bike when I was a kid. My greatest rides have been with her. You can relax now; she'll take us to where we need to go."

Saltire push-started his motorcycle and cruised down the dirt road just as the sun was sliding past 4:00 p.m.

CHAPTER FOURTEEN

The Second Sun

O ctavio, Reynaldo, Sergio, and Xochitl pulled alongside Lake Laguna de Chapala in the Colonial Heartland of Mexico. Octavio exited his white pick-up truck, removed his outer garments, and requested his sons to pay their respects to Lake Laguna de Chapala—a Sacred Mayan/Toltec Pilgrimage Outpost. The were-eagle—Paloma's body double—lifted the latch to her cage and flew toward the lake.

Wearing only his briefs, Octavio approached the lakeshore by tagging the tops of smooth shaped rocks with his left toe. (These rocks will be used to activate memories when Octavio manipulates them in his hand later.) Octavio solemnly initiated an ancient Mayan-Toltec Rite. He began by stating his observation of the Toltec God Tlaloc of Tollan/Tula Hidalgo, Mexico.

> "First Principle, Original Intent,
> Primordial essence divine.
> From the eternal Living Word of God,
> You are The Spirit of the Voice."

And with that, Octavio slipped into the freezing cold lake. Partially submerged, Octavio used his hands to pour water over his head. He does this motion several times, all the while repeating what he knows to be true of Noelle's *Seminal Being* Soul.

Reynaldo and his brother Sergio strolled over to their father, carrying cotton blankets. The sons admired Octavio and thought of him as a loving father, husband, and friend. They had witnessed the impact their mother's death had on their father and vowed to each other to honor and respect their father's wishes no matter what.

Octavio relaxed, allowing his entire body to sink under the water. His sons stopped and stood, poised in anticipation of their father's return. Further down the water's edge, Xochitl sat down on a piece of driftwood and carefully examined the rocks nearby. Minutes passed before Octavio rose slowly out of the lake and walked over to his sons. Facing the young men, he extended his limbs into the shape of a human X. Each son took a blanket and patted Octavio dry. Wrapping another blanket securely around their father's waist, all three men returned to the pick-up truck. Xochitl followed with a collection of rocks and sun-dried sticks bundled neatly in the front of her blue button-down shirt.

Octavio removed his wet briefs from under the dry blanket and put his clothes back on. He then changed places with his son Reynaldo and set up a makeshift blanket-bed next to Saltire's magnificent fish. Xochitl, choosing to ride with her uncle, grabbed a small pillow from inside a workbench, fastened it to the truck bed, and cuddled up next to him.

In her mother Leah's absence, Xochitl was co-parented by Paloma Balam Celestino—Saltire's elder half-sister—at his Mayan-Toltec Estate on Lake Pátzcuaro, Michoacán, Mexico. Paloma's help allowed Saltire the flexibility to become a successful businessman, all while training to become a member of the elite Toltec Secret Eagle Knight Council. Most noteworthy to the neighboring community was Xochitl's longstanding status as the Master of Ceremonies at Saltire's Annual *Days of the Dead* Festival. Every year at sundown on November first, Xochitl unleashed Victor Ruis Celestino's dancing horses and freestanding Chilam Balam—four were-jaguars—as part of an initiation ceremony into the Toltec Secret Eagle Knight Council.

Xochitl was, in a sense, related to Noelle. Her soul was an aspect of the same *Seminal Being* Soul of Immokalee's mother, Ollin Tularosa Chisholm. Ollin was one-third Hohokam Indian from Arizona, one-third Northern Toltec from the Santa Monica Mountains in Malibu, CA, and one-third Quallatown Cherokee Indian from the Great Smoky Mountains on the North Carolina side.

Even further back, in the year 980 AD, Xochitl's *Seminal Being* Soul had inhabited a Doe. The Doe later became the Magical Deer Mother called "Tah Tay Mahjrahlee." When the time came, she became the scout for the Toltec King-Priest Ce Acatl Topiltzin-Quetzalcoatl during his escape to Chichen Itza.

As Reynaldo was driving away, the giant were-eagle dive-bombed and then snatched up a smooth rock from the lakeshore of Laguna de Chapala. It then circled back around to Octavio's pick-up truck, placing the rock next to the other water-bearing stones inside her cage. The were-eagle then entered her cage and dropped shot the pin device, securing the lock with a talon. Its piercing eyes then stared upwards at the blazing sun, shedding its double, known to mystics as "The Second Sun." This was the sun's *Seminal Being*—the spiritual body of the rock that we've come to revere as "Mother Earth." It began to follow Octavio's pick-up truck like a hot air balloon.

Emilio was speeding down the Motorway #15 in Rosita's Mercedes, passing one car after another. He was anxious to get to Saltire's Mayan-Toltec Estate and hoped to cut through the Colonial Heartland of Mexico before dark. As he took a hit of marijuana from his wooden pipe, Emilio started a conversation with Chargo on his car phone. "Do you have her? Emilio asked.

"Yep! She's right in front of me, still chomping on a half-eaten heart." Chargo said gleefully.

"You know that's not the heart—"

"What do you want me to do about it?"

"Don't know. I'll call you later. Stay off the phone."

Dahlia and Rosita slept soundly as Emilio drove. Rosita was curled up in the back seat, while Dahlia was slouched over in the passenger seat, her head practically in her lap. They appeared to be enjoying themselves until Emilio abruptly swerved Rosita's car to the far left to avoid squashing an armadillo.

"Slow down, Emilio! What are you doing? Dahlia yelled in Spanish.

Emilio backed off on the gas pedal.

"I'm taking one of these beers, Emilio you want one?" Rosita asked nonchalantly.

Emilio nodded his head enthusiastically.

Rosita popped the top and handed him the beer can. She asked, "So, what do you imagine Saltire has planned for his American friend?"

"Hey, maybe he likes her!" Dahlia piped.

"Well! Noelle better not get her hopes up. The day another American is a part of this family is the day I'll declare Civil War!" Rosita said as she caressed the back of Emilio's neck.

Scowling at her mother, Dahlia fired back, "Mother! Why are you acting this way? Afraid she might end up with one of your brothers?"

"Yeah! Like that will ever happen," Emilio scoffed.

"Why not?" Dahlia persisted.

"Noelle ain't no Dahlia!" Emilio said jeeringly.

The look on Dahlia's face was one of disgust.

Saltire and Noelle were within an hour of arriving at his Estate when he elected to take an alternative route. He chose a less-traveled side road so Noelle could have a more intimate experience of the green and purple desert's stark terrain.

"This desert is a place of great magic and beauty," Saltire told Noelle. "It has been my teacher for many years. Now I intend that it be yours as well."

Saltire and Noelle soon came upon a region of charred and barren land. Miles upon miles of scorched desert lay before them.

Noelle leaned forward, and with great concern, whispered, "What happened here?"

"A firestorm. I was here the night the desert caught ablaze. The lightning struck in several places, and I was not equipped to stop the flames. The fire would've reached my place if Tlaloc hadn't snuffed it out."

Saltire continued to motor across the winding desert road, which took him southwesterly to his home. It would be an hour before the desert showed signs of new life.

"Hey, look, it's all growing back!" Noelle exclaimed.

Traditional Mayan/Toltec papier-mâché facemasks adorned the pine trees outlining the front driveway leading up to Saltire's estate. They had been placed in the lower branches for Saltire's guests to don during his party. As the partygoers entered, seven dancing mares greet them. Each horse was tattooed in body paint and wore a 400-year-old Mayan/Toltec *Days of the Dead* multi-colored mask and costume. The mares were performing to a 19th-century Mexican choreographed routine around the large bas-relief fountainhead, which was adorned with images of Ceiba trees, jaguars, eagles, and human skulls.

To the rear of the property, musicians dressed in skeleton facemasks and costumes were tuning their instruments. Edmundo, Paloma's love interest, was managing the buffet tables arranged in a semicircle on the backyard terrace. In final preparation for the evening's festivities, the house staff began igniting the large torches surrounding perimeter of the estate. The flickering flames enlivened the atmosphere. And, as the neighboring families and their children started to filter in, they oohed and aahed at the spectacle.

Reynaldo pulled up in front of a 17th-century Spanish-style church in Pátzcuaro, Mexico. The sun was settling down for the night. Octavio rolled up his makeshift blanket-bed wedged alongside Saltire's swordfish. Reynaldo then assisted his father and Xochitl as they stepped down from the truck bed.

"You boys stay here," Octavio said. "I want to see if the Monsignor has something for me."

Octavio entered Temple Del Saguaro and returned carrying a small vial of Holy Water, a crystal heart, and a picture of Christ Jesus. Octavio then asked Xochitl if she wanted to stop by the cemetery and leave Rueben, her deceased twin brother, a gift.

"I want Rueben to have this heart; it will make him very happy," Xochitl said, respectfully.

Octavio responded in kind. He immediately drove over to the nearby cemetery, and the two hustled over to Rueben's headstone. Octavio recited a short prayer of gratitude while Xochitl remained seated on the ground. Xochitl asked Rueben if she could plant the crystal heart by his tombstone and sat quietly for his reply.

"His spirit told me to plant it under the rosebush," Xochitl said a moment later.

Octavio knelt down, scooped out a handful of grass and dirt, and watched as Xochitl buried the crystal heart in the ground. Xochitl then covered the crystal heart with the earth and grass and patted it in place.

Xochitl speaking directly to her late baby brother, said, "There, there, Rueben."

"Okay, say, Bye! Bye!" Octavio whispered sweetly.

"Bye! Bye! Ruben. I love you!"

Octavio and Xochitl walked hand and hand back to his pick-up truck. Upon returning, Octavio set the were-eagle free, removed Paloma's cage from his truck bed, and deposited the birdcage on the curb next to a mature Ceiba tree.

Emilio arrived at Saltire's Mayan-Toltec Estate and parked Rosita's Mercedes near the main gate at the edge of the property.

"Can you believe this? Look at all these people? Reckon he knows any of them?" Rosita inquired while surveying the guests.

"I thought he was hardly ever here," Emilio reported.

"Can we just go and have a good time?" Dahlia petitioned. She was looking exhausted from all the negativity.

Dahlia got out of the car and wandered over to greet some of the neighboring guests she recognized from prior years. Rosita and Emilio followed haphazardly stopping every chance they could to gather light snacks and drinks at the buffet tables. Finally, with Dahlia out of sight and with no one nearby who could make any sense of their conversation, Rosita expressed her great disappointment over the were-cougar mishap.

"What happened? What the hell happened today? I'm serious; how difficult can it be to get rid of this girl?"

Emilio pointed out what Rosita had overlooked, "She's nothing like the other ones. She's different."

"You're right," Rosita agreed. "Come to think of it, none of the other girls ever made it to his party."

"That I wouldn't know."

"Isn't it obvious what they're doing? They're initiating her," Rosita said.

"What?" Emilio shouted.

"Yep, That's it! Yesterday morning, when Saltire showed up, I overheard him telling Dahlia that Paloma felt she'd found the tenth member of the Council. Do you have the slightest idea—"

"No, why don't you clue me in," Emilio said, shuffling his feet on the ground.

"You're out of luck."

Emilio hesitated, turned around, and snatched Rosita by the arm.

"Shut up! Just keep your mouth shut," Emilio snarled.

Emilio moved behind Rosita and shoved her forward and away from all the partying guests.

In a designated clearing to the left of the backyard terrace, hordes of children wearing Saltire's Traditional Mayan/Toltec papier-mâché facemasks were running and playing in-between the adults.

Off to the right, the seven dancing horses were magically trotting unattended over to Xochitl, who was standing center stage on a platform replicated to look like the Temple of the Morning Star at Tula, Mexico. Alongside Xochitl, musicians playing Mexican instrumental music were deliberately positioned in front of several Toltec Atlantean Warrior statues.

CHAPTER FIFTEEN

White Horse Falling

altire had one more stop to make before reaching his Mayan-Toltec Estate. The day bowed down to the night as he pulled his motorcycle up onto a dirt path that led to the Temple Del Saguaro Cemetery. The cemetery was laden with personal items: glyphs, flowers, photographs, special foods, and toys intended to honor the deaths of recently deceased children. The spirits of children and adults, who had crossed over into the fourth dimension, were acknowledged and summoned forth on the first or second of November.

Saltire slowed his motorcycle to a halt, and Noelle quickly disembarked. He then took her hand, and the two-headed over to his son's headstone.

"Where's Xochitl's mom? Noelle asked.

Saltire kept walking, but his demeanor had become solemn.

"She left us when the twins were ten months old." He said. "For some people, appearances are everything."

Stopping just short of a terraced pyramid tomb, Saltire noticed one lone flower cart unattended. He gathered up, in his arms, several garlands of orange marigolds (cempasuchiles). In exchange for the flowers, he left a 1966 Ralph Lauren Safari-style watch on the cart's handle. Saltire had been coming to visit Ruben's burial place since Ruben's passing. Sometimes he gave the flower merchant a one hundred dollar bill. Other years, he offered beautiful antique gifts in exchange for the flowers. He was a patron of Temple Del Saguaro Cemetery and frequently covered the funeral costs of the family's who had lost children unexpectedly. Anything he could do financially to alleviate further suffering on their part was his aim.

Saltire and Noelle walked down the dirt path and over to a modest headstone. Squatting down next to Ruben's burial place, Saltire presented an offering using two of the garlands. Noelle crouched down next to him in anticipation.

Saltire turned to Noelle and announced, "Here lies Xochitl's twin brother Rueben; he died before his first birthday. Xochitl barely remembers him, but not a week goes by when I don't stop to think of who he might have been."

Noelle's eyes remain stationed on Rueben's headstone sheltered by a rosebush. Saltire reached into his motorcycle jacket and pulled out a "Cabbage Patch Kids – Koosas Lion Cat" cloth-doll. The doll had a handwritten note pinned to its chest. Note read:

CHILAM BALAM, PLEASE RESTORE RUEBEN'S SEMINAL BEING SOUL.

Saltire placed the Lion Cat cloth doll in Noelle's hands and said, "Here Noelle, you place it near the rosebush; he'd like getting a gift from a new friend."

Noelle glanced up at Saltire; she then gently set the cloth doll at the base of the rosebush and directly above Xochitl's crystal heart mound.

Noelle started to giggle, "I feel dizzy, and I see things; it looks as though the Lion Cat doll is breathing."

To Noelle, the doll looked as if it were alive. Saltire inched forward, positioning himself directly behind Noelle.

"Can you match its rhythmical breath?" Saltire asked encouragingly as he placed a garland around her neck.

"Okay, I think I can do that."

Noelle then began to imitate the Lion Cat doll's quick pulsating action. Noelle gazed past the toy and noticed the rosebush was now accompanying the doll's breathing motion.

"Oh no, where am I going?" Noelle questioned.

Saltire does not reply. Instead, he slapped Noelle between her shoulder blades, and she fell backward into his lap.

Noelle ventured deeper and deeper into her subconscious and landed back in Los Angeles, CA; it is the "Ides of March" in 1993. One and a half years had passed; Noelle lived in a first-floor one-bedroom apartment near the "Farmers' Market" off Fairfax Avenue in Los Angeles, CA. She lived alone and slept on a queen-size box spring and mattress in the front living room. The bed was placed in an awkward position; it was pressed up against a wall, hindering easy access to and from the kitchen. An antique wooden table at the foot of the bed supported a tiny black and white TV. To the right of the bed next to the front window, a champagne-colored French Revival chase lounge looked overdressed and out-of-place. Cheap canvas shades were drawn to shut out the sunlight and noisy foot traffic. There was absolutely nothing inviting about the place.

It was sunset, and a rosy glow filled the living room and kitchen. Noelle, still wearing her painting cloths—black spandex shorts and a white T-shirt—was sorting through grocery bags on a 1960s-style kitchen table. The phone rang as Noelle put a carton of milk and a block of cheese in the refrigerator. She quickly finished putting away the remaining perishables—a dozen eggs and a quart of yogurt—in the fridge before placing the touchtone phone to her ear.

"Hello, hello!" There was a long silence and then, "Oh! Hi Benoit, what's up?"

Noelle just listened while she continued to put the rest of the groceries in the walnut stained kitchen cabinets.

"What do you mean Avery had a bad fall?" Noelle asked. "What happened?"

Benoit told Noelle he was calling from the hospital in Salem, MA.

"You're at the hospital? Which hospital? . . . Is he in a coma? . . . 'They're saying he has a five percent chance of making it.' " Noelle said, repeating verbatim Benoit's last remark.

Noelle's face was turning ash-gray as Benoit confirmed her worst fears. She flung her arms out desperately in the direction of the kitchen table in an attempt to stabilize herself. Noelle was devastated.

"I have to go now, I have to go!" Noelle told Benoit, her words barely audible as she put down the receiver.

Immobilized by the news of Avery's bizarre accident, Noelle's breathing became impaired when a mass, the size of a navel orange, seized her throat. Noelle clutched the obstruction with both hands and frantically yanked at the skin on her neck in an upward motion. In an attempt to dislodge the massive lump in her throat, she uncontrollably started circling the kitchen floor. After ten seconds, Noelle stopped resisting and experienced a total emotional meltdown; she collapsed onto the linoleum floor, crawled over to the side of the bed and released a primordial scream.

The *Flashback Sequence* reawakened in Noelle the Prophetic Dream she experienced on November 1, 1992. It was morning, and the sun was filtering through a thicket of oak trees encircling a lush carpeted meadow. Noelle, wearing a blue denim shirt over black leggings, seemed to be part of an assembly sitting transfixed under a massive two-hun-dred-year-old oak tree—the symbol for the storehouse of cosmic wisdom, it attracted lightning, and the power of the Gods.

A man was standing in front of the congregation talking, but Noelle was unable to comprehend what he was saying. There was a late 19th-century brick building situated along the Marina in Salem, MA, on the meadow's far side. Noelle noticed, out of the corner of her left eye, a large white shape jerking in and out of a third-story window.

Noelle nudged the woman next to her and whispered, "Look over there; what is it?"

As the two women turned their heads, the white shape zooms into view; Noelle started giggling. A white horse was lunging in an out of the 19th-century brick building's third-story window. Wide-eyed and smiling, the horse turned its eyes to Noelle. Noelle and the woman covered their mouths; uncontrollable, insatiable laughter had taken them over.

Suddenly, the white horse tumbled out of the third-story window and began its descent to the street below. The white horse's legs were flailing in a hopeless attempt to counter the impact of the fall. Noelle leaped up and ran full-steam across the meadow toward the falling horse. A red toy fire truck was seen winding its way down the road to the 19th-century brick building. The white horse had landed; it was lying motionless on its back. As Noelle approached the injured horse, the miniature fire truck morphed into a regular standard-sized truck. Noelle knelt down by the horse's neck and just before she touched it, she heard, "It's too late!" Then her mind went blank.

The start of Noelle's *Flashback Sequence*, occurring at the cemetery in 1994, which sent her back to a telephone conversation, was consistent with how she experienced past events. However, when Noelle relived the emotional trauma caused by the bizarre accident that took Avery's life, her memory brought to light the prophetic dream she had six months before the actual event—Avery falling to his death. In her subconscious, Noelle foresaw the imminent fate of Avery as if she were viewing it through a Mutoscope-hand-cranked circular flipbook.

From my viewpoint, I couldn't help but remember Avery's Seminal Being *Soul relationship to Immokalee's* Seminal Being. *In the prior incarnation, his "Original Intent" had inhabited Nicolaus Renato Intaglio III, an Italian American born in Gloucester, MA, in the year 1890. Nicolaus had only been married to Immokalee Awinita Chisholm for a short time before being shot and killed in WWI. The trauma of the shot to his skull was now seeking resolution through the life of his current* Seminal Being's *incarnation in Avery.*

Compounding the Karmic Debt between Noelle and Avery was the ancient history that Avery's Seminal Being *Soul had with Emilio's father, Kumukite "were-wolf" Delgado—the sole surviving link to the last Toltec King Huemac who ruled over the Tollan/Tula nearing its end.*

The edge of night had taken dominion over the Temple Del Saguaro Cemetery. A group of Mexican children went racing by in traditional *Days of the Dead* facemasks and costumes. The sound of party favors and laughter returned Noelle to the year 1994; she was cradled in Saltire's arms. His outstretched hand was a few inches from her heart; he was sending love and healing energy to her heart chakra.

Noelle's eyes open slowly, looked past Saltire's strong jaw line and peaceful demeanor, and focused on a bevy of birds migrating in a southerly direction in a crescent formation—the configuration denoted one capable of immense sacrifice; one who had surrendered their self-interests, expecting no reward.

"I've often wondered if the soul is eternal; if it incarnates to fulfill a divine purpose?" Noelle asked quietly.

"Your soul is an aspect of the *Seminal Being* Soul of which you are apart. The *Seminal Being* is a Virtue. When you have accepted this, you will integrate with other souls born with the same Intent—your designated virtue. And in doing so, you shall activate your 'Soul's Intended Future' and see it fulfilled."

As Noelle was lifted to her feet by Saltire, her tears evaporated. Saltire reached around Noelle and held her momentarily in a loving embrace. His appearance had shape-shifted into that of Ce Acatl Topiltzin-Quetzalcoatl; the 10th-century Toltec King-Priest of Tollan, Mexico. Noelle, in turn, morphed into the noble likeness of the Toltec Atlantean Warrior and High Priestess Quetzal Hunahpu, the King-Priest's most loyal adept in 987 AD.

CHAPTER SIXTEEN

One Intention

The moonlit sky, illuminated by stars, cast an ethereal glow on the "Temple of the Morning Star" at Tollan/Tula of Hidalgo, Mexico. The celestial lights enhanced the stone faces of four Toltec Atlantean Warriors that kept watch on the top platform of the pyramid. Sixteen Huichol Indians sang and danced in a trance-like state to the sounds of percussion instruments and flutes. The elder of the indians, transfigured by face paint, removed himself from the group and revealed a sacred codex from a terra-cotta ceramic vessel (a tankard). He began to translate through song the hidden meaning to the other indians.

Gathered around a centralized bonfire, the sixteen Huichol Indians breathed in the vital life force inherent in the flames. As One Intention, the indians mimicked the fire's flickering flames. Sparks flew, and the Bonfire Spirits spoke as the sacred text, and its message jogged upward and awakened the Mayan and Toltec Deities. Each line spelled out in Roman Capital Letters streamed upward like the tail on a kite in flight. The Bonfire Spirits and the Elder indian sang in unison, part of Quetzal Hunahpu's Prophetic Resurrection Hymn of 987 AD.

> *"Eagle Knights to summon Dancing Movement,*
> *Loathsome creatures signal terror.*
> *Mirrors of the Gods will, too, intervene,*
> *The Morning Star is ill at ease.*

Beholden is the Master of Intent,
To the fate of the one transfixed.
Immutable Wind, living memory,
Restores what has been forgotten.

I am a rock in the River of Light,
Emerging as Falling Waters.
Transcending fear, the serpent learns to fly,
Quickening her soul retrieval.

Now the Door of Life opens up to all,
Toltec Atlantean Warrior.
Let my presence transform your body and mind,
I AM that you shall be reformed.

Refrain: As Archetypal Creative Order,
Retrieving souls is our passion.
We are the archrivals of ill-intent,
Our kind will not be extinguished."

Saltire's annual party was well underway. A raging bonfire in the backyard launched flames twenty feet high into the air; as the blaze grew in size and strength, the image of a were-eagle materialized. Several guests took notice and were mesmerized when the shape-shifting were-eagle emerged from the flames as Paloma Celestino.

Rosita and Emilio were in the tack room, adorned with horse gear and saddles, located in a secluded area inside the horse stables. She was lighting up a marijuana cigarette while attempting to seduce Emilio. Emilio was ignoring her; he was on the phone talking to Chargo.

"Chargo, where are you? Put the phone up to your mouth; I can't hear you! No! Go straight there! We'll hookup before sundown."

Emilio hung up the phone and spun around, shrugging off Rosita's advances. Rosita, still fishing for positive affirmations, made every attempt to win Emilio over.

"Darling, don't be cross with me; I haven't done anything to deserve this."

"No? Well then, let's test your little theory!" Emilio said angrily. "Some of my constituents have informed me that your family owns some of the most fertile lands in Central America. Not to mention the special relationship they've had over the centuries with Mexican dignitaries."

"What on earth are you talking about?"

Emilio's demeanor was becoming increasingly aggressive toward Rosita. "And you're going to stand there and tell me you know nothing of the clandestine operations of your own family!"

At the conclusion of his cross-examination, Emilio demanded to know where Dahlia stood in all this. "Satisfy my curiosity, would ya? What's Dahlia in-line to inherit?"

Rosita, stunned by Emilio's blatant disrespect bit her upper lip and closed her eyes before she spoke. "My daughter knows absolutely nothing about any such landholdings," Rosita insisted. "And, since I'm not a part of the Council, I don't have firsthand knowledge of their activities!"

Aware Rosita was telling him the truth, Emilio changed his tactics. "Tell me, what do you know about your brother?"

"Which one?" Rosita gasped.

"The one that's not the bastard!"

Ashamed by Emilio's rude remark, Rosita does her best to keep Saltire out of the inquisition.

"Octavio had taken charge of the important family matters after my father's passing. Now it seems, he's deferring those matters to Paloma and Saltire." Rosita, casting her eyes downward, for one brief moment, got present to Octavio's plight. "He's dying for God's sake; can't you leave him alone?"

Unmoved by Octavio's health crisis, Emilio played to the desires of Rosita's heart. "Who's got the rights to all the landholdings?"

Rosita did her utmost to deflect Emilio's attack but found him to be too persuasive. The fear that he would no longer see her as desirable caused her character to cave in.

"Saltire most likely!" Rosita reaffirmed.

Emilio paced nervously back and forth and then suddenly erupted, "Who decides who gets what and when?"

"What's it to you!" Rosita, sounding defiant, responded in kind.

"In the inner workings of your family, tell me who has the final say?"

"No one!"

"I don't believe you. I'll be getting back to you on this one."

Rosita had not grasped the gravity of the situation. She was a pawn in a dangerous game of chess, one that involved her entire family. It was too late for her to distance herself from Emilio. He wanted answers, and he demanded her total cooperation or else she would most likely suffer.

Rosita hopped up on top of a Mexican Colonial desk and hung over her head. She was exhausted from the squabbling. After a brief pause, she offered up the family secrets, disclosing who is to get what and why.

"Regardless of what you find out, it still all comes down to Xochitl," Rosita said. "She's the person preventing Dahlia from inheriting the family's fortune. Originally, it was to go to the eldest grandchild, my daughter; and she was to disperse the holdings equally amongst the other children. But that all changed when Xochitl was born."

"I suspected as much," Emilio confirmed.

Sensing Rosita's level of duress, Emilio had but only a few more questions.

"What's with Noelle and the kid? There's absolutely no reason why they weren't killed!"

"Well, it didn't happen now, did it? And, now we have to start over!" Rosita complained.

"I don't think you have the right to complain," Emilio pointed out. "You should see what Noelle did to my sister. That bitch sliced her eye open!"

Rosita, unsympathetic to Mela's dilemma, had become impatient with Emilio.

"So get your sister on a truck, and let's finish what we started. If you want to destroy my brother, we'll have to kill 'em both."

"And where do you see this happening?" Emilio asked, flipping his hands in disgust.

"After tonight, wherever they go, we go, Mela goes. Saltire brought Noelle here for a reason."

"So you said," Emilio muttered.

"They'll be on the move tomorrow, so let me handle it. I'll find out where he's headed."

Suddenly, and for no apparent reason, the iron caste torchlights in the horse stable were turned off. The tack room was black as night, with only a sliver of light shining through a small window.

"Shhh!" Emilio shushed loudly.

Rosita's eyes scanned the room in pursuit of some invisible force. Emilio heard the sound of high heels clattering down the length of the horse stables, and pointed to a window.

"Find out who it is and get rid of 'em," Emilio ordered Rosita.

Frightened, Rosita rushed over to the window and twisted her body through it. Emilio was left to face the intruder alone. He bolted into the adjoining office and hid under a large antique oak desk. Emilio waited and held his breath. After a few minutes, the person who stepped into the room was not at all who he expected.

Reynaldo and Sergio were actively grilling local vegetables and meats over an open pit. Octavio was off to their side. In secrecy, Octavio sprinkled sacred magical herbs and oils over the top of Saltire's magnificent one hundred and fifty-pound swordfish.

The magical herbs and oils were ancient Mayan-Toltec remedies that altered a person's perception; it made Silent Knowledge more readily accessible by downloading spiritual distinctions into the individual's crown chakra. As I grew more proficient at listening from spiritual discernment, I realized I could master a whole myriad of healing practices dependent upon the level of integrity I operated from.

Xochitl was with her Aunt Paloma, maintaining order at the buffet tables. She was prepping everyone's plate with a flower garnish while informing the guests of its intrinsic value. They responded with a show of pleasure and amazement.

"Xochitl, there's your Papi. See, he's over there at the fire pit with Octavio and Noelle. Go ahead, I'll take over." Paloma insisted.

Xochitl wiggled her way through the crowded tables and joined the trio, who were immersed in conversation. Looking up at Saltire, Xochitl tapped her father's arm.

Saltire said, "I see you, sweet pea, just give me a few more minutes, please."

Meanwhile, Octavio turned to Noelle and asked teasingly, "Noelle, you and the swordfish have something in common, any idea what that might be?"

Noelle looked to Saltire for the answer, but he just shrugged his shoulders.

"Give up?"

Highly amused, Noelle was poised and ready for the answer.

"Well, like Saltire's fish here, you too are an endangered species."

"Oh, I get it," said Noelle. "Out of the frying pan and into the fire?"

After light-hearted laughing, Octavio asked Noelle to get two cold brews for him and his brother. Noelle obliged, taking Xochitl with her to the buffet tables.

Saltire shielded Octavio with his body from the loud reverb of the Mexican music nearby.

"This afternoon, I saw the aspect of Noelle's *Seminal Being* that's preventing her from becoming self-actualized and wholly aware of her "Original Intent.""

"Is it a presence we can perceive, or will it require the assistance of tribal dancers?" Octavio asked with great interest.

"Best if we signal the dancers!" Saltire recommended. "We need all the assistance allowed."

"What about the Huichol Indians? Do we know what they've been doing?"

Saltire, confident in his remote viewing capabilities, provided his brother with an update.

"I saw them earlier at the Temple of the Morning Star. The Elder indian was reading Quetzal's Prophetic Resurrection Hymn. I then saw it being considered by Dancing Movement. He/she was at the Akashic Records; it appeared that the hymn was being synthesized into an Intent."

"Other than the Elder indian, who else can decipher Quetzal's hymn?" Octavio asked.

"Noelle."

"Come again."

"Noelle can. She's the only other soul who knows how to decipher the meaning of Quetzal Hunahpu's Prophetic Resurrection Hymn in the manner in which it was intended.

"How are you going to go about this?" Octavio inquired.

"I can shift Noelle's point of perception. This will increase the likelihood of her recognizing her Great Aunt Immokalee's as a soul aspect of herself. Once Noelle integrates her soul with Immokalee's, their Primordial Self, *"Seminal Being,"* will allow Noelle to receive the meaning inherent in the Intent that governed Quetzal Hunahpu in her final hours."

"That's right," Octavio nodded. "It was Immokalee who unearthed the Quetzal's codex when she first arrived in Malibu."

"Immokalee also preserved the contents of the book, *The Spirit of the Voice*, before moving to New England," Saltire confirmed.

"Let the true nature of our American initiate be seen!" Octavio voiced emphatically.

Octavio instinctually turned his head toward the guests and became aware that Noelle and Xochitl were on their way back from the buffet tables. He quickly changed the subject.

"First things first, I'd like you to make a pit-stop at the horse stables. I can't seem to locate mom. Wasn't she supposed to have waited until your signal?"

"Yeah, well, talking to her is like being in a wind tunnel, in one ear and out the other."

Octavio chuckled while taking an inventory of the guests, "Not good! I see Dahlia, but no Emilio!"

"You don't suppose he's engaged in a repeat performance, one reminiscent of last year?" Saltire joshed.

"This guy's got to go. That's all there is to it!" Octavio said.

Noelle and Xochitl returned carrying two beers, a diet soda, and a cup full of lemonade.

Saltire nodded in approval. He took a draft beer from Noelle and instructed Xochitl to stay with her uncle.

"I've got some business to attend to; you two stay here with Octavio unless he tells you otherwise."

Saltire walked away through the crowds of guests, in the direction of the horse stables.

The striking Blonde Lady, alias Saltire's stepmother Melita, ran past the seven dancing horses as their masks and costumes were being removed and smacked headlong into Saltire.

"It worked! He fell for it!" Blonde Lady said, gleefully.

"How so?" Saltire inquired.

"After I shut down the lights, it got pitch-black, and I was able to walk past the stalls and into the tack room undetected. Rosita was just leaving through the window, so I crouched down until I knew she'd taken off."

Saltire snatched up his stepmother's hand and twirled her around to the beat of the music. He kept dancing as she elaborated.

"Well, you can imagine my dilemma." Blonde Lady said. "I had to wait a good while before I could present myself as Rosita. I had to make her re-entrance believable. You know, like she'd forgotten something."

"Yes, go on."

"I did as you instructed; I called out to him after I heard him rummaging around in your office."

"What happened next?"

"He snuck up behind me, kissed me on the back of my neck, and asked if I saw anybody."

Glancing down at his stepmother's feet, Saltire couldn't resist, "I think it's a bit premature to call this a total success. Tell me, where have you misplaced your shoes?"

Blonde Lady placing her hand over her mouth, said modestly, "I let him take my shoes off. I didn't know what else to do. He took them, the bastard, and wouldn't give 'em back!"

Saltire noticed Octavio waving. Saltire took it to mean he wanted his attention. Saltire started escorting Blonde Lady over to the buffet tables while she continued talking his ear off.

"Wait, I'm not finished. While I was looking around for my shoes, he left and went back into the tack room. It was then that Emilio pretended to be you! He called out for Noelle a few times, then picked up the house phone, and I could have sworn I heard him talking to someone."

Saltire, smiling inquired into his sister's whereabouts, "Where did you say Rosita was when all this was going on?"

"Don't have the faintest; I did see trails of smoke from just outside the window, though."

The two stopped dancing, and Saltire thanked his stepmother, Melita, the Blonde Lady, for the dance. Before leaving, she had one last thing to say to Saltire.

"Bet you had no idea he could throw his voice to sound just like yours!"

With a gleam in his eye, Saltire replied, "Can he now? Well, that puts an interesting spin on things, now doesn't it?"

Saltire then told Melita to adjust her blonde wig, get some dinner, sit down at a table, and not speak of this matter to anyone. He pardoned himself and bolted past the horse stables where the seven dancing horses were being hosed down for the night. Tattoos made of gypsum clay crumbled and liquefied under their hooves. Saltire treaded lightly past the horse stalls and directly into the office by way of the tack room.

"Emiliooo! Emiliooo! Come out from under the desk!" Saltire whispered in a singsong voice.

Emilio crawled out from under the Mexican Colonial desk; his hands were tucked inside Blonde Lady's shoes. Rat-a-tat-tat the shoes fired a warning signal on the desktop.

"No, Emilio, There's no battle to be won here this evening. Give me the shoes, and I'll make sure they get to their rightful owner."

Emilio tossed the shoes at Saltire and he managed to capture them before they hit the wall.

"By the way," Saltire continued. "You wouldn't by chance have any idea how much longer you intend on tormenting my family?"

Saltire's sharp-edged intention to rid his family of this menace permeated the room. Emilio, unable to utter another word, sought to escape through the adjoining room. On his way back into the tack room, Emilio slipped past Saltire. Yet, Saltire knew he had him at a disadvantage and seized the opportunity to inspect him from head to toe to get insight into Emilio's hidden agenda. Saltire then watched from his office as Emilio left the tack room through the same window Rosita made her escape.

What showed up was more along the lines of a negative thought-form. Emilio had apparently, at one time, sought the companionship of the diabolical Toltec Deity Black Tezcatlipoca. As with all compromised souls, he had entered into a parasitic arrangement that ultimately would cost him life's vital energy. This was the spiritual path he was on, and he would have to own up to his active role in the splintering of his own Seminal Being *Soul, of which he was a part—or remain ignorant to its existence. I could sympathize with Emilio, yet I envied him not.*

Before leaving, Saltire paused for a moment at the window; taking in a whiff of the residue of Rosita's marijuana cigarette. "Why, Sis, who'd of ever guessed?"

Octavio, Xochitl, and Noelle were finishing up serving Saltire's magnificent swordfish to those guests gathered around the bonfire. Octavio took Xochitl by the hand and led her over to a standing microphone situated front and center on the platform replica of the Temple of the Morning Star. Xochitl patiently waited for instructions from Octavio. Lifting her off the platform, Octavio placed Xochitl's feet firmly on the seat of a wooden folding chair behind the microphone. He whispered in Xochitl's ear, the two announcements that she was to deliver.

"Our mixed-heritage American, Noelle, will be joining us amongst the reeds. Please put forth your sincere intentions for her transfiguration." Xochitl said, definitively.

Xochitl did her utmost in reproducing Octavio in both tone and intonation; she received cheers for her effort from the guests.

Noelle was standing alone under a small covered porch that opened into the family room and kitchen. The porch was complete with a bentwood rocking chair, hammock, porch swing, and stick basket. Holding a large walking stick, Saltire strolled over to Noelle.

"Xochitl and Octavio are going to the Lake Ceremony. You, on the other hand, are coming with me!" Saltire pointed to a stack of walking sticks stashed in a tall woven basket made from reeds.

"Choose your destiny," he said.

Noelle reached for a long smooth walking stick but suddenly rejected it for a small gnarly-looking one.

"Brilliant!" Shouted Saltire. "This was father's."

Saltire stepped off the porch and gestured for Noelle to follow. Past the horse stables and then onto a dirt footpath, the two gracefully slipped inside the pine forest and vanished.

Octavio, Xochitl, and one hundred or more of Saltire's guests all gathered at the lakeshore. Everyone was there to enjoy and participate in the "night vigil" honoring children who had recently passed. Boats decorated with candles and flowers traveled between the Pátzcuaro docks and the Island of Janitzio. Packed to the brim with chanting locals, the smell of incense, and the ringing of bells, these magical boats beckoned the universe's Intent and sought out disembodied spirits. Tugging at Octavio, Xochitl requested her uncle take notice of smoke pouring into the atmosphere.

"Tio, isn't that where the very first were-eagle was sighted a long, long time ago?"

Octavio shaking his head in amazement, replied, "Xochitl, you have the memory of an elephant.

"Yes, it's true, that is the place where our ancestors the Toltec first recognized the were-eagle as the vehicle by which Intent—the Spiritual Virtue—made its presence known."

"Is Papi there now with Noelle?"

Octavio leaned down, picked Xochitl up in his arms, and said, "Your Papi is taking Noelle to the place where she can see from the vantage point of her *Seminal Being*. There, she will crossover from this realm into another."

Xochitl's eyes dropped as she asked, "How will we know if Noelle has left this world and incarnated into a better one?"

"Into a better one?"

"Yes! Into the sacred skull—the place where she can begin to fulfill her soul's Intended future?"

Octavio lifted his eyes to the night sky and replied, "Baile Movimiento, the Dancing Movement of our Milky Way will appear and fill Noelle's soul with "JOT"—Divine Light—and we shall see the Aurora Borealis put on a display."

CHAPTER SEVENTEEN

The Intent That Love Is

altire and Noelle were traveling along a dirt footpath through a grove of pine trees. Noelle was becoming nervous and excited, "I see smoke up ahead. Are we going in the right direction?" Noelle asked.

"We are." Saltire said.

No sooner did Saltire reassure Noelle when they broke through a thicket and onto a flat top capped mountain. A large gathering of locals was dancing freeform to hypnotic, overlapping melodies resonating from the drums. Further away, in a remote corner, a much smaller group was twirling as one pulsating, spiral dance movement.

Noelle immediately hid underneath a small pine tree. Saltire quietly followed Noelle and maneuvered himself right behind her.

"Go ahead, Noelle; seize the moment, this moment!" Saltire instructed.

Gazing at the ground, Noelle took a step forward, hesitated, and then walked to the shoulder of the multilayered dance movement. She felt her body moving in rhythm with the drums while being pulled into the coalescing group. Noelle's mind collapsed and merged with the sounds of the drums.

Eyes glistening like silver crystals, Saltire watched as Noelle was lifted into the shape of a Saint Andrew's cross (X). Stretched out in this horizontal position, Noelle was being carried to the center of the spiral. When she reached the focal point, "The Point of Recognition," Noelle shifted her perception and entered a waking dream of her *Seminal Being's* making.

Noelle saw herself standing off stage in a Theater Palace, built in the year 1910, in North Carolina. She was standing in front of a set of crimson-colored, velvet drapes. Directly behind her, and within inches, was Immokalee's soul. Twelve beings: half-man, half-animal creatures in silhouette, walked on their hind legs in front of the stage and formed a semicircle. With their backs to the arena, they looked upon a stone disk, twelve feet in diameter and three feet in depth, rotating counterclockwise twenty-two feet above the ground. Dancing Movement, the multidimensional living spirit comprised of iridescent shades of emerald-green, was pacing back and forth in front of the twelve silhouettes.

All of a sudden, a booming voice from above the rotating disk put forth the question.

"Who is willing to save mankind?" Who is prepared to give of their life and risk being extinguished?"

Immediately, Dancing Movement leaped off the ground and landed on the stone disk.

The stone disk is a metaphor for the early stage of an embryo's creation in the womb. It occurs before three months' gestation. During this span of time, the soul—which inhabits the Infant—arises with and inside of the given Intent, or Virtue. Therefore, if you abort the fetus, you have taken away the Intent of that soul, not to mention the possibility that could have been.

Noelle was then pulled and stretched, like a stick of salt-water taffy, into the crown chakra of Dancing Movement. As she entered inside, so did Immokalee's soul. Together, they perceived the outer world through the eyes of Dancing Movement. The divine messenger instantaneously configured itself into the shape of an X. As one being, the three souls were enclosed in a cone of steely white light. Suddenly, from the zenith of the cone, a cascade of sounds and syllables tumbled down in sequential order, creating the phrase:

THE

INTENT

THAT

LOVE

IS

IN

THE

MOMENT

IT

IS

ACTED

UPON

Noelle saw the spiritual distinction being spelled out in Roman Capital Letters. She was readily available now to comprehend its deeper meaning but seemed unable to do so.

Octavio lifted his head to the night sky, "Look, Xochitl, Noelle is in a dance with Baile Movimiento."

Xochitl's eyes looked upon the stars as they reorganized themselves into unusual geometric configurations. Xochitl giggled as she put her hand above her head in an attempt to grab hold of an arrangement. The pine forest at Lake Pátzcuaro was acting as a sound chamber, amplifying the intention of the "Drum Ceremony." Noelle was slowly lowered to her feet and gracefully exited through an opening in the group.

Saltire greeted Noelle affectionately, "Noelle! Noelle, hold up a second. Aren't you going to tell me what happened?"

Noelle doesn't stop to answer Saltire; instead, she continued back down the footpath from which they came. After a few minutes, she halted and turned around. Looking intensely into Saltire's eyes, Noelle said, "I saw my Great Aunt Immokalee standing right behind me. I know it was her because I've studied her photos, the ones in her artist book. If you don't believe me, I can show you."

"I believe you. Who else did you encounter?"

Noelle moving around excitedly, reported, "An emerald green androgynous creature pulled me into the top of its head. As soon as I figured out where I was, a stream of sounds and symbols came crashing down over me in the shape of Roman Capital Letters. The letters spelled out a phrase that I don't fully understand. This is what it said:

"THE INTENT THAT LOVE IS IN THE MOMENT IT IS ACTED UPON."

Saltire's eyes started to glisten, and they began to spin clockwise.

"I don't feel like myself anymore," Noelle said shyly. "I feel the presence of another voice."

"You have been reformed inside Baile Movimiento," Saltire declared. His vision for you is transforming your DNA even as we speak. From my vantage point, your *Seminal Being* Soul, your original intent became an aspect of the divine messenger Baile Movimiento's Intent."

Noelle turned in the direction of Saltire's estate and began to walk back through the pine forest just as Saltire's guests were leaving.

"Noelle, have you been listening?" Saltire asked.

Noelle touched to tears, replied, "Yes! I've heard everything you've said. It's just a bit much to take in. And, when you tell me, my DNA is changing . . ."

Noelle broke down crying; she was shaking from limb to limb. Saltire quickly snatched up Noelle's hands, and while holding them tightly, informed her of her present state-of-affairs.

"You're all right, Noelle! You're becoming a "Master of Intent." From this point forward, it's you as an Intent which will determine what exists and what does not!"

CHAPTER EIGHTEEN

Noble Savage Transforms

The last remaining guests were leaving Saltire's party through the main gate. Emilio had flagged down Reynaldo and Sergio, who were attending to the bonfire, and suggested that they come with him for a smoke. Inside Saltire's estate, Blonde Lady anxiously waited for him by a baby-grand piano situated off to the right when one entered the family room from the entrance inside. Rustic yet inviting, the room featured a large limestone fireplace, which served as the focal point for four leatherback chairs with matching footstools, two colorful Mexican fabricated loveseats, and one bentwood rocker. The area was ideal for entertaining about a dozen friends and relatives. A single piece of a hand-honed cypress raised-panel bench and an antique chest of drawers were pressed up against the wall closet—an emergency exit if ever needed. The back staircase, with its simple wrought-iron railing, led to an upstairs pantry next to a small bedroom and bathroom with a shower. The floor was formed from sizeable three-inch-thick rectangular limestone blocks, covered in part by a large handmade palm leaf area rug, which made moving across the cold surface more enjoyable. Surrounding the family room were four recessed windows with double-door cypress shutters. Six Mexican iron lock plate torches provided additional lighting.

Across from the fireplace and kitty-corner to the baby-grand piano, Paloma, Rosita, and Dahlia were preparing dessert on top of a 19th-century antique Mexican repoussé credenza. Multi-colored scoops of sherbet were displayed inside a large Gorky Gonzalez Majolica bowl adorned with homemade sugar cookies. The sweets were offset by a Celestino brand of hot dark chocolate.

Situated just off to the side of the fireplace, Octavio was relaxing in the Bentwood rocker with his eyes closed. Xochitl entered the family room from the kitchen carrying an antique sterling silver pitcher filled with spoons.

"Xochitl, did I tell you to bring that pitcher in?" Rosita scolded.

Xochitl stopped in her tracks. She looked confused and slightly embarrassed.

"Well, go ahead. Put it on the credenza behind the coffee cups."

Dahlia seeing that Xochitl couldn't reach that far without first being picked up, offered to do it for her. Xochitl handed the pitcher to her beloved cousin and scampered over to her Octavio. He immediately made room for her in his rocking chair.

"Where's Papi? Isn't he coming?" Xochitl asked.

"Yes, my dear. He'll be here shortly," Octavio said.

Reynaldo and Sergio came clamoring into the family room through the small covered porch; they were joking around and laughing at each other's buffoonery. Dripping wet, the young men crossed the limestone floor and served themselves a bowl of sherbet before heading up the back staircase to change into drier clothes. Without hesitation, Paloma grabbed a mop from the kitchen and began to wipe away their wet footprints. When the two young men were halfway up the staircase, Paloma threw the mop in their general direction. Sergio, sensing something heading straight for his head, caught the mop in mid-air, turned around, and cleaned away the watermarks left on the steps.

Saltire placed his walking stick back in the rack and entered the family room through the same porch entrance. Noelle hesitated and remained outside when she heard Blonde Lady address Saltire in a friendly manner.

"Saltire, I'm going to be staying in town for the night. I wanted to know if we are still hooking up for a sunrise breakfast."

"Come, let's take it out front." Saltire suggested.

While walking Blonde Lady through the great room and over to the vestibule, Saltire explained that things had become a bit more complicated.

"Mom, you can knock it off now; you did great!" Saltire said.

"I thought there was more for me to do tomorrow, wasn't that part of the plan?"

"I can't get into it right now." Saltire said, abruptly. What's important is fulfilling the Intent of our forefathers. I'll call on you if I need to."

Saltire's stepmother, looking like a fading Hollywood star of the 40s, sashayed through the front door and over to her 1957 Safari Jeep parked to the far right of the bas-relief fountainhead. In a blink-of-an-eye, Saltire's stepmother shape-shifted, from the distinguished looking blonde woman in her mid-forties, into her everyday demeanor as Melita, a silver haired woman in her early seventies. Driving away slowly, she turned down an alternate dirt road to bypass the traffic jam that had formed from the last of the departing guests.

Walking stick still in hand, Noelle grew impatient and entered the family room through the covered porch. Noelle looked uneasy as she crossed the floor and placed the walking stick up against the back staircase banister where a pair of sandals lay. After taking a moment, she inquired into the portraits gracing the walls.

"I've seen these markings before at Rosita's—are those tattoos covering their faces?" Noelle asked.

Seated firmly in one of the leatherback chairs closest to the kitchen entrance, Paloma imparted the meaning of the signature markings in the gallery of the Celestino family portraits.

With eyes latched onto Noelle, Paloma said, "The one to your left was my grandmother, Icoquih, which in English means "Venus." Back in those times, my entire family would paint their faces and bodies with clay before entering into spiritual battle. The war paint signaled Nagual's Intent."

Noelle stepping closer to the portrait of Icoquih, asked for clarification, "I'm sorry, I'm not familiar with the term, Nagual."

"Forgive me for interrupting," Octavio interjected. "A Nagual is a title of recognition of the individual who has become a Master of Intent."

Sounding anxious and wanting to drop the subject altogether, Noelle said, "Maybe later we can discuss this?"

Paloma excused herself and left the family room for the adjoining kitchen. Rosita and Dahlia sat down together on one of the loveseats. Octavio waited until the room was quiet before he spoke of his family's origins.

"We are the original cave dwellers that descended from the mountains. We established the Metropolis Teotihuacán in 350 AD. When the Empire fell into ruin during the eighth century, we moved as a family and built the city capital of Tollan.

"So your family is comprised of masons and artists?" asked Noelle.

Octavio sounded pleased and replied, "Yes! Only to be Toltec—"Master Builders and Artists of the Spirit"—implies you practice specific disciplines and shifts in consciousness to further spiritual development in the collective consciousness."

"I've never heard of the Toltecs before. Where are they now?"

"All around you!"

Xochitl wiggled out of Octavio's lap and called after Paloma just as she was reentering the family room with another platter of assorted homemade cookies.

"The statues, don't forget to tell her about the Toltec Atlantean Warriors!" Xochitl implored.

Xochitl helped herself to a handful of cookies, two for herself and three intended for Octavio.

"I was just getting to that," Paloma said as she crossed the floor, offering everyone some more cookies with their hot chocolate.

Xochitl skipped back over to Octavio, handed off the three cookies, and then hopped back in her uncle's lap.

Rosita was leaning up against the credenza when Paloma placed the remaining platter of cookies down upon it. Ignoring her younger sister's poor attitude, Paloma turned back around and spoke to Noelle. Paloma was a soft-spoken woman who moved gracefully from side to side as she traced her family's bloodline to the 10th century AD.

"The first two hundred and fifty years Tollan thrived; but where there's an upswing, there's always a downturn. By 987 AD, Tollan had become polluted with Toltec Warriors practicing the Black Arts. The Deity Black Tezcatlipoca referred to as Smoking Mirror, had been recruiting many of the younger warriors—convincing them it was in their best interest to join forces with the people from the north "Chichimecas"—and seized Tollan for their own gain. Upon hearing this treasonous plot to overthrow the city's capital, my family—the keepers of Silent Knowledge—were summoned by the Priest-King Ce Acatl Topiltzin-Quetzalcoatl. They were told to secure the sacred codices in the tunnels beneath the Toltec Atlantean Warrior statues."

Rosita was determined to redirect the conversation to a less informative one. She rose up from the loveseat, crossed the floor, and then began scooping out the assorted colored sherbet into bowls. With her back to Noelle, Rosita asked, "Noelle, aren't you having any?"

Noelle walked over to Rosita, accepted her ration of sherbet, and took a seat at one of the footstools near Octavio.

All too familiar with Rosita's interference antics, Paloma continued.

"When the Civil War destroyed the ideals of the citizens living in and around Tollan in the 10th century, we fled to the last stronghold we'd come to know, Chichen Itza. There amongst the sacred jaguar and the blessed eagle, our ancestors, the Toltecs, co-mingled their bloodlines with the existing Mayans. From that time forward, a chosen group of men and women became Jaguar Knights and Eagle Knights 'Masters of Intent'—able to create the desired outcome from seeing the end result first."

Noelle was still contemplating Paloma's story when the slam of a bedroom door from off the back staircase interrupted her thought process. The family room was uncomfortably quiet when Emilio descended the back staircase. Buttoning up his shirt, he demanded that Dahlia fetch him a cup of hot chocolate and bowl of sherbet.

"Don't do it! Don't do it!" Octavio chirped in a parrot-like voice. Xochitl began giggling.

"What are you giggling about, you Parvulo Chingadera!" Emilio hissed, trying to insult and humiliate Xochitl in front of her family.

Octavio directed his comments to Dahlia, who was standing by the antique chest of drawers. "It's a curious thing, the two of you. I don't suppose you have any idea what you're doing?"

Dahlia blushed as she crossed the floor and handed Emilio the bowl of sherbet, forgetting all together with the hot chocolate he had requested.

Emilio leaned up against the baby-grand piano and directed his comments to Noelle.

"Any talk of my family?"

"Why, were they Toltecs too? Noelle innocently responded.

"At one time, we were all part of the Royal Court at Tollan."

Octavio questioned Emilio's facts. "Delgado? I'm not familiar with the Nahuatl translation of your surname. Would you happen to know its origin?"

"When the Spanish invaded Mexico in 1521, they enslaved or killed everybody in sight," Emilio replied proudly. "The women in my family were clever enough to stay alive; they gave the soldiers what they wanted."

"That would make you Aztec, not Toltec." Octavio clarified. "The remaining Toltecs at Tollan fled for the Occidental Mountains centuries before the Spanish invasion."

"That's irrelevant!" Emilio snarled. "The ancestors of the Aztecs were Toltec!"

Right in that instant, Paloma suspected that Emilio had a deep connection to Noelle. She felt that an aspect of Emilio's Seminal Being *had been Chantal's husband, Karl Wendel Wolfrick. Paloma also sensed that Emilio had another soul aspect tied to his* Seminal Being—*this was Chantal and Immokalee's grandfather, on their maternal side, of whom the Cherokee Elders nicknamed "Saltman." Strengthening the belief that Emilio and Noelle had a deep connection were those who would concur that the Delgado families are the sole surviving descendants of the last Toltec King Huemac, who ruled over the great Citadel of Tollan. The Delgado family's vendetta against the Celestino family went back as far as 987 AD. His family was credited with creating the rival "Black Jaguar Cult" of Tezcatlipoca at Tollan Mexico that ousted Ce Acatl Topiltzin-Quetzalcoatl at that time.*

Octavio continued to pry Emilio for details, hoping to find a possible tie to the Celestino family. "Where'd you say your family was from?"

"What's it to you?" Emilio grunted.

"I was just wondering if we're related?"

Feeling confined by Octavio's line of questions, Emilio continued to defend his family name.

"My family came from Alta, CA and relocated to Tollan over one thousand years ago. As a matter of fact, they helped build your beloved Temple of the Morning Star."

Octavio, with eyes glistening in recognition, suddenly recalled the name given to Northern Toltecs.

"Noble Savage Transforms," he said.

Emilio reeled from within and shouted, "What'd you call me?"

"Calm yourself down," Octavio advised. "You know as well as I, the Northern Toltecs were referred to as Chichimecas by the Aztecs; the name simply means *Noble Savage Transforms.'* "

Emilio leaned down, picked up his dessert bowl, and carried it over to the antique chest of drawers. After depositing his empty bowl, he turned around and addressed Noelle, "Do you believe in werewolves?"

Noelle said jokingly, "Only when I'm in North America."

Octavio cracked a smile and changed the subject altogether. "Emilio, will you be joining us tomorrow—"

"And where might that be?" Emilio asked.

"At the Temple of the Morning Star."

"What time?"

"I find it's always most active at twilight," Octavio said. "So can we count you in?"

"Absolutely!"

Meanwhile, Rosita and Paloma had reconvened in the kitchen. They prepared a pot of freshly brewed hot dark chocolate from their family's cocoa plantation in Southern Mexico. Rosita confided to her older sister Paloma that she hated it when Octavio and Emilio expressed their dislike for one another.

"I know what Octavio is doing, but it won't work." Rosita boasted. "Dahlia is going to marry Emilio this spring whether he likes it or not. Besides, at the rate he's going, he won't even be around to object!"

"Don't bet on it!" Paloma said. "If you can strike from a distance, it doesn't matter how formidable your enemy is."

Not up for the verbal contest. Rosita turned her head and cast her eyes downward. Paloma left the kitchen with the pot of hot chocolate between her hands and began offering refills to anyone interested. She was serving the hot chocolate to Xochitl when Saltire dashed into the family room. In his hand, he was holding what appeared to be a golden were-eagle egg.

"The strangest thing just happened. I was walking back when from out of the sky an egg fell into my hand." Saltire motioned for an answer to the incident, "Anyone?"

Everyone in the room engaged in a discussion. Xochitl was the first to question what sort of egg fell down from out of the sky. Her father told his daughter it appeared to be a were-eagle egg. Paloma, Rosita, and Dahlia gave a stab at the correct answer from the kitchen, but to no avail. Emilio, confident he knew the why and the reason for the emergency landing, predicted a gloomy interpretation of the were-eagle's erratic behavior.

"Exotic endangered species, like the were-eagle and were-jaguar, are in demand at an alarming rate. These species can bring in hundreds of millions of dollars if properly handled," Emilio said with authority.

"That's fascinating, and?" Saltire beckoned.

"She knows her time is up, and she wants to protect what little cargo she still has," Emilio argued. Emilio knew from where he spoke. He had spent the better part of ten years in the illegal wild animal trading business. Emilio sold his were-jaguars, were-cougars, and were-eagles to the Mexican cartels operating in and around Central America. Emilio's international business grossed ten times the profits of his competitors. He hired his friends to be spies and informants, animal catchers, and food handlers. He knew where the cave dwellings and the fresh waterholes were harboring sacred artifacts and bones. Emilio believed that if you captured a were-creature at one of any number of sacred caves, cenotes, or temple ruins, you would be harnessing magical earth spirits who possessed invincible strength, speed, and remote viewing capabilities. In other words, you had an advantage over your opponent. Your forces, those that answered to you directly, could know in advance the current whereabouts of any subject.

Octavio offered no insights into the discussion. The case had gone cold in a matter of minutes. Noelle remained seated on the footstool, listening intensely to the inquiry.

Saltire abruptly turned in Noelle's direction. "We haven't heard anything from you?"

"I think it's a sign of some sort. I think Octavio's pet eagle wants our attention."

"What makes you think it's his."

"It's the same one that confronted me this afternoon. It's his!"

"You keep saying eagle, it's a were-eagle! There's somewhat of a difference." Saltire emphasized.

"The point I'm trying to make is, the were-eagle seems to have an affinity for this family. It clearly trusts you, trusts you enough to protect its offspring."

"Go on." Saltire encouraged his American initiate.

"Well, aren't eagles considered by many ancient civilizations to be messengers of the Gods?"

"I suppose," sensing no objection from the group, Noelle continued to piece together the relationship between the were-eagle and the Celestino family.

Noelle was on her feet, moving her head around ever so slightly. She was feeling more agitated by the second. Little did Noelle know that she was instinctually dodging interference from the invisible force of Black Tezcatlipoca. Under no circumstances did the Toltec Deity want Noelle to remember her soul affiliation with Quetzal Hunahpu—let alone acquire her magical-skill set at this particular time.

"Listen, what if one of your deities was attempting to contact someone in your family through the half-human, half-animal creature?" Noelle insisted.

Octavio's eyes glanced over at Saltire and then quickly back to Noelle.

"Yes!" said Saltire.

"What's the divine message?" Octavio asked. "Take your time."

Noelle began pacing around the family room, taking giant steps and keeping her eyes focused on a few feet in front of her.

In an attempt to mislead Noelle, Emilio cried out, "The sky is falling! The sky is falling!"

Noelle remained unfazed and immediately identified something consistent in the family portraits: two quetzal birds' ramparts were hitched together by a rattlesnake tail.

"Can you all wait but a few? I'll be right back," Noelle said enthusiastically.

Noelle ran from the family room, sailing through the covered porch over to the smoldering bonfire, and turned around. Her eyes scanned the façade of Saltire's Mayan-Toltec estate and landed on the Family Crest fastened below the second story windows. Flapping in the wind was the Celestino's "Coat of Arms." Like a whip-cracking over Noelle's head, it acted as a spiritual force recalibrating her assemblage point to a distant time and space. Contemplating the quetzal bird ramparts emerging from the single rattlesnake tail, Noelle drew upon her *Seminal Being* Soul—the Original Intent and First Principle that had previously influenced Quetzal Hunahpu's soul in the 10th century.

I watched in amazement as my *Seminal Being* Soul spoke to its intended recipient, Noelle Intaglio Leandre. Noelle, in turn, used this very moment to gain insight into her purpose in relationship to the Celestino family and the Toltec Secret Eagle Knight Council—the collective body of ten members; the likes of which modern civilization had never seen.

Noelle rushed back inside the family room and said emphatically a stanza from Quetzal Hunahpu's Prophetic Resurrection Hymn.

> *"Transcending fear, the serpent learns to fly.*
> *Quickening her soul retrieval.*
> *Now the door of life opens up to all.*
> *Toltec Atlantean Warrior."*

Recognizing that Noelle successfully shifted her perception from ignorance to awareness, Saltire and Octavio seemed satisfied that she could move on to the next level in her initiation. Saltire moved within a few feet of Noelle and placed a smooth round object in her hand.

Noelle, with an expression of great excitement shouted, "Look! This isn't an egg at all; it's a stone!"

Emilio, looking totally disgusted, said to Noelle. "Looks like your theory just got shot out of the sky. You fool!"

With her newfound clarity, Noelle directed her comments at Emilio and said to him what she could not express to Avery when he was alive.

"I'm afraid you're not so original, Emilio." Noelle voiced assuredly. "You remind me of my ex-fiancé. Muy Egoista! He also enjoyed coveting other peoples' accomplishments, and then seizing ownership of their achievements."

Unable to resist, Emilio muttered, "I bet he's better off than you!"

"Only if you think being dead is to your advantage," Noelle retorted.

Emilio, noticeably perturbed by Noelle's underhanded comment, stepped away from the baby-grand piano and knelt down over the adjoining bench. On the piano bench, an antique checkerboard with black jaguar knights and golden eagle knights confronted each other in a game of chess. Emilio replaced the black jaguar queen with a clay-colored were-cougar figurine; the statement was intended for Saltire.

"My feline to your knight." Emilio challenged.

Saltire left Noelle's side and joined Emilio in his version of chess. Saltire pointed at Noelle, who had returned to the footstool, and said, "My endangered species to your loathsome creatures."

Loathsome creatures are an aphorism—an observation that contains a general truth. In this case, the maxim alludes to Emilio and Rosita's mutual loyalty and commitment to Black Tezcatlipoca's Smoking Mirror. I could sense tension mounting within Noelle's chest cavity.

Shrills of laughter engulfed the family room; Emilio and Rosita were not amused. Aware that Saltire was referring to him as one of the two 'loathsome creatures,' Emilio looked to Rosita for moral support. Rosita, not aware of the direct insult, sat quietly on one of the loveseats.

"Look on the bright side," Saltire said, half-kidding to Emilio. "Once you know how a person does or does not synthesize information, you'll be able to predict his next move."

Reynaldo and Sergio were in the backyard dousing the bonfire with buckets of water. Trying their best not to get wet, the young men moved slowly and assuredly. The were-eagle watched from a cave in the nearby volcanic cliffside sheltering the cenote. Without warning, she took flight and dove directly over the bonfire, releasing an enormous were-eagle feather. Reynaldo snatched the feather out of the air and entered the family room via the porch.

"Hey dad, look what just fell out of the sky!" Reynaldo said.

"Ah, splendid! The last ingredient, may I have it?"

Reynaldo took the were-eagle feather over to his father and dropped it on his lap.

"This is the finest were-eagle feather I've ever had the privilege of holding," Octavio said, puffing out his chest.

"Two feathers does a wand make!" Xochitl confirmed.

Emilio walked over to the antique chest of drawers. He helped himself to another bowl of sherbet and then accused the Celestino family of gross misconduct.

"You people are so full of it!"

"How so?" Octavio asked.

"Each year, I've had to listen to some crazy fabricated tale. This year it's the were-eagle who flings rocks and feathers instead of eggs in an attempt to communicate some dire message. What will it be next year, the tiny river snail that wiggles its way out from under the jaws of the slimy salamander as it desperately hippity-hops upstream?"

"Emilio, calm down!" Dahlia pleaded.

"No, I won't calm down!" Emilio shouted. "Your friends consider you to be decent folk, but I know different."

Usually, in favor of Emilio's insults, Rosita raised her hand in objection. She felt the room's temperature rising and wanted desperately to leave before one of Emilio's outbursts.

"Clay figurines in the hands of 'loathsome creatures'; what more can one say about these energy seeking suckers?" Saltire reinstated.

Emilio's eyes shifted over to Rosita. Head bowed, her eyes were plastered on the floor. Again, Rosita said nothing in Emilio's defense. From the beginning, Emilio had wanted desperately to be a part of this family. He sought to dominate and then destroy it by attempting to kill little Xochitl out at the waterfall basin in Yelapa. When that misfired, Emilio set in motion another scheme that would kill both Noelle and Xochitl. Octavio had known for awhile that Emilio was a danger to his family, so he decided it was best to know his whereabouts at all times until he was excommunicated.

Staring coolly at Rosita, Saltire requested that she join him for a private meeting out by the cenote.

Octavio, in an attempt to rid himself of Emilio's company, said ungraciously, "Don't you have family in the area, Emilio?"

Emilio took the hint and joined his fiancé Dahlia in the kitchen.

Octavio rose from the bentwood rocker with Xochitl's arms and legs wrapped about his torso.

"Okay, everyone, it's time to call it quits," Octavio said.

Placing Xochitl down on the floor, the two went trotting past the kitchen to their left, in the direction of the vestibule. Before disappearing, Octavio looked over his shoulder and stated, "Come on Noelle, this way."

Noelle picked up the remaining bowls of sherbet and teacups of hot chocolate off the floor and deposited them into Dahlia's hands. Only then did she follow Octavio out of the family room.

Paloma, Reynaldo, and Sergio finished straightening the family room, and then went into the kitchen. Emilio and Dahlia, it appeared had already left the kitchen in favor of the Great room.

Saltire vacated the premise, headed past the smoldering bonfire, and in the direction of the cenote and the aviary, which were both protected by forty-three-foot volcanic cliffs. On his way, Saltire snapped off a thin branch from a pine tree. With a swish, he sliced the air with the tip of the switch, exhibiting great finesse and swordsmanship.

Rosita rushed after her brother, making her way through a maze of green hedges and on through to a barrel-vaulted entrance. Saltire ducked behind a limestone pillar and watched as his sister speeded past him. Rosita continued down the length of the cenote in search of Saltire. A hot breath of air landed on the back of her neck and sent a shiver down her spine. She turned around abruptly. Saltire was but a foot away from Rosita when she demanded answers.

"Let's get on with it!" Rosita yelped.

"I thought it best not to embarrass you in front of our guests," Saltire said, aware of her demeanor. "You know Sis, I've been watching you over the past few years, and I don't get it."

"What's there to get?"

Saltire slid past Rosita and walked her in a grand circle around the cenote.

"Emilio distracts to destroy others," Saltire said matter-of-factly. "He's poisoning this family one female at a time."

"Emilio isn't poisoning anyone. You're paranoid; you need help!" Rosita shouted.

Saltire swooped in within inches of Rosita's face and asked, "Who's in need of help?"

Rosita avoided his intense gaze, and when she attempted to leave, she found both her feet stuck to the dirt footpath leading back to his estate.

"Let me go!" Rosita screamed. "I mean it, I'll hurt you!"

Saltire, showing no signs of distress, informed his sister of an ancient truism. "What is meant to harm another, our ancestors will use to assist."

Rosita, gnashing her teeth, screamed again only more fervently, "Let go of me!"

"Not until you agree to listen."

"Oh, for the love of God! Will you kindly get to the point?"

"I know you and Emilio are hell-bent on destroying this family and all the good we've accomplished to date. Surely you must have gathered by now that Baile Movimiento is engaged in a healing process to restore the integrity of Noelle's soul."

"Heal her from what, herself?" Rosita snickered.

"Through the process of Karmic Debt Removal-soul retrieval, Noelle has been healing the debilitating effects of trauma," Saltire confirmed.

"Good for her!" Rosita said sarcastically.

"I'm not about to stand by and watch you and your boyfriend destroy her God-given right to incarnate into a better life condition."

"What about me, aren't I entitled to a better life?"

"There's to be no more 'bloodletting' in this family, do you understand me!" Saltire proclaimed.

Rosita abruptly shoved Saltire aside, stepped through the barrel-vaulted entrance, and hurried back toward his residence.

CHAPTER NINETEEN

The Spirit of the Voice

Octavio was leaning against the upstairs hallway just outside Xochitl's bedroom. Out of sight, he listened with a look of contentment as he overheard her asking Noelle if she had a good time at her father's party, "Aren't you glad you came? It was fun, wasn't it?" Xochitl said enthusiastically.

"It was a lot of fun," Noelle agreed. "Your father seems so familiar."

Xochitl giggled and concurred, "You're like one of us!"

"Don't tell anyone, but I wish I could stay here forever."

Rosita, Emilio, and Dahlia were hanging out by the front door landing. Emilio was the first to walk casually over to Rosita's Mercedes stationed by the main gate. Dahlia, looking askance, remained strong as her mother followed Emilio over to her car.

"Throw him your keys Rosita and be done with it!" Saltire yelled through the front door.

Rosita handed her keys to Emilio, walked around to the passenger side, and got in. The two promptly drove away into the night.

Emilio and Rosita's relationship was to be a series of missteps, one more detrimental than the other. Neither party had integrated past transgressions; as such, they were spiraling out of control.

"I'm done!" Dahlia said to Saltire. "This is unacceptable!"

Octavio and Noelle descended the sweeping front stairway and moved across the vestibule to join Saltire and Dahlia at the front door landing. Dahlia made a gesture to leave, but Octavio asked that she walk with him around the bas-relief fountainhead. Dahlia took her uncle's hand, and the two set out on a private excursion.

Octavio and Dahlia made a big circle around the fountainhead, appreciating each Ceiba tree, jaguar form, and eagle shape, as well as a human skull. During their walk, Octavio kindly asked for Dahlia's aid in a matter pertaining to Xochitl.

"I'd like you to handle something for me," Octavio said. "You are to look after Xochitl until Saltire and Noelle return. My sons will be close by if you need a hand. Paloma is going to take me to the hospital; I need to be at my birthplace, Morelia. It's there that my soul will take on a life of its own and reunite with my *Seminal Being* Soul—Primordial Self."

Dahlia was visually impacted by the news of Octavio's failing health, yet she remained optimistic. She assisted her uncle as he shuffled back over to Saltire and Noelle, standing next to one another. Octavio's speech was slow and specific. He directed his request to Saltire.

"You and Noelle are to leave tonight for Tula. You'll need to get her belongings then meet me in the carriage house. I have the sneaking suspicion we haven't seen the last of those two."

Dahlia felt she must remind her uncle of a potential oversight, "Let's keep in mind, Emilio thinks we're all leaving here at dawn."

"Your mother believes she's got him and all of us under her control," Saltire said.

"What else can I do?" Dahlia asked wistfully.

"Make them think that we're all still here!" Octavio replied.

Directing his remark to Noelle, Octavio continued, "Noelle, you come with me."

Rosita had her head partially outside of the passenger side window. Emilio, in the driver's seat, noticed the rearview mirror becoming a non-reflective surface. In the mirror, he saw a silhouette of a figure floating toward him. The shadow-like black figure with yellow stripes across its face was Emilio's spiritual mentor, Smoking Mirror. Black Tezcatlipoca proceeded to remove a layer of one of his yellow-colored facial bands and drop it through the rearview mirror and onto Emilio's lap. Fascinated by the intruder, Emilio picked up the yellow strip and held it up to Smoking Mirror to see what would happen. The diabolical Toltec Deity took his pointed index finger, reached through the rearview mirror, and scribbled down the markings of an evil spell. In a growling whisper, Smoking Mirror sounded out the words in his vision:

"Cat comes running,
Eclipsing the light of the moon.
Your movement makes no difference,
Atlantean!"

Noelle was inside the carriage house front entrance, assisting Octavio as he shuffled cautiously over to a large standing fireproof metal cabinet. Octavio pressed his hands up against the cabinet and offered Noelle some final instructions.

"The most valuable experiences we can create for ourselves and others are multifaceted. They arise from the Field of Imaginings, reinterpreted by the eye in the form of "Imaginal-Vignettes®""—infinite numbers of inverted triangles which are pictorial representations of a sequence of seminal forms that, given the right conditions, will manifest. If you ever are fortunate enough to see even three of them in a cluster, you must initiate contact."

"Haven't I seen these inverted triangles before?" Noelle asked.

"On one occasion perhaps, but it seems you have no memory of it. If you did, you wouldn't feel the need to have asked."

At a loss for words, Noelle threw her leather-beaded pouch in the air and then caught it behind her back. In doing so, she compromised the integrity of the objects inside as they brushed up against one another. Octavio snatched the pouch out of her hand as it was being tossed about.

"Stop damaging the integrity of the gifts you've been given," He sounded off. "Don't you know that everything you do goes out into the Universe and has an effect on everything else? I should think that you, of all people, need no reminding."

Noelle looked startled by Octavio's last remark. He took no offense and turned his back to her. Stepping forward, Octavio opened the metal cabinet filled with family relics.

"You're going into uncharted territory tomorrow, but you will not be alone," Octavio reassured her. "Every aspect of your *Seminal Being* Soul, from every incarnation, will be available to you. You have the power within you to retrieve fragmented soul aspects and unite them with their Original Intent—the Virtue that all of you were meant to represent to the world."

Turning back around and holding a mesa—a ceremonial basket— Octavio went on to say, "Inside this realm called 'Intent,' it is paramount that you temper your soul's intention so that it will be strong enough to withstand any opposition."

Octavio then gestured for Noelle to carry the mesa back over to the front entrance of the carriage house. Walking very deliberately, he continued to give her specific instructions. "Flip the lid and locate a symbol of an ideal you hold dear. Go ahead, pick an object."

Noelle reached into Octavio's ceremonial basket and pulled out the tip of a petrified were-quetzal bird tail feather. She then placed it inside her leather-beaded pouch filled with three other sacred objects: copal incense, the diamond-pointed quartz crystal wand—newly shaped into an octagon, and the smooth clay figurine of the were-cougar.

"Good! Now all you have left to do is find one more item, preferably in liquid form. Then it's imperative that all five objects show up tomorrow during your 'soul retrieval'—waking dream—Ceremony!"

Before Noelle had the opportunity to question Octavio they were greeted by Paloma. She had been waiting patiently by the carriage house front entrance. The Holy Bible and the Popol Vuh were protruding from inside her shoulder bag. Eyeing the Popol Vuh, Octavio was reminded of a critical action he forgot to mention.

"Noelle, once the dream begins, you must see each of the objects before they reach you."

Sounding concerned, Noelle asked "What happens if they bump into me or notice me first?"

"Your chance of propelling yourself forward and into the world given by Intent will significantly be diminished. The objects you've collected have power to alter your trajectory. It's even possible you could die."

"Are you saying I might die tomorrow?"

Then again, if you succeed, something quite remarkable might show up."

"What? What will show up?" Noelle asked hopefully.

"The Spirit of the Voice!" Octavio said with confidence.

Emilio bringing the Mercedes to a halt yelled in Rosita's ear, "What are we doing?"

"We're turning this car around! That's what we're doing," Rosita replied.

Emilio floored the accelerator, spun the Mercedes back around, and then instructed Rosita to call Saltire's Estate from the car phone. No one picked up, so she left a message.

"You need to let us back in. We're staying the night!" Rosita insisted.

Dahlia was peering out of one of the second-story windows, with Xochitl in her arms, when she called out to Saltire, "Wait! That was Mom! She wants us to buzz her in."

Saltire turned back around. He'd been anticipating their return and walked over to Dahlia. While removing Xochitl from Dahlia's arms, Saltire told her precisely how to handle the situation.

"If they ask you about tomorrow, just say as far as you know, everyone is leaving first thing in the morning."

Dahlia nodded and bid them adieu.

Saltire and Xochitl quickly descended the sweeping front stairway, jogged through the vestibule, and headed over to the carriage house to fetch Noelle.

Paloma and Octavio were to the far left and at the rear of the carriage house. Saltire entered through the front entrance, signaled to his brother, and quickly took Xochitl and Noelle over to a secret garage door. He popped and turned a large wooden knob, and the garage door lifted, revealing a spectacular collection of vintage cars and motorcycles.

"Comfort or speed?" Saltire asked.

Noelle glanced over at Octavio. Contemplating his medical condition, she opted for speed.

Dahlia could be seen turning off the iron light fixtures throughout the second-story hallway. She continued to scurry as she shut all the bedroom doors, except for Rosita's. The entire upstairs was eerily shrouded in a charcoal-gray. Dahlia moved into position near an open window facing the fountainhead. In the distance, she heard two cars speeding away.

Paloma was behind the wheel of Octavio's truck while Saltire, in his 1992 red Alfa Romeo Spider, safely navigated his way over the bridge. When they both reached the irrigation canal, they split up. Paloma and Octavio left using a dirt road that cut through the vegetable garden before taking the central thoroughfare, one-half mile from Saltire's property line. Saltire, Noelle, and Xochitl took their chances on the "scabes"—old Mayan road. The rarely, if ever, traveled route (made of loose dirt and debris) ran alongside the nearby wetlands and veered right, abruptly after three miles. After which it merged with the main thoroughfare.

Dahlia pressed the upstairs buzzer, allowing Rosita and Emilio back onto Saltire's Property. Running down the front stairway and through the vestibule, she dashed into the kitchen and pulled a white sheet of paper from the copy machine. She then ran back into the vestibule, taped a note to the front banister, and jetted upstairs to her bedroom. Note read:

QUIET PLEASE, WE'VE ALL GONE TO BED.
SEE YOU AT SUNUP.

Emilio and Rosita entered by way of the front door. Dahlia had left it unlocked. Emilio noticed the white sheet of paper hanging from the banister and snatched it before Rosita had a chance to read it.

"What? What does it say?" Rosita quibbled.

Emilio tossed the crinkled note at Rosita and went upstairs.

"No, wait!" Rosita shouted and then ran upstairs after him.

Emilio and Rosita met in the upstairs hallway. Rosita pleaded with Emilio, sighting the dangers infighting will bring upon them. Emilio was unwilling to budge. He pushed Rosita to the side and entered Dahlia's bedroom, closing the door loudly.

From midnight till dawn, Saltire drove at breakneck speed to get to the ancient ruins of Tollan/Tula, Mexico, before it opened its doors to the public. Noelle was looking out the passenger window and trying to make sense of her surroundings. Xochitl was asleep, curled up on Noelle's lap, allowing her head to rest on her right shoulder. After Saltire was confident Xochitl was sound asleep, he initiated a conversation. It was designed to grant Noelle greater insight into her nature.

"All your life, you've been storing energy for this moment," Saltire informed Noelle.

"How have I been storing energy?" Noelle inquired.

"Through impeccability, you are what Toltec Eagle Knights refer to as 'fertile ground.' "

Deeply moved, Noelle questioned, "I'm fertile ground for something?"

"That's correct," Saltire lowered his voice so as not to awaken his daughter. "And, by not engaging in reckless sexual behavior, you've managed to cultivate enough personal energy to deflect and defeat your oppressors."

"My oppressors?" Noelle asked, seeking clarification.

Saltire declined to answer. He needed Noelle to start making her own connections. He went straight to the heart of the matter—her *Seminal Being* Soul and its many aspects.

"What do you know about incarnation?" Saltire whispered.

"Not much, just that some religions believe in it and others don't."

"And you? Any thoughts on the matter?"

"Personally, I think the soul is immortal."

"If your soul is immortal, then what's it comprised of?"

Taking a moment to consider the question, Noelle looked peacefully at the passing landscape.

"I don't know exactly," Noelle said, looking perplexed. "I've been thinking about what you said earlier. You said all those faces floating by in the mirror were aspects of me. What did you mean by that?"

"They are aspects of your *Seminal Being's* Soul seeking to be integrated. Through trauma, your Original Intent fractured in each of the lives it inhabited. A living soul is a facet of the greater divine essence which, at one time, was complete and whole at the inception of Its Original Intent."

"That would mean before a traumatic event fractured my *Seminal Being* Soul, it functioned as a world unto itself."

Saltire nodded.

"This makes me think of one of the aspects I saw floating by in the mirror. It was of my Great Aunt Immokalee."

"Go on. Do you know much about her?"

"Not much," Noelle replied. "Just that she was part Cherokee Indian from North Carolina and was raised by her older sister, Chantal, after their parents died in a storm while working on a fishing schooner."

"Anything else?"

"Well, I know she was briefly married in 1913 to Nicolas Renato Intaglio III, an Italian American born in Gloucester, MA. Mom says he died in WWI and that Immokalee suffered a mental breakdown and miscarriage shortly after receiving the horrific news." Noelle, while grappling with her emotions, remembered Immokalee's presence earlier that evening.

"You know this may sound strange, but I've always felt a close connection to my great aunt. I carry around her artist book wherever I go."

It was the crack of dawn on November 2, 1994, when Emilio stirred from his sleep. He left Dahlia's bedroom, sauntered down the upstairs hallway, and knocked on Saltire's bedroom door. While he waited for a response, he placed Black Tezcatlipoca's yellow facial band over the bridge of his nose and ears. The spell was cast.

Rosita opened her bedroom door and hollered for Dahlia to awaken. Dahlia, cracked open her door—told her mother she was getting dressed and asked her to hold on a minute.

Emilio knocked on the door again, then without hesitation, he opened it and walked in. Saltire's master-bedroom suite was a testimony to the indigenous peoples of Mesoamerica. Beautifully handcrafted cherry-red Mexican Colonial oak furniture and gorgeous handcrafted artwork captivated one's imagination. Over his king-size, raised-paneled headboard was a breathtaking six-foot-wide by eight-feet-long "Prairie Stars" Zapotec wool rug. Recessed windows with faded blue double-door shutters were the primary light source on three of the interior walls. A large built-in closet in the far-right corner of the bedroom shielded the granite-tiled master bathroom from extreme weather. Interior lighting was minimal and remained in the classic tradition of tin wall-mounted sconces. The flooring carried the limestone block theme from downstairs. Three throw rugs depicting sacred geometric patterns provided warmth and comfort for Saltire's bare feet during the winter months.

Rosita left her bedroom and headed over to Saltire's master bedroom after noticing his door was left wide open. Dahlia followed her mother down the upstairs hallway and stood near the doorjamb. Emilio took a thorough look around and then, realizing he had been duped, spun around and locked eyes with Dahlia.

Dahlia squealed, "What did you do to your face?"

"They left last night, didn't they?" Emilio sniped.

Dahlia remembered something Octavio had told her as a child. "Never throw lighter fluid on a raging fire." She said nothing.

In the process of leaving Saltire's master bedroom, Emilio, in his haste, sideswiped Rosita, knocking her to the floor. Pivoting in a burst of anger, he grabbed the back of Dahlia's hair and flung her body to the ground. When Emilio assaulted Dahlia he smashed all the clay figurines hidden inside his black leather moneybag rendering them useless for any future spell casting.

"I'm going to kill 'em all!" Emilio shouted.

Emilio's entire body was in the process of shape-shifting into the malevolent Black Tezcatlipoca jaguar. Hunched over, he took on the posture of the menacing animal readying itself for battle. Reeling in pain, Dahlia peeled herself off of the cold hard floor and yelled, "Get the hell out of here! Get out of here!"

Rosita, fearing that Emilio had succumbed to the evil demon, momentarily abandoned Emilio and endorsed a longstanding belief held by her father.

"What Ce Acatl Topiltzin-Quetzalcoatl has blessed, no one may curse," Rosita proclaimed.

Ignoring Rosita's warning, Emilio took a few steps, then turned and faced the open window above the parking area to the right of the fountainhead. Eyes gleaming, Emilio proclaimed Black Tezcatlipoca Smoking Mirror's Prophetic spell.

"Cat comes running;
Eclipsing the light of the moon.
Your movements make no difference;
Atlantean!"

In a last-ditch effort to save her pathetic relationship with Emilio, Rosita picked herself up off the floor, shuffled past him down the hallway, and returned to her bedroom.

"Emilio, take my keys," Rosita pleaded. "Take my keys."

Dahlia, appearing shaken, began her descent down the sweeping front stairway. Emilio scurried past her, with Rosita's car keys in hand, and slid across the vestibule, and then through the front door. Emilio hurried over to Rosita's Mercedes, entered it in haste, and put the car in reverse. With the car phone in hand, he left Chargo a message: "Get her to the Temple at Tula. The bastards left last night. They must already be there. Call me on this number when you get this message."

Dahlia and Rosita had followed Emilio outside. They were unable to make out everything he was saying, but they knew it was not in their best interests.

With a scowl on her face, Dahlia said to her mother, "How is it that we let it get to this? Dear God, please stop him!" she implored.

Seated in a chair next to Octavio's hospital bed in Morelia, Mexico, Paloma was quietly turning the pages of the King James Version of the Holy Bible. Octavio was weak and near death; a slow intravenous-drip fed his devastated body with antibiotics. Paloma located her favorite passage in the Bible. She read out loud, for the benefit of herself, Octavio, and Noelle, Psalm 51:10-12:

> *"Create in me a pure heart Oh God,*
> *Renew a steadfast spirit within me.*
> *Do not cast me from your presence,*
> *Or take your Holy Spirit from me.*
> *Restore to me the joy of your salvation,*
> *And grant me a willing spirit to sustain me.*
> *Now and evermore, Amen."*

Octavio motioned with his hand for Noelle's copy of *The Spirit of the Voice*. Holding the sacred book to his heart, Octavio sent forth one of the great spiritual truths of life to the Temple of the Morning Star atop of the pyramid at Tollan/Tula, Mexico.

"A soul is a creature of the spirit,
A species true unto itself.
Resuscitate 'The Spirit of the Voice,'
Be silent, observe, and reflect."

Thirty minutes outside of Mexico, the ancient ruins of Tollan, which means "Among the Reeds," lay silent and still under the rising sun. The temple platform was covered in puddles. A spectacular twin rainbow touched down on either side of four impressive Toltec Atlantean Warrior statues. A were-eagle—Paloma's body double—flew in the sky, forming a figure-eight flight pattern.

Saltire turned his Alfa Romeo toward the Temple of the Morning Star, a pyramid platform upon which the four, fifteen-foot Toltec Atlantean Warriors stood in a row. They once served to support the roof of the sacred temple. As Saltire approached a red streetlight, a preteen boy appeared from out of nowhere and walked over to Saltire's passenger seat.

"Would you like a souvenir? Please, I give you special price!" the boy spoke in broken English and directed his question to Noelle.

Noelle put her hand up and waved the kid away. Realizing there are no coincidences, Saltire handed Noelle a one-dollar bill and the change from his pants pocket. He told her to go ahead and buy something. As the light turned green, Noelle signaled for the boy to return with his souvenir tray. She quickly gave him all the money in her hand in exchange for a vial of holy water with an illustration of Ce Acatl Topiltzin-Quetzalcoatl on the front and Christ Jesus on the back. Noelle took the vial of holy water and placed it inside her beaded-leather pouch.

The blessed water was now grouped along with: the copal incense, discovered at the burned-out beach house; the smooth clay figurine of the were-cougar, returned to her by Octavio; the diamond crystal wand, from Victor's Rock Garden, now in the shape of an octagon; and the petrified were-quetzal bird tail feather that she chose from Octavio's Mesa.

Saltire pulled away slowly out of the intersection.

Noelle turned and addressed Saltire, "I thought I'd bring along an old friend for the ride."

Saltire smiled and then said, "It's time you thought about attaching your pouch to your belt. It's imperative that you maintain your focus. Don't let any of these five objects get loose, or that could be disastrous for us both!"

"Disastrous?" Noelle was taken aback.

"Be ever vigilant." Saltire said, in all seriousness. "Your enemy has been my adversary for a very long time. He will try to thwart our opportunity to restore the Integrity of our *Seminal Being* Soul—our Godly Soul."

Saltire whipped his sports car into a reserved parking space closest to the ticket booth, and the three promptly enter the historical ruins.

CHAPTER TWENTY

Point of Recognition

T ula was about to open its avenue to the public. Saltire, Noelle and Xochitl moved swiftly in amongst a forest of truncated pillars, just a few feet up from ground level. Xochitl in the lead was zigzagging her way toward a bright beam of light. Saltire hollered after Xochitl and told her to wait up! Xochitl stopped abruptly and did a little boogie dance.

"Xochitl is the genuine article, isn't she?" Noelle said smiling,

"As you Americans put it, she's my pride and joy."

Saltire and Noelle flanked Xochitl as they continued along the pillared promenade.

"We're now at the foot of 'The City of the Gods,'" Saltire declared.

Saltire then pointed out to Noelle three Huichol Indians standing between the four Toltec Atlantean Warrior statues at the top of a Temple Pyramid. Noelle squints but was unable to make out their physiology.

"Quiet your mind and focus your attention to where they are; propel yourself forward; put yourself physically there." Saltire instructed Noelle.

Noelle stopped walking, raised her head, and lowered her eyes to a forty-five-degree angle.

"Yes, okay, I can see them clearly now." Noelle assured Saltire.

The three Huichol Indians appeared as off-white shimmering inverted triangles—Imaginal-Vignettes®.

"Let's pick up the pace; Xochitl go ahead start us off," Saltire said.

Xochitl was out in front again running to her heart's content. Noelle jetted off and relaxed into a steady jog behind her. Saltire picking up the rear said, "Remember, keep breathing; whatever you do, keep the flow of breath circulating during this phase of initiation."

Noelle's breathing was becoming forced as she and Saltire approach the Temple of the Morning Star.

"If the indians are gone when I get up there, then what?" Noelle needed to know.

"They won't leave until your Intent has interceded."

"Yes! But how will I know if this has happened?"

"You'll first feel a jolt, and then a swift current of wind will lift you off your feet. When this happens, pay close attention to the surrounding landscape; it retains the action scenes and you'll experience them in silence. Harness your emotions, then speak, this will make all the difference."

Noelle was processing Saltire's description of what she could expect to experience when she made her final sprint past Xochitl to reach the base of the Temple Pyramid first. Exhausted, Noelle grabbed both her knees and bent over.

The rising Sun put forth its Intent in the form of a massive solar flare; Baile Movimiento—Dancing Movement's, shadow, crossed over the Toltec Atlantean Warriors statues. Poised at the top of the Temple of the Morning Star were three Huichol Indians. They took note as Saltire and Xochitl joined Noelle at the base of the Temple Pyramid.

Noelle, Saltire, and Xochitl stood respectfully at the foot of the temple. Noelle, weak at the knees, wobbled to the ground. Saltire crouched down and met Noelle at her level.

Saltire, "Why do you suppose Octavio insisted that I bring you here?" Noelle looked at him intrigued. "It wasn't for the scenery, it was, so that you become the spectacle—Quetzal's prophetic vision in the flesh."

Noelle stood up and looked around.

"We've prepared you the best we know how; however, we have a slight problem," Saltire informed Noelle.

"What? What's the problem?" Noelle asked looking troubled.

"We've arrived twenty-four hours ahead of the designated time. The total solar eclipse doesn't occur until 8:19 a.m. the third of November. Alignment, as you will soon find out, more often than not determines one's fate."

Intuiting that the stakes were indeed high, Noelle said, "Well let's not just stand here. Give me something to do!"

Saltire then told Noelle the why and the wherefore. "We members of the Council pray in extreme circumstances because prayers, by their very nature, don't have mass and can move at the speed of light. Prayers by design are both heard and answered in the manner in which they are intended. It all happens at a 'Point of Recognition.' "

Standing at the base of the Temple Pyramid, Xochitl had spotted a were-cougar blindly racing toward them from out of the tall reeds surrounding the ancient ruins. Xochitl affirmed her father's worst suspicions; he placed his daughter behind his body and out of sight.

"What have you done?" Saltire accused Noelle.

Noelle glanced down at her beaded-leather pouch and realized her persistent fidgeting had loosened its drawstrings and let the were-cougar figurine wiggle loose. Under Black Tezcatlipoca, Smoking Mirror's spell had caused her actions to conjure up the real were-cougar—Emilio's younger sister, Melato resurface.

In a split second decision, Noelle lifted her eyes to the Temple's zenith and leaped off the ground running. Noelle, in a state above suspicion and doubt, darted headlong up the Temple Pyramid's large stone steps.

Noelle reached the flat-topped landing of the Temple and spun around frantically in every direction in an attempt to protect herself from the were-cougar. She was standing alongside the four Toltec Atlantean Warrior statues. The three Huichol Indians were nowhere in sight. Then, like a helicopter rising above a skyscraper, the were-cougar hurled itself through the air in preparation for a kill.

"NO!" Noelle's soul forcibly cried.

The were-cougar was thrown back in mid-flight and tumbled down the side of the Temple.

He began shape-shifting from one Toltec Deity into another. There was Chalchiuhtotolin Blood-Jeweled Fowl, Long-Nose Turkey, then Black Tezcatlipoca Smoking Mirror, then Tlaloc the Deity of thunder and rain, and then Ce Acatl Topiltzin-Quetzalcoatl appeared, just as he had looked on the eve of the Sacred Temple's decimation by fire in 987 AD. The King Priest rose to his feet, and immediately became Saltire Daghda McKenna Celestino.

In the far distance, another were-cougar was seen patrolling the area. Mela had evidently missed the opportunity to challenge Noelle and further her spiritual development. The were-cougar shape-shifted back into Mela and she slinked away looking demoralized.

Mela T. Delgado had played the role of double agent brilliantly. She had exposed Emilio's ties to Black Tezcatlipoca's and thwarted his intention to decimate the Celestino family. Mela was, however, fully aware that she would be required to perform this act as the agent provocateur in the upcoming year during the Days of the Dead Festival. It was imperative that Mela complete her own training, if ever she planned on becoming a member of the Toltec Secret Eagle Knight Council. The were-cougar in the Mayan and Toltec cultures was thought of as an "agent provocateur" to an initiate engaged in spiritual test and ordeals. If you successfully survived its attack, you move up a ring on the spiritual ladder to the Sun, the God of all things seen and unseen; the God of Silent Knowledge.

Noelle physically shaken by the were-cougar attack, lumbered over to the edge of the flattop landing and sat down. In a moment of silence, Noelle shifted her perception and entered into a waking dream; one in which her *Seminal Being* Soul would shed light on the mystery that sustains life.

It was mid morning and the fog draped over the Santa Monica Mountains in Malibu, CA was slowly lifting. (Malibu was an actual location that was rumored to have had Toltec migrations after the burning of Tollan in 987 AD). Noelle was photographing the shoreline when a silver flash of reflected light hooked her imagination. She went over to investigate and found her octagon quartz crystal wand protruding from the shoreline. In an attempt to remove her wand, she stumbled upon her petrified were-quetzal bird tail feather tumbling in the waves. The tail feather rushed past Noelle forcing her to turn and take note of something peculiar in the sky. Before running up the beach toward the Santa Monica Mountains, Noelle placed the tail feather and crystal wand in her empty beaded-leather pouch attached to her belt.

Floating nearby, only partially hidden by a cloud was a dark and distinguished-looking Native American Warrior, bare-chested, in torn blue jeans. As Noelle scurried up from the beach, she watched as the Warrior glided across the face of one of the mountains then vanished. Noelle crossed the Pacific Coast Highway and made her way up a steep winding path made of pressed sand to a flat top precipice. Unable to pull herself up and onto the plateau, Noelle turned around and leaned back underneath an overhang. Suddenly, the aroma of burning copal incense caused Noelle to turn her head over her right shoulder. At that very second, the Warrior's left hand reached down to assist her. Grabbing hold of his hand, Noelle was elevated in one swift movement.

Standing atop the plateau, the indian Warrior took several strides over to a sacred circle made from ocean rocks and tiny balls of copal incense. Facing Noelle, he signaled for her to step inside the sacred space. As Noelle entered the circle, she picked up one incense ball and placed it inside her beaded leather pouch. Immediately, the indian Warrior started to dance and twirl around Noelle; in the process, he transformed into a "Cherokee Eagle Dancer." Dressed in deer hide, eagle feathers, and brightly colored paint, he moved faster and faster as if to the sound of drums beating. A thundercloud appeared directly over Noelle and released buckets of rainwater. Casting her eyes downward, Noelle spotted the vial of holy water with the images of Ce Acatl Topiltzin-Quetzalcoatl and Christ Jesus bobbing and turning in a puddle.

Overcome with emotion, Noelle's knees gave out, and she started to fall backward. The dancer gracefully caught Noelle and held her in a state of suspension. Without provocation, Noelle was transformed into her Great Aunt Immokalee at the age of thirty-five. When Immokalee opened her eyes, the dancer had shape-shifted into Dancing Movement. Immokalee peered deep into the emerald-green eyes of the "divine Messenger." Together they levitated way above the Toltec Atlantean Warrior statues. The sky broke open, and the raindrops retreated back into the clouds.

With Immokalee's attention fixed on Dancing Movement, she asked, "Who are you?"

As the ground beneath Noelle began to turn clockwise, a thundering voice from out of a huge churning cloud proclaimed:

"LOVE, JUST LOVE!"

Multicolored rays of light streamed forth from Dancing Movement, as he/she became a fractal pattern in shades of emerald-green and indigo-blue. Within seconds, an intricate maze of gypsum gray tattoos appeared on another one of Noelle's incarnations, one that goes back over one thousand years. Noelle had shape-shifted from Immokalee into the Toltec Atlantean Warrior, Quetzal Hunahpu. The markings on Quetzal's face signaled that the Intent of her soul's *"Intended Future"* was in the process of being fulfilled with and inside of Noelle Intaglio Leandre's *Seminal Being* Soul.

By actively being of service to the Toltec Secret Eagle Knight Council (by way of her relationship with Ce Acatl Topiltzin-Quetzalcoatl), Quetzal created the clearing that would give birth to her future self as Noelle; which in turn allowed her Seminal Being *Soul to live on with the aspirations of its own fulfillment. Noelle contained within her soul a self-contained World unto Itself. As with all human beings, she was an endangered species, a* Seminal Being *Soul – a living facet who would later become an aspect of the greater cosmic source, That is "Love, Just Love."*

As Quetzal Hunahpu, Noelle was able to propel herself twenty-four hours into the future. Her face to the sun at 8:19 a.m. on November 3, 1994 during a total solar eclipse at the ancient ruin of Tollan/Tula in Hidalgo, Mexico, Noelle aligned her will with an Intent far greater than her own self-interest. By doing so, Noelle reclaimed lost vital energy in two of her previous lifetimes. The total solar eclipse was reflected in the eyes of Quetzal and the image of Black Tezcatlipoca began its smoldering decent into oblivion under the protective sky of Mother Earth. In this extraordinary moment in time and space, Smoking Mirror lost all power and influence over the Toltec Atlantean Warrior. Consequently, Noelle was then able to communicate to Quetzal directly, and Quetzal to Noelle, through a spontaneous exchange of hidden truths.

After Noelle shape-shifted fully into Quetzal, she called out to her:

Sacred Bird, One Marksman Lord Eternal,
Make known your soul's Intent to me.
Spoken Prophetic Resurrection Hymn,
Reveal our natural virtue.

Quetzal responded in kind, reminding Noelle of their *Seminal Being Soul's* eternal motto:

> *As Archetypal Creative Order,*
> *Retrieving souls is our passion.*
> *We are the archrivals of ill-intent,*
> *Our kind will not be extinguished.*

The year 1994 became still; no longer an agent provocateur in the memory vortex of Noelle.

A rider approached an archway made of brick and mortar covered in vines. A pine tree switch was quietly tapping the timbers of a century old wooden fence when the sound of Octavio's voice was heard.

> *"Tethered hearts fashioned by 'Divine Promptings,'*
> *Lattice structures sourced from Intent.*
> *Artistry in the Silence of Knowledge,*
> *Forms an archetypal Order."*

The Sun burst through the archway as Noelle positioned her Andalusian Classic Dun stallion, Lexicon, onto a shelf of loose bedrock. Separated by rivers of tears, the gypsum gray line drawing of the Toltec Atlantean Warrior on her face was interrupted and set apart randomly. A new image had emerged.

> *High above Saltire's Mayan-Toltec Estate, on November 2, 2015, Noelle was seen as an inclusion; as an integrated Seminal Being Soul; as the threefold aspect of her Divine Natures – Quetzal Hunahpu (Spirit to Animal), Immokalee Awinita Chisholm Intaglio (Animal to Human), and Noelle Intaglio Leandre (Human to Spirit). The effects of trauma stored in her "body memory tissue" had disappeared.*

Xochitl, age twenty-nine, was tending to the aviary alongside Saltire's estate when her Belgian Malinois puppy, Ceiba, began barking. Immediately she looked in the dog's direction and started running towards Noelle.

"Noelle! Noelle!" Xochitl yelled at the top of her lungs.

Lexicon crumbled the bedrock beneath his hoofs and galloped alongside an irrigation canal, through the vegetable garden, and over to Xochitl. Exhausted from their journey to the *Otherworld*, Xochitl took a hold of the reigns and lead Lexicon and Noelle over to the horse stables.

A man wearing a spirit facemask of the Toltec Deity Tlaloc descended the sweeping staircase, walked through the vestibule, and flung wide the antique bronze front door enhanced with the Celestino family Coat of Arms. The elements had been kind to Saltire, age sixty-seven. Only his sideburns and a few lines around the eyes showed the slightest sign of aging. Snatching a switch from an oak tree sheltering the bas-relief fountainhead adorned with Ceiba trees, jaguars, eagles, and human skulls, Saltire headed toward the main gate.

Xochitl, while taking off her gardening gloves, asked Noelle, "Should I call after him?"

"No, Xochitl," Noelle softly replied. "Let him go; he often likes to be alone before Octavio and his guests arrive."

Paloma, as the impressive were-quetzal bird swooped down from above and dropped a small rock behind Saltire's back. Without hesitation he turned around and snatched the rock out of the air. Saltire lifted his facemask, and looked lovingly at Noelle; they were to begin their Soul's Intended Future together.

THE END

Joan Parrish Morency

Joan Parrish Morency has lived in Southern Nevada for over twenty-four years. She is the owner of Epiphany Artistic License, Publisher and Talias Visual Art & Design Studio. Joan began her professional career as a backdrop artist for commercial photographer in the Greater Boston Area in 1985. By 1996, Joan's artistry received recognition and with it came a myriad of painting projects in Las Vegas, Nevada. Introduced to the Japanese in 1999 as one of America's finest "European Aged Wall Specialists," she was contracted to design and execute the wall finishes for the massive village inside the "Venus Fort" luxury shopping mall in Tokyo, Japan.

After a severe auto accident in 2000, Joan found solace in her first love, movies. In the summer of 2002 she began writing a movie treatment, which then developed into a novel. *Seminal Being: Mirrors of the Gods* is the first novel, second chapter, in the *Seminal Being Trilogy*. Joan, the founder of Imaginal-Vignettes®—short stories and novels in the field of Art and Entertainment—is passionate about cultivating stories that restore the integrity of the Soul, while healing the debilitating effects of trauma.

CPSIA information can be obtained
at www.ICGtesting.com
Printed in the USA
BVHW041206230821
615022BV00010B/667